BLOODY BILL ANDERSON

BLOODY BILL ANDERSON

The Short, Savage Life of a Civil War Guerrilla

ALBERT CASTEL AND THOMAS GOODRICH

University Press of Kansas

Published by the University Press of Kansas (Lawrence, Kansas 66045), which was organized by the Kansas Board of Regents, and is operated and funded by Emporia State University, Fort Hays State University, Kansas State University, Pittsburg State University, the University of Kansas, and Wichita State University

Library of Congress Cataloging-in-Publication Data

Castel, Albert E.
   Bloody Bill Anderson : the short, savage life of a Civil War guerrilla / Albert Castel and Thomas Goodrich.
      p.   cm.
   Originally published: Mechanicsburg, PA : Stakepole Books, c1998.
   Includes bibliographical references and index.
   ISBN 0-7006-1434-6 (pbk. : alk. paper)
   1. Anderson, William T.   2. United States—History—Civil War, 1861–1865—Underground movements.   3. West (U.S.)—History—Civil War, 1861–1865—Underground movements.
4. Quantrill, William Clarke, 1837–1865.   5. Guerrillas—Missouri—Biography.   6. Soldiers—Missouri—Biography.   I. Goodrich, Th.   II. Title.
   E470.45.A53C37 2006
   973.7'42092—dc22   2005036177

British Library Cataloguing-in-Publication is available.

Printed in the United States of America

10 9 8 7 6 5 4 3 2 1

CONTENTS

Preface
vii

Acknowledgments
ix

Prologue *This is the Way We Do Business*
1

Chapter One *The Last Man You Will Ever See*
7

Chapter Two *I'm Here for Revenge*
19

Chapter Three *Such a Damn Outfit*
31

Chapter Four *Let the Blood Flow*
41

Chapter Five *There are Guerrillas There*
63

Chapter Six *You All are to Be Killed*
79

Chapter Seven *The Lord Have Mercy*
87

Chapter Eight *Reserved*
99

Chapter Nine *How Do You like That?*
111

Chapter Ten *Good Morning, Captain Anderson*
123

Epilogue *The Spirit of Bill Anderson Yet Lives*
131

Notes
145

Bibliographical Essay
159

Index
165

Maps appear on pages 8, 22, 90, and 92.

PREFACE

Why a book about William "Bloody Bill" Anderson? Let us answer that question with another question: Why not a book about him? His career was, to say the least, an eventful one, and for a brief but spectacular period he played the leading role in the most viciously violent arena of the entire Civil War, with the result that even before he died he had passed from life into legend—where he remains.

"My name is Anderson. They call me Bloody Bill."

So says an actor at the outset of the film, *The Outlaw Josey Wales*. Viewers know what these words signify. They understand immediately why Josey Wales, a Missouri farmer whose wife has been murdered by Kansas raiders, joins Anderson's guerrilla gang. He wants revenge. With Bloody Bill he will get it.

Much has been written about Bill Anderson. With one exception, though, all of these writings have taken the form of either short articles or somewhat longer accounts of Anderson and his doings in biographies of William Clarke Quantrill and general histories of the guerrilla conflict in Missouri during the Civil War. The exception is Donald R. Hale's *They Called Him Bloody Bill: The Missouri Badman Who Taught Jesse James Outlawry,* a slender paperbound volume published in 1975. It contains much useful information and has been of assistance in the writing of this book. But it is not, nor was it intended to be, a full-fledged account of Anderson's career. Instead it devotes 70 of its 118 pages, many of which consist of illustrations, to Anderson's activities during the summer and fall of 1864 and only 12 to what he did prior to then, with the remaining 30 pages dealing mainly with what happened to Anderson's grave and to the postwar escapades of some of his followers. Thus this book represents the first attempt to present a complete account, insofar as available sources allow, of Bloody Bill's prewar life, of how he became a guerrilla, and of the war that he and his men waged—a war that for some of them never ended until they died.

In making this attempt, we encountered two major problems, both common to all serious historical endeavors but especially difficult given the nature of our subject. One was obtaining an adequate supply of authentic and reliable sources. But this is a matter best discussed in the bibliographic essay at the end of this book, and the interested reader is referred to it.

The second major problem had to do with achieving objectivity in dealing with matters that remain controversial and about which people still have strong feelings. Compounding this problem was that one of the authors tends to be more critical than the other of the Missouri guerrillas and what they did. As it turned out, our conflicting attitudes proved beneficial rather than harmful in that they compelled us to try to reconcile them by compromise and thereby attain a greater balance in what we wrote.

Aiding us in compromise was our agreement with what B. James George Sr., the son of a Missouri guerrilla, wrote in a 1958 letter to Dr. Richard S. Brownlee, author of the then newly published *Gray Ghosts of the Confederacy: Guerrilla Warfare in the West, 1861–1865*[1] "Many, many of the guerrillas were neither neurotic nor psychotic, nor did they come out of the war with any such tendencies. . . . It was my pleasure and pride for many years to have known a large number [of them] and very few were mentally sick. They were just human beings, I would say."

Yet in the same letter George also admitted that the guerrilla war in Missouri "attracted men of unsavory nature and reputation," and he gave as his example Bill Anderson, whose deeds he described with the words "bitter bloodshed."

What follows is the story of that "bitter bloodshed." It is often an ugly story, sometimes a tragic one, but at all times it is dramatic, for nowhere was the Civil War so savage as it was in Missouri, and nowhere did it produce a protagonist more savage than Bloody Bill Anderson.

ACKNOWLEDGMENTS

First and foremost we wish to record our gratitude to full-time lawyer and part-time historian Charles F. Harris of Wichita, Kansas, for providing us with valuable source materials pertaining to the Kansas phase of Bill Anderson's career; for his excellent article in the *Missouri Historical Review* on the collapse of the Kansas City military prison, in which one of Anderson's sisters was killed and the other two injured; for his astute and persuasive critique of a new but flawed contention as to the cause of that collapse; and for obtaining what we had concluded would be impossible for him to obtain—photographs of a tintype of Bush Smith Anderson and (assuming that in fact it existed) of the silk cord with which Anderson kept count of the Union soldiers killed by him. His assistance was given willingly out of a love for history, and he has every right to say that he played a key role in the preparation of this book. We hope that he finds it to be of such a nature that he will wish to say this and say it proudly.

We also wish to convey our thanks to Betty Pierce and Lorlei Metke for the data and other materials relating to Thomas Goodman and Maj. Ave Johnston that they provided. They made it possible to provide a much fuller portrait of both of these men, especially Goodman.

Larry and Priscilla Massie of Allegan Forest, Michigan, gladly helped with illustrations. So, once again, thank you, Larry and Priscilla. Thanks, too, to Donald R. Hale of Lee's Summit, Missouri, who unselfishly shared information about Bill and Jim Anderson and also allowed us to "lift" the photo of Bill Anderson's gravestone.

Finally, Albert Castel most sincerely thanks Linda Moore, Judy Leising, and "Squeaky" Barnett of the Hillsdale College Library for their highly professional and always courteous help, and the same to Richard Wunsch and his associates at the Volume I Used Bookstore in Hillsdale, Michigan, where the photocopier (temperamental though it may be) and the close proximity of the post office greatly facilitated his historical endeavors.

THIS IS THE WAY WE DO BUSINESS

FAYETTE, MISSOURI: MORNING, SEPTEMBER 24, 1864

Pvt. Tom Benton of the Ninth Missouri State Militia Cavalry stood beside the road leading to the garrison's camp on the northern outskirts of Fayette, Missouri. The morning sounds were gone now. On nearby farms the cocks no longer crowed and in neighboring pastures cows had ceased their lowing. Even the chirping music of songbirds had faded as the sun began to bear down. It was going to be a hot day.

Normally sentry duty was boring. Not this time. Benton felt uneasy, even apprehensive. There was something in the air. It was intangible and unnameable yet for those very reasons all the more ominous. His eyes scanned the landscape with quick, nervous glances. The vista was familiar, but it was the unfamiliar that he looked for. Again he stared up the dirt road that led from the town; again he saw nothing out of the ordinary. The same held true for the timber along the creek to the east and the cornfield to the west, where the dry, brownish-yellow stalks rustled softly whenever stirred by a breeze. Good. But this only meant that whatever was out there had not arrived yet—not that it wasn't coming. His tenseness increased.

Benton was just a private. He had no office with maps on the wall, he read no dispatches, he had no "dark connections" in the form of scouts and spies. Nonetheless he sensed that today something was going to happen, something so terrible that he did not want to think about it yet could not think about anything else: an attack on Fayette by bushwhackers.

That is what made it so terrible. Bushwhackers were not soldiers, at least not in the normal sense. They killed because they liked to kill, and they were merciless. If they came to Fayette, Tom Benton and his fellow militiamen would have only two choices if they wanted to live: fight or escape. To surrender meant a hideous, nasty death.

Benton wanted to live. Should the attack come his way, he would fire his rifle to give warning and then run for it. He knew he could not make it to the camp—it was too far away, and the attackers would be riding horses. His best hope was the big brick building some 250 yards up the road west of the garrison's camp that was being used as a hospital. But if he couldn't make it there, either, he would hide in the cornfield.

In town the hands on the courthouse clock pointed to 10:20. It was Saturday, market day, and scores of people from outlying farms and hamlets swarmed through Fayette's business district, buying and selling, visiting friends and relatives, and, if they were men, having a drink or two, or maybe more, at one of the saloons. Fayette numbered barely a thousand inhabitants, but it was the seat of Howard County and the biggest town in that particular subregion of central Missouri. Why, it even had a female seminary. To be sure, because of the war the school no longer had any students. Instead, the three-story brick building had been turned into a hospital for sick or wounded members of the garrison. All the patients able to stand had rifles handy, and Benton counted on those convalescent soldiers to cover him if he had to flee. Like Private Benton, like the forty-five troops posted in and around the log huts of the camp, and like the thirty soldiers and pro-Union civilians stationed in the big stone, massive-columned courthouse, they were waiting.

They were waiting because a spy had reported that an attack might be coming, and if it came, it would come "soon." Of course, such reports or rumors had arrived before and each time proved false. But there was reason to think that this one stood a good chance of being true. For the past week or so a lot of bushwhackers had been roaming about central Missouri, ambushing army detachments and wagon trains, waylaying stagecoaches, ransacking villages, robbing people, and killing—always killing—ruthlessly and sometimes in ways that made death a deliverance. Consequently, on orders from the district commander, Lt. Col. Daniel Draper had set out from Fayette several days ago with Maj. Reeves Leonard's battalion of the Ninth Missouri Militia Cavalry to track down and slay as many of the "wolves" as possible. The departure of this force reduced the town's garrison to only 150 soldiers plus some civilian volunteers, commanded by a young lieutenant named S. S. Eaton. If there was going to be an attack, it would be hard to pick a better time than "soon."

High overhead the clock in the courthouse tower tolled the half-hour when its hands pointed to 10:30. Off to the south, a dust cloud rose above the trees along the road to Rocheport. Was it Draper and Leonard returning? They came in columns of four, riding slowly up Main Street toward the courthouse square. As they drew nearer, it could be seen that they wore blue Union uniforms.

Figure P.1 Howard County Courthouse, Fayette, Missouri.
COURTESY OF ROBERT H. BRAY.

Everybody relaxed. There would be no attack. Up at the camp, sitting in his tent, Lieutenant Eaton resumed writing a letter.

Standing on the sidewalk watching the column file by was a black man wearing a blue uniform jacket. Suddenly one of the horsemen drew a pistol and shot the man. These men in blue were bushwhackers!

As civilians scurried for cover, the soldiers and armed citizens in the courthouse opened fire. Breaking into a gallop, the attackers dashed through the square and toward the camp. Only a few tarried to fire their revolvers at the courthouse, shattering windows. A hail of bullets from long musket barrels—all that could be seen of the defenders—answered them. One rider, a man with a flowing red beard, jumped from his horse, ran to the courthouse entrance, then blazed away at the heavy wooden doors. When his pistol was empty, he dodged back through the smoke and disappeared. So, too, did the other assailants. Nothing could be gained by popping revolvers at invisible foes in a stone building.

Sweeping up the road where Private Benton had been standing sentry, some seventy-five attackers halted in a ravine, spread out in a battle line, then charged toward the log cabins up on the ridge, screaming and firing as they came. Orange-red flashes spewed from loopholes in the cabin walls. As usual when fired downhill at an advancing enemy, most of the bullets went too high. Even so, some saddles were emptied, in others men swayed, and horses stumbled and fell. The charging line halted, milled about, then retreated to the shelter of the ravine.

A few minutes later another charge took place. With shouts of "Scalp them! Scalp them!" the bushwhackers got close enough to leap from their mounts and run forward to knock the chinking from the logs and set the log cabins ablaze. Inside one of the cabins a frightened voice cried out, "Don't fire your revolvers until they get among us!" Fortunately, the attempt failed and with it the second assault. So did a third sally, but it was merely a feint designed to cover the removal of as many dead and wounded from the field as possible. That accomplished, the attackers formed into a march column, then headed westward along the Glasgow Road.

Silence settled over Fayette, a silence that seemed strange, almost eerie, after the din of the battle. Had the enemy gone? Or were they getting ready to strike again from a different direction and with even greater ferocity? Lookouts up in the courthouse cupola shouted down that they saw a long cloud of dust moving west toward Glasgow. Soldiers began emerging from the cabins, the hospital, and the courthouse. Civilians likewise came out from their hiding places. Many felt as if they were awakening from a terrible nightmare. But the broken glass on the sidewalks, the dead men and horses lying in the streets and fields, and the smell of gunpowder smoke, gray wisps of which still floated among the trees, told them that this had been no dream. It had been as real as the sun shining bright and hot above, and when the bells of the courthouse clock sounded 11:30, they realized that it had all happened in less than an hour.

Details of soldiers looked for enemy dead and wounded. They found five of the former, none of the latter. They placed the corpses in a row on the street. Their own loss seemed to be just one dead and two wounded. Then someone remembered Private Benton. Where was he?

The answer lay in the cornfield. His body was mangled by bullets. His scalp had been nailed to a fence. With it was a note: THIS IS THE WAY WE DO BUSINESS.

Rage rose in the soldiers' throats and burst forth in howls of primeval vengeance. Galloping into town, they rode their horses over and over the five bodies, trampling and mashing them into the dirt.[1]

Such was the war in Missouri in 1864. It did not take place on the same scale as in Virginia or Georgia, where the contending armies numbered in the tens of thousands and casualties were counted in equal measure. But what it lacked in size, it more than made up for in sheer viciousness and horror. And while elsewhere Federals fought under the stars and stripes and Confederates beneath the stars and bars, in Missouri both sides served the same banner: a black flag, crimsoned with blood.

It was a different war in Missouri—a very different war.

CHAPTER ONE

THE LAST MAN YOU WILL EVER SEE

THE GLASGOW ROAD: AFTERNOON, SEPTEMBER 24, 1864

The pungent reek of blood hung over the long line of horsemen riding westward from Fayette. Some of the wounded remained mounted, slumping in their saddles. Many more lay twisting with agony in wagons and buggies taken, along with their teams, from Fayette itself and farmhouses along the way. Head wounds, gut shots, mangled arms and legs dripped blood, splattering the yellow dust of the road. Never before had they suffered such heavy losses: eight dead, more dying, and a couple dozen wounded, some badly. Never again, they resolved, would they attack an enemy they could not shoot but who could shoot them. Their object was to kill, and you could not do that if *you* got killed.[1]

Almost all of them were in their late teens or early twenties and natives of western Missouri, in particular the counties bordering the Missouri River—the "Big Muddy." With few exceptions their families had come from Virginia, Kentucky, and Tennessee to grow in the fresh, fertile soil of Missouri the same crops that they had produced in their home states, tobacco and hemp. Prior to the war the more prosperous had owned slaves—not many, as a rule, but some. Before the war, too, back in the mid-1850s their fathers, uncles, and older brothers had tried to turn the newly opened territory of Kansas into a slave state. They believed that Kansas naturally belonged to them, separated as it was from Missouri only by a line drawn on a map, and they resented the Yankees coming in from New England, New York, Ohio, and other Northern states with the avowed purpose of making it a free state where slaves, and thus slave-owners, would not be tolerated. They struggled to prevent this from happening, and Kansas became "Bleeding Kansas" as both sides fought, raided, and massacred each other. For a while it seemed that the Missourians—Border Ruffians, as they were called—would prevail thanks to the advantage of proximity, but in the end they went down before the overwhelming numbers of the

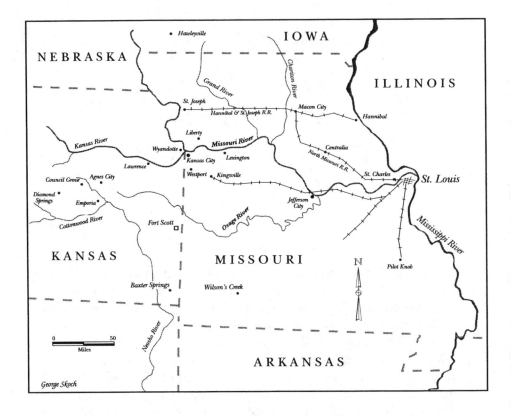

Northern settlers, who turned Kansas into a Yankee fiefdom, an antislavery stronghold.

The Kansas conflict also brought a new political party into being in the North—the Republicans, dedicated to banning slavery from all the western territories as the first step toward eventually eliminating it in the South itself. In 1860 they carried every Northern state except one and so elected Abraham Lincoln president. "A house divided against itself cannot stand," he declared, and when he added that the nation must either be all free or all slave, there could be no doubt that he meant for it to be all free. Seven states of the lower South seceded and formed the Confederate States of America, soon to be joined by four others from the upper South. Southerners believed that in leaving the Union, they were merely exercising their constitutional right, not to mention the right of revolution and the right of self-defense. Most Northerners, Democrats as well as Republicans, regarded secession as rebellion—a rebellion that had to be suppressed if the Union and "government of the people, by the people, and for the people" were to survive.

And so the war came. Many Missourians, especially in the western part of the state, wished to join the Confederacy, but a great many more remained loyal to the "old flag" or took refuge in passive, ambiguous neutrality. Furthermore, Union states bordered Missouri on the east (Illinois), the north (Iowa), and the west (Kansas and Nebraska), whereas only sparsely populated Arkansas to the south provided a direct link with the Confederacy. Outnumbered and out-flanked, prosecessionist Missouri forces under Maj. Gen. Sterling Price failed, despite initial successes, to gain control of the state during the summer and fall of 1861 and had to retreat into Arkansas. Only partisans, guerrillas or bush-whackers, as they commonly were called by others and themselves, remained to challenge Federal domination.

In the beginning they consisted merely of small, local, ad hoc bands defending and retaliating against the persecutions of Missouri Unionists and the depredations of Kansas jayhawkers, who, under such leaders as Jim Lane and Charles "Doc" Jennison, ravaged the western border counties. Rapidly, though, they grew in strength, skill, and effectiveness until they were able to go on the offensive, harassing Federal occupation troops, terrorizing Unionists, and mak-ing raids into Kansas itself. The inevitable outcome—inevitable because of the very nature of guerrilla warfare when waged as part of a civil war—was an ever-ascending spiral of violence as reprisal begat reprisal, murder begat murder, and atrocities begat atrocities, with neither side giving nor asking for quarter.

Also, to begin with, most of the bushwhackers were motivated mainly by a desire to fight for what they deemed to be their rights and avenge what they considered to be their wrongs. They thought of themselves as Southerners and believed that the Confederacy was needed to save the South and its way of life from Yankee thralldom. And they knew what that would mean from personal experience. Few among them did not carry in their minds and see in their dreams blue-clad soldiers ransacking and burning houses, ragged and starving families begging from door to door, jayhawkers torturing and killing old men, Union militia and regular Federal troops shooting or hanging captured com-rades on orders from their commanders to treat guerrillas as outlaws, bodies floating facedown in creeks, their hands chalk white and nearly severed by a futile struggle to get free of the piano wire that bound them. Sometimes the house and families were their own, the tortured and dead men their fathers, grandfathers, brothers, friends, or neighbors. Only one response could be made to such deeds, and they gave it—that and more.[2]

But in doing so they paid a price: degeneration. For many—too many—the thirst for revenge became mixed with a lust for loot, causing the difference between guerrilla and bandit to blur, then all but disappear. At the same time, a growing number of bushwhackers—probably not a majority but certainly a large minority—began killing for the sheer thrill of it or callous, cold-eyed thugs who, to quote what a Confederate general wrote about Missouri partisans after observing them in Texas, "regard the life of a man less than [that] of a

Figure 1.1 Bloody Bill Anderson. COURTESY OF THE STATE HISTORICAL SOCIETY OF MISSOURI.

sheep-killing dog." For such as these, bushwhacking ceased to be a means to an end and instead became an end in itself. "You need not consider me a Confederate officer," declared George Todd, one of the top guerrilla chieftains, to a captive a few days before the attack on Fayette. "I intend to follow bushwhacking as long as I live."[3]

Thus the men riding along the Glasgow Road. Some still wore Federal uniform jackets, the disguise by which they had come close to catching Fayette's garrison off guard. Most, though, were clad in loose-fitting, low-cut, large-pocketed hunting shirts ornately embroidered across the front and around the cuffs with green garlands and red and blue flowers, the loving handiwork of mothers, sisters, and girlfriends but rarely a wife—bushwhacking did not lend itself to connubial ties. All colors of ribbons dangled from felt hats cocked on one side by a crescent- or star-shaped pin to which was attached a plume or squirrel tail. Pants tucked into knee-high, Mexican-spurred boots completed the costume, except for the most important feature of all—a pistol belt with two holstered revolvers and often a couple more thrust into the belt. They were, typically, five- and six-shot .36-caliber Colt Navies—the best, because they were the most accurate and reliable handguns of the time. The bushwhackers did not carry so many of these weapons out of vain bravado but for the very practical reason that they wanted to be able to keep firing rapidly without stopping to reload, a tricky and risky business on horseback in the midst of a fight, even if you had, as they did, preloaded spare cylinders, in those large shirt pockets. In their hands the revolvers were not simply tools of war but instruments of execution.[4]

This was especially true for the man riding at the head of one portion of the column. Dressed entirely in black—hat, velvet shirt, pants, boots—he was lean and sinewy and looked taller sitting in the saddle of his large black horse than his actual height of five ten. Long, thick, dark-brown hair, a thin mustache, and a short pointed beard framed his narrow, high cheekboned face. The eyes—cold, blue-gray, unfathomable—struck one observer as a "cross between an eagle and a snake." In sum, he looked like what he was: a killer—a point driven home by the scalps of Federal soldiers dangling from his horse's bridle.

His name was William T. Anderson, but Unionists and secessionists alike called him Bloody Bill. By autumn 1864 this man had incarnated the savage war raging across Missouri, a savage war about to reach its savage climax.[5] How and why did he become this? The answer—at least as much answer as can be attained—lies back in time and in another place.

AGNES CITY, KANSAS: NIGHT, JULY 3, 1863

Bill Anderson and his younger brother Jim stood in the dark at the side of the building, long steel-gray revolvers in their hands. They said nothing. There was nothing to say. They knew what they were going to do, and it was too late to turn back even if they wanted to. They didn't.

Bill and Jim had come to Kansas in the spring of 1857, along with their mother, Martha, a brother named Ellis, and three sisters, Mary Ellen, Josephine, and Janie. There they had joined their father, William Anderson Sr., on his land claim and helped build a log cabin some thirteen miles east of Council Grove near the fringe of the western frontier. For Anderson Sr. this was yet another beginning in a life of beginnings that had seen him wander from his native Kentucky into Missouri, next up to Iowa, and then back to Missouri, from where he journeyed to California in quest of gold. Like most, he did not find it—at least not much—and after a year or two he returned to his family and farm outside of Huntsville, Missouri. Then in 1855, soon after Kansas was opened up to settlement, he went there and acquired his claim, which was located on the east

bank of Bluff Creek beside the Santa Fe Trail, the passageway for wagon cara-
vans bound to and from New Mexico. Still in his mid-thirties, he was not old,
yet he was no longer young as age was reckoned then. It was time to settle
down. If he and his family could not make it in Kansas, there might not be
another chance, certainly not as good as this one appeared to be.

And they did make it—not big, but enough. By 1860, according to the
United States census, the Anderson homestead had an estimated value of
$1,000, which was above average for the time and place. In addition, Anderson
engaged in the freighting business and operated a grocery store on the Santa Fe
Trail, selling provisions to passing wagon trains. To be sure, his family still lived
in a log cabin—one room with a sleeping loft—but such dwellings were standard and by no means indicated poverty, given that the same census credited the
Andersons with possessing one horse, two milk cows, two oxen, and 320 acres
of land, half of which was owned by young Bill and appraised at $500. Like-
wise, the Andersons being from Missouri did not cause problems, even though
the vast majority of settlers in the area were midwestern Northerners. On the
frontier the main concern was Indians, not Border Ruffians, and the sole violent
incident that was purported to be politically motivated occurred on September
14, 1856, during the height of the "Bleeding Kansas" troubles, when a band of
men calling themselves Freestaters raided the village of Neosho Rapids, killing a
woman in the process. No one could rightly blame Southerners like the Andersons for this outrage, and none did. [6]

But if the Andersons stayed clear of political involvements, they failed to
escape hard luck or resist the enticing temptations of the frontier, where semia-
narchic conditions offered all sorts of opportunities to those who had enough
courage, yet not too many scruples, to grasp them. First Ellis, the second oldest
son, had an altercation with a drunken Indian; he shot him through the head
and fled to Iowa, from where it was reported falsely that "he got in a row . . .
and was killed." Next, in the latter part of 1860, Mrs. Anderson died when a
lightning bolt struck her while she was gathering wood chips. She was thirty-six,
and she left six children behind, the youngest a boy only a year old named
Charles. And then Bill, the eldest son, succumbed to the temptations.

Born in Kentucky in 1839, on coming to Kansas with his family, he initially enjoyed the reputation of being a "good boy, steady as a clock." For a
couple years he worked for Eli Sewell, who had a ranch on Elm Creek, west of
Council Grove. When he reached twenty-one he acquired his own claim and
seemed, like his father, to be making it. Then he started accompanying wagon
trains on the Santa Fe Trail. After several trips he became "second boss" of one
of those trains. Soon after it set out, however, he and the top boss returned to
Council Grove and claimed that they had "lost" the train because the horses
and mules had strayed. If true, their tale indicated gross negligence. More
likely, they had sold the animals and pocketed the money.

Suspicion that such was the case increased when Bill began taking ponies into Missouri, then returning with horses, which he sold around Council Grove. Where and how did he obtain the ponies? An interesting question, particularly for ranchers with ponies missing from their stables.[7]

The coming of the war did not put an end to Anderson's "pony business." Instead, he expanded it to include all-around banditry—or as it was called in Kansas, jayhawking. He was being far from unusual in doing this. During 1860 and on into 1861 Kansas experienced severe drought, the "granddaddy" of many more to come. Weeks and months passed with little or no rain, and not a flake of snow fell throughout the winter. Crops withered in the fields, streams stopped running and rivers dwindled to a muddy trickle, wells dried up, and cattle had to be butchered before they became too scrawny to eat. Only food sent in large quantities by relief societies in the East prevented mass hunger, even famine. Thousands of people left Kansas, which in January 1861 finally achieved statehood. Thousand of others would have done the same had they not been too destitute to leave. Among them were large numbers of men who followed the same course taken by Bill Anderson—a course that became all the more appealing when the chaotic conditions created by the war provided a ready-made excuse to carry out plundering forays into western Missouri in the name of suppressing rebellion and liberating slaves. Nor was jayhawking confined to the eastern side of the border. In August 1861 Kansas governor Charles Robinson sent a posse into Johnson County when its inhabitants complained that they feared jayhawkers more than invasion by Missourians, and in his January 1862 message to the state legislature, Robinson declared that the whole state was "overrun with thieves and highway robbers."[8]

Among those hard hit by the drought and accompanying depression was Arthur Inghram Baker of Agnes City. Indeed, for all intents and purposes Baker *was* Agnes City. He had founded the place in 1856, naming it after his mother, and he owned all of its buildings, with the main one being his two-story stone house, the finest dwelling for many miles around. Furthermore, he had been the postmaster, justice of the peace, and a probate, then a district judge. Last, but hardly least, he possessed land holdings valued at $6,000—$1,000 in personal property, "one of the best corn fields" in Kansas, a large cattle herd, and along with practicing law he operated a highly profitable provision store near his house at the Rock Creek crossing of the Santa Fe Trail, eight miles east of Council Grove. Manifestly, Baker, a native of Virginia and just thirty-seven in 1861, was a person of substance and status.

Yet he wanted more of both—a lot more. To that end, in January 1861 he became the owner and editor of the *Council Grove Press* and purchased that town's only hotel. This proved to be a mistake. Owing to drought and war, neither the newspaper nor the hotel attracted sufficient patronage, with the result that in the fall of 1861 he had to sell them at a large loss. At the same time his

Figure 1.2 Jim Anderson. COURTESY OF CARL BREIHAN.

Agnes City farm suffered a total crop failure and lost many of its cattle. Intensi-
fying these woes and quite likely contributing to them, in March 1861 his wife,
Susan, died at the age of thirty-four, leaving him a widower with a young
daughter.

Little wonder then that by late 1861 Baker was a despondent and desperate
man—so much so that soon after the failure of his newspaper and hotel enter-
prises, he decided to join those other Kansans who were "stealing themselves
rich in the name of liberty," and he took up jayhawking. He induced a group of
young men in the Agnes City area to accompany him on a raid into southwest
Missouri—one of them was Bill Anderson and another, according to some
sources, was Jim Anderson, now eighteen and a partner in his brother's "pony
business."

Their foray ended in fiasco. While they were camped along Drywood Creek
in Missouri, a Union patrol came along and, evidently thinking that they were
bushwhackers, attacked them. All escaped except a man named John Ratcliffe,
who was killed, and Baker, who was captured, accused of attempting to join
Brig. Gen. James S. Rain's unit of Sterling Price's army, and incarcerated in the

military prison at nearby Fort Scott, Kansas. Here he languished in durance vile until March 24, 1862, when he came before a military commission—only to be released because the officer prosecuting his case preferred no charges against him. Those in a position to know subsequently asserted that he owed his freedom to the "influence of friends," with the most influential one being U.S. Senator James H. Lane of Kansas, the Republican political boss of the state and an occasional "general" whose plundering, burning sweeps through western Missouri during the summer and fall of 1861 gained him the well-deserved title of "King of the Jayhawkers." Although nominally a Democrat, Baker had supported Lane politically and, it is safe to assume, financially as well, especially after being arrested.[9]

Meanwhile, Bill Anderson resumed his former activities around Council Grove and also began conducting raids into Missouri, where his main, although not exclusive, victims were Unionists. Given his family background, no doubt Bill possessed Southern sentiments, but his motive for engaging in bushwhacking along with jayhawking was financial, not ideological. Thus, when he attempted unsuccessfully to recruit a neighbor named Charles Strieby for one of his Missouri expeditions, he stated, "I don't care any more than you for the South, Strieby, but there is a lot of money in this [bushwhacking] business."[10]

Early in April, Baker returned to Agnes City and promptly published a letter in the *Emporia News* declaring that his "object in going to Missouri was not to act in antagonism to my Government, but, on the contrary, [I] was advised by those who have the welfare of the Nation and Kansas at heart," and that it was "impossible for me to be a secessionist" because "all I love best on earth is here"—his family, his home, and his business and financial interests. Evidently this explanation satisfied the people around Council Grove and Emporia, or at least most of them, for he was not subjected to any persecution or harassment despite Kansas being a place where, in the words of a *New York Tribune* reporter, the "mere suspicion that one is disloyal may result in his being shot."[11]

What Baker most needed and wanted, now that he was again a free man, was a new wife. With that object apparently in mind, he began making trips to the Anderson cabin, only five miles away, to visit Mary Ellen, who at fifteen had attained marriageable age. So frequent were his calls and so warm (if not intimate) did his relationship with Mary Ellen become that her father assumed that they soon would be married. Hence, when in early May word came that Baker had instead become engaged to Annis Segur, a seventeen-year-old schoolteacher, the senior Anderson exploded with rage, as did Bill and Jim. Baker, they believed, had betrayed Mary Ellen and in so doing dishonored both her and her family.[12]

Adding injury to insult, Baker then formed and led a posse in pursuit of Lee Griffin, a cousin of the Anderson brothers and a member of their gang, whom he rightly suspected of stealing two horses from his future father-in-law, a farmer named Ira Segur. Tracking the pilfered equines eighty miles to the west of Council Grove, Baker found one of them on a ranch, the other in the possession of a Mexican suspected of belonging to the Anderson gang. He took the horses and the Mexican back to Agnes City, then obtained a warrant for the arrest of Griffin.

For the Andersons, father and sons, this was the ultimate offense. On May 11 they rode to Baker's house and threatened to kill him unless he withdrew the accusation against Griffin. He refused, and since he had a number of armed friends and employees backing him, the Andersons returned home to await a more favorable opportunity.

William Anderson Sr. decided not to wait long. The next morning, having primed himself with whiskey, he grabbed a double-barreled shotgun and rode to Baker's house, where he yelled at him to come outside. When for obvious reasons his quarry stayed put Anderson stormed into the house and, ascertaining that Baker was in a bedroom on the second floor, started up the stairs. Baker stepped out of the bedroom onto the landing and let loose with his own shotgun. Anderson tumbled back down the stairs, a bubbling red hole in his chest. Whether or not Baker was aware that Anderson, prior to entering the house, had stopped off at Baker's store for another slug of whiskey and that a close friend of Baker's—to be precise, Eli Sewell, Bill Anderson's former employer —had removed the caps from his shotgun, rendering it harmless, is unknown.

Bill and Jim made no immediate attempt to avenge their father. Incredible as it may seem, according to some sources Bill even "made up" with Baker. But if so, then Baker did not trust him and suspected, with good cause, that the Anderson brothers were merely biding their time. Therefore, he obtained a warrant for Bill's arrest on charges of horse stealing, presumably hoping that this would lead to his getting "short shrift and a long rope," the fate that had befallen the Mexican found with one of Segur's horses.

A posse led by Charles Strieby—whom Bill had tried to recruit for bushwhacking in Missouri—soon located and arrested Bill, then took him before a justice of the peace. But instead of a quick guilty verdict and a legalized lynching, the official, no doubt to Baker's dismay, released Bill on bond. That night Bill and Jim headed for Missouri and safety. Three weeks later a stranger with a wagon and team showed up at the Anderson homestead and took Mary Ellen, Josephine, and Janie to Missouri as well. They left behind the graves of their mother and father—and possibly that of their infant brother, Charles.[13]

The Andersons had not made it in Kansas.

Hence, Bill and Jim Anderson now stood in the shadows beside Baker's store on the night of July 3, 1862. They intended to kill Baker and do it in such a way that before he died, he would wish that he never had been born.

A stranger and at least two other men, one of whom was Lee Griffin, accompanied the Anderson brothers. The stranger was now at Baker's house, telling him that he was the boss of a wagon train and wanted to buy whiskey for his teamsters so that they could celebrate the Fourth of July in proper style.

Baker should have been on his guard. In fact, he *was* on guard, having heard that the Andersons were lurking in the vicinity, and he had therefore taken the precaution of placing extra cartridges on the sills of every window in his stone house. Nevertheless, he responded to the stranger's request by saying that he would go to the store and get the desired whiskey. Strapping a brace of pistols around his waist, Baker set out for the store, followed by the stranger and George Segur, the sixteen-year-old brother of Baker's new wife, whom he had married two days after killing William Anderson Sr.

On reaching the store, Baker unlocked the door and went inside with the stranger and young Segur. While the latter lit a lamp, Baker offered the stranger a drink of whiskey but then saw that the bottle was empty. Taking the lamp, he pulled up a trap door and descended stairs leading to a cellar, where he refilled the whiskey bottle from a barrel. As he closed the gurgling tap, he turned around and saw Bill and Jim Anderson.

"I was not expecting you here now, Bill," Baker muttered.

"But you do see me, Ingrham Baker," Bill replied, "and I am the last man you will ever see, God damn your soul!"

Faced with death, Baker did not blink. He whipped out a pistol and fired, striking Jim Anderson in the fleshy part of a thigh. Even as Baker pulled the trigger, Bill Anderson's revolver roared, and a bullet left Baker moaning on the cellar floor. Bill and Jim then went back up the stairs, shot and wounded young Segur, and dumped him down into the cellar with Baker. Next they closed the trap door, piled boxes and barrels atop it, and set them afire. For a while they watched, their faces glowing crimson in the light of the crackling, leaping flames. When sure that Baker and the boy were doomed, they left the now-burning store and proceeded to torch Baker's house, from which his wife and several other occupants had fled on hearing the gunshots and seeing the store burn. After setting fire to Baker's barn for good measure, the Andersons and their companions rode rapidly through the night back toward Missouri, stopping at each stage station to obtain fresh mounts, thereby easily outdistancing a pursuing posse led by Charles Strieby. As the sun began to rise, they reached Missouri, their mission of retribution accomplished.[14]

In the morning the men searching the smoldering remnants of Baker's store found his body in the cellar. The head, arms, and legs had been reduced to ashes. Yet flames had not killed him. Instead he had shot himself in the head so as to avoid being burned alive. Young Segur, by crawling through a small window, had managed to escape from the cellar—but not from death. That afternoon he died after telling the tale, between gasps of pain, of how Bill Anderson, assisted by brother Jim, had claimed his first victims.[15]

They would be far from his last.

CHAPTER TWO

I'M HERE FOR REVENGE

WESTERN MISSOURI: JULY 1862–APRIL 1863

On returning to Missouri, Bill and Jim Anderson became, if not so already, full-time bushwhackers. At first they operated in Jackson County, to the south and east of Kansas City. But not for long. Early in the fall William Clarke Quantrill, chieftain of the largest and most successful partisan band in western Missouri, received complaints that the Andersons were robbing pro-Southern as well as Unionist civilians. At once he sent forth a detachment that apprehended Bill and Jim, took away their horses, and warned them to be more discriminating henceforth in their depredations or else they would be killed.[1]

Following this humiliation—for which they never forgave Quantrill—Bill and Jim shifted their operations to other sections of western Missouri, in particular the area between Lexington and Warrensburg. They belonged, declared an editorial in the *Lexington Weekly Union* of February 7, 1863, to a guerrilla gang composed mainly of men from Kansas, one of whom had been Lee Griffin prior to his being killed "a short time since." The captain of the band, also a Kansan, was a man named Reed, and "they all claim[ed] to be southern men," thereby securing the "sympathy and protection . . . of the disloyal" wherever they went. In fact, though,

> They are the basest robbers ever left at large in a civilized community. They are the men who killed Gaston, Barker, Iddings, Phelps, King, Myres, and McFaddin—who have robbed every loyal man in that whole country [between Lexington and Warrensburg], of money, silver plate, blankets, horses, and everything else which could be turned into money. They boast of their deeds of daring and murder, their robbery of the mail and express at various times, and there is no act of villainy or cold blooded murder, where a dollar could be made, which they will not do.

The editorial continued, "we confidently expected to overtake them," but "winter has nearly passed" and "summer soon will be here again, and our troubles will be upon us, unless they are captured."

In spite of the *Weekly Union*'s warning, not only did the winter pass without the Andersons or any of the other Kansans-turned-bushwhackers being captured, but even before the official arrival of summer they participated in one of the most spectacular raids of the entire war.

THE SANTA FE TRAIL: MAY 1863

No one in Council Grove had expected bushwhackers to show up there, 120 miles from the Missouri line by way of the Santa Fe Trail. Yet on the afternoon of May 4, 1863, there they were, two or three dozen strong, sitting on their horses outside the town and gazing at it like wolves contemplating their prey.

Among them were Bill and Jim Anderson. Quite literally they had come home. The previous night the band had camped at Bluff Creek, and their faces must have been grim as they beheld what was left of the family cabin: nothing. Like the dwellings of many other Missourians who had resided along the Santa Fe Trail and were known or suspected of being pro-Confederate, it had been destroyed by Kansans determined to eradicate all traces of treason from their land (and in the process perhaps acquire some useful plunder).

On the other hand, when Bill and Jim crossed Rock Creek, they no doubt broke into satisfied grins. Agnes City, like Arthur Inghram Baker, also was no more. All that remained were the stone foundations of Baker's house and store and some fire-charred timbers. They had done a thorough and permanent job some ten months prior.

Word that bushwhackers were approaching on the trail had reached Council Grove the night before, with the result that the authorities had sent a message to Fort Riley asking for military help, and a "few determined men" had made ready to defend the place. But instead of a horde of yelling, revolver-firing guerrillas charging into the town, only two of them quietly trotted their horses up the main street. One was Dick Yager, subsequently described by the *Council Grove Press* as "one of the worst guerrillas in Missouri, equaled only by Quantrel [*sic*] himself." Yager, however, came not to rob, burn, and kill. What he wanted was a dentist for his bad toothache. Knowing Council Grove from prewar days as a teamster on the Santa Fe Trail, he rode to the office of Dr. J. H. Bradford, dismounted, and went inside while his companion remained outside to keep an eye on things.

"Take out this tooth," he told Bradford. "It hurts like hell!"

"All right," Bradford replied, "but if I take care of the tooth, will you leave the town alone?"

"Yes," Yager agreed. "Just get this damned tooth out!"

Figure 2.1 William Clarke Quantrill. COURTESY OF
CARL BREIHAN.

Bradford thereupon extracted the tooth, and Yeager and the other bush-whacker then rode out of the town; whether or not he paid Bradford is unknown, but it is doubtful that the dentist pressed him on the matter. One did not do that with a patient armed with four revolvers and a reputation for know-ing how to use them.

The bushwhackers passed the night in a camp near Council Grove, drink-ing and visiting with acquaintances from the town. In the morning they marched west about fifteen miles to Diamond Springs, where they sacked a store, murdered its owner, and shot his wife in the arm. Surely this last was unintentional. Killers though they were, the bushwhackers were Victorians, brought up to respect women—at least, those who were white and respectable. Besides, they knew, as did the Federals, that violence directed against the enemy's womenfolk would expose their own to the same. It was a line that no one on either side wished to cross—not yet, anyway.

From Diamond Springs the raiders continued west on the Santa Fe Trail until they reached the crossing of Cottonwood River, where they set up camp. On May 6, a sixty-man posse led by James L. McDowell, U.S. marshal at Leav-enworth, surprised the guerrillas and scattered them in every direction. Yager and the Andersons escaped, but ten others were captured. These men, along with seven "secesh" later arrested at Council Grove, were turned over to Federal sol-diers, who soon shot the prisoners as they were "attempting to escape."

With his posse's horses being too exhausted to pursue the remaining guer-rillas, McDowell dispatched a courier to Emporia with instructions to form a

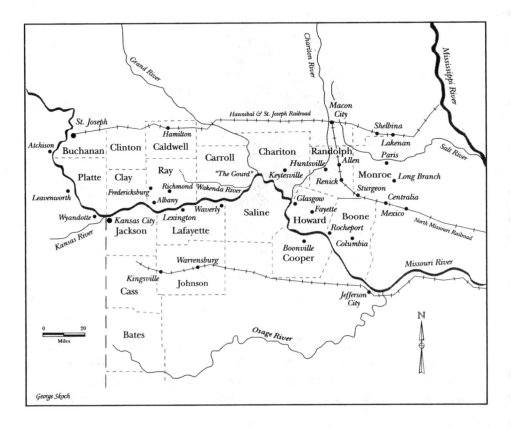

George Skoch

force there and use it to intercept them at another point on the Cottonwood. Anticipating such a move, Yager evaded it by swinging farther south to the Neosho River, crossing it, then returning north to the Santa Fe Trail. There his band resumed its rampage, killing two men, looting stores and houses, holding up another stage, and stealing fresh mounts at every opportunity before disappearing back into Missouri on the morning of May 9. Although they had suffered heavy losses (five more guerrillas were captured and killed after fording the Neosho) the raiders had penetrated nearly 150 miles into Kansas and exposed the vulnerability of that state's defenses—something that was not lost on Quantrill, who began mulling over plans for a far more ambitious raid, one that would teach the Kansans a lesson they never would forget.[2]

Other than that Bill Anderson participated in Yager's foray and survived it, as did brother Jim, nothing is known of his role, although it can be safely assumed that he did his share of plundering and killing. So far since fleeing Kansas, he had done nothing to set himself apart from scores of other bushwhackers. Except for the brief period he headed a small gang in Jackson County, he had not become one of the numerous and petty guerrilla "captains." There is no mention of him whatsoever in the Federal military reports covering the period from May 1862 to May 1863, and the sole extant newspaper reference to him (and Jim) is the one in the *Lexington Weekly Union* previously quoted. Obviously, while he had become a "known" bushwhacker by the spring of 1863, he was far from famous or, to use the common expression of the day, "notorious."

Soon, though, this would change.

WESTERN MISSOURI AND EASTERN KANSAS: MAY–JULY 1863

As the editor of the *Lexington Weekly Union* had predicted, the advent of summer brought "troubles." In fact, the war along the border rapidly attained a ferocity that equaled, if not surpassed, that of 1862. Bushwhacker incursions into Kansas became so frequent and devastating that late in May, Kansas newspapers reported that all of the state's border counties from the Kansas River south to Fort Scott were virtually depopulated. At the same time, Kansas "Red Legs"—so-called because of the red leather leggings they wore—ravaged Missouri's western counties, robbing and killing with little or no attempt to distinguish between Unionists and secessionists.

Federal troops seemed incapable of protecting Kansas against the guerrilla raids. Likewise, the bushwhackers failed to deter the Red Legs; nowhere is there a documented instance of their engaging their Kansas counterparts in combat or even attempting to do so. Perhaps, as some charged, a tacit, secret understanding existed between the two whereby they would "live and let live"—or, to be more exact, steal and let steal. Certainly such an understanding would have been logical in view of the fact that since both parties were well-armed, well-mounted, and skilled in partisan tactics, they would have had little to gain and much to lose by fighting one another.[3]

But if the bushwhackers stayed clear of the Red Legs, they showed no such restraint when it came to harassing Union troops and terrorizing Unionist civilians. By July a series of deadly ambushes, climaxed by the rout of a 150-man detachment of the Ninth Kansas Cavalry near Westport on June 17, in which fourteen of the soldiers were killed, had so cowed Federal forces in Jackson County that they rarely dared to venture forth from the fortified towns that they garrisoned. This gave the bushwhackers almost total domination of the countryside, and they used it to plunder, burn out, and often torture and/or murder pro-Union civilians. Scores of Unionists either sought refuge in the towns or fled into Kansas, Iowa, and Nebraska. Like the border counties of Kansas, much of Jackson County became nearly depopulated, and many of the few farmers who remained did not bother to plant crops.[4]

Conditions in adjoining Lafayette County were better, yet bad enough. There, reported the garrison commander at Lexington on July 15, bushwhacker bands led by "Poole and Anderson" swept through a German settlement fifteen miles from that town, murdered five people, one of them a girl, and wounded nine others. They also strung up a prominent local Unionist but spared him when friends intervened on his behalf (that is, they gave the raiders sufficient money). Finally Anderson captured and then paroled a militiaman to be exchanged for "one notorious William Ogden," a guerrilla being held prisoner in Kansas (perhaps a member of Yager's raiding party who for some reason had not been shot while "attempting to escape"). If Ogden was not released, Anderson had warned, then the militiaman's "life is to be forfeited."[5]

This is the first reference to Anderson to be found in all 128 volumes of the *Official Records of the Union and Confederate Armies.* It tells us two things: first, that Anderson, following the Yager raid, returned to the Lexington–Warrensburg area; second, and more important, that he now headed his own band and thus had finally become a guerrilla "captain," recognized as such by both Federals and other bushwhackers.

Moreover, Anderson's was a comparatively large gang, with between thirty and forty members, many of them from Kansas. As to its character, what it did in the attack on the German settlement tells us much, but more can be surmised from a look at the young man who would become Anderson's top lieutenant: Archie Clements.

Only eighteen in 1863 and from near Kingsville in Johnson County, where Union militia had burned his home and killed his brother, Clements was called "Little Archie" because of his diminutive stature—barely five feet. But what he lacked in size he more than made up for in ferocity. None of the bushwhackers had compunctions about killing enemies; it went with being a bushwhacker and was simply a matter of doing unto others what they would do unto you. Little Archie, though, liked to kill and to kill just for the sake of killing. After awhile not even that contented him, so he started working his victims over with a knife, sometimes after they were dead, sometimes while they still lived. He enjoyed that, too.[6]

Two weeks and some days after shooting up the German settlement in Lafayette County, Anderson's band showed what it was capable of doing in another county, this one in Kansas.

"THE JUNCTION," WYANDOTTE COUNTY, KANSAS: JULY 31–AUGUST 1, 1863

Except on its northeast corner, where the Missouri River makes an abrupt upward bend, Wyandotte County, Kansas, is separated from Jackson County, Missouri, by only a road, called for obvious reasons the Stateline Road. Hence it was a simple matter for Anderson's gang to cross into that county on the night of July 31 and head west. Four miles from the town of Wyandotte (now Kansas City, Kansas) the gang came upon and destroyed a wagon train bound for New

Figure 2.2 Archie Clements. COURTESY OF THE STATE
HISTORICAL SOCIETY OF MISSOURI.

Mexico. Continuing on, the bushwhackers soon reached "the Junction," a cross-roads between Wyandotte and Shawnee Mission. Here they attempted to rob a recently constructed stone house. But the owner, despite being wounded, managed to fight them off with the aid of several other men, wounding two of the raiders in return.

Frustrated and infuriated, the raiders vented their feelings by pillaging a neighboring house, burning the home of a Shawnee named Big Knife, and murdering a Wyandotte County commissioner. They then dashed back into Missouri, stopping only long enough to torch four more houses and slay another man.

In the morning Union cavalry picked up their trail, followed it across the Stateline Road, and surprised them in their camp, killing four and scattering the rest. One of the dead bushwhackers, a man attired in a Federal uniform, had been shot repeatedly while astride his horse, yet had not fallen. When the soldiers got close enough, they discovered why: he was strapped to his saddle. Some of the guerrillas did this to prevent falling to the ground, should they fall asleep during long night rides. Evidently this one preferred to die rather than be wounded, captured, and then hanged—the fate recently suffered at Fort Leaven-worth by the "somewhat notorious" Jim Vaughn, who had been apprehended in, of all places, a Wyandotte City barbershop. At this stage of the war the Federals rarely took bushwhackers prisoner except to execute them, and even if that had not been their policy, they would not have spared a "bushman" wearing their uniform.[7]

For the bushwhackers, the Wyandotte raid could be deemed a failure, for whatever it gained them in the way of money, loot, and the satisfaction of burn-ing out and killing some Kansans, it did not compensate for four dead and at least two wounded comrades. Moreover, although it enhanced Anderson's status as a "notorious" guerrilla chieftain, his family was about to pay a heavy price for that notoriety.

KANSAS CITY, MISSOURI: AUGUST 13, 1863

> The large three-story brick building in the Metropolitan Block, McGee's Addition, owned by G. C. Bingham, Esq., and occupied for the last two weeks as a guardhouse, fell in yesterday afternoon, carrying with it the adjoining building south. There were in the building at the time nine women prisoners, two children, and one man. Four women were killed, the balance escaped without fatal injuries.
>
> —*Kansas City Daily Journal of Commerce,* August 14, 1863

On June 16, 1863, Brig. Gen. Thomas Ewing Jr., brother-in-law of Gen. William T. Sherman and former chief justice of the Kansas Supreme Court, assumed command of the District of the Border, comprising West Missouri and most of Kansas. That very same day, Quantrill's band carried out the devastat-ing Westport ambush, slaying fourteen soldiers. This humiliating disaster steeled Ewing's determination to escalate the campaign against bushwhacking by doing what military leaders before and since have done when unable to sup-press guerrillas by direct methods: Attack them indirectly through their families, friends, and sympathizers in the civilian population. Starting in July, per his orders, Union troops arrested nine western Missouri women on charges of spy-ing for and otherwise aiding Confederate partisans. Among them were Mary Ellen and Josephine Anderson, now, respectively, sixteen and fourteen. Ten-year-old Janie Anderson, at her request, went with her sisters, having nowhere else to go.[8]

The Federals took the female prisoners to Kansas City and locked them up on the second floor of a three-story brick structure called the Thomas Building on the east side of Grand Avenue between Fourteenth and Fifteenth

Streets in what was known as McGee's Addition. The building was practically new, having been erected in 1859, and until recently had been the residence of its owner, George Caleb Bingham, the famous painter, who added the third story for his studio.

In an adjoining building being used as a guardhouse, the soldiers, in order to obtain more space, removed the partitions and posts that the center girder supporting the second floor rested on. The guardhouse building began to sag against the prison building, subjecting it to a great and growing pressure. Cracks appeared in the first-floor walls, and plaster dust began falling. Notified by a guard of the danger, the provost marshal sent a soldier to inspect the building. While he was doing so on the afternoon of August 13, it suddenly collapsed, burying the female inmates and one man beneath a huge pile of bricks and timber. Rescuers pulled the crushed corpses of four women from the rubble. One was that of Josephine Anderson. Mary Ellen and Janie survived, the former crippled and disfigured for life, the latter with two broken legs, an injured back, and a lacerated face.[9]

News of the incident enraged the bushwhackers. They believed, and always would believe, that Union soldiers had deliberately undermined the prison building in a vicious scheme to kill the prisoners. Anderson's violent reaction soon revealed its singular purpose. Hitherto he had killed ruthlessly, but as a means to an end: revenge against Arthur Inghram Baker, plunder during a raid, to terrorize Union troops and civilians. Now, though, killing—especially killing enemy soldiers—became an end in itself, one driven by a bloodlust so strong that sometimes Anderson would foam at the mouth and sob because he could not continue pumping bullets into still more blue-uniformed victims.[10]

Out of the wreckage of the building on Kansas City's Grand Avenue came not only the mangled bodies of young women. It also sparked the emergence of "Bloody Bill" Anderson, a man who lived for death and who shortly before he himself died declared: "I have killed Union soldiers until I have got sick of killing them."[11]

LAWRENCE, KANSAS: AUGUST 21, 1863

As dawn broke on August 21, 1863, William Clarke Quantrill reined his horse to a halt on the crest of a ridge overlooking Lawrence, Kansas. Twenty-six, blond, blue-eyed, lean and wiry, the guerrilla captain was a striking figure. Less than three years earlier he had lived in Lawrence, where he went by the name of Charley Hart and belonged to a gang that rustled cattle and "jayhawked" slaves in Missouri—to be sold back to their masters. Forced to flee Lawrence late in 1860 when the authorities issued a warrant for his arrest, he sought and found refuge in Jackson County, Missouri, by luring three Kansas abolitionists into a deadly trap on the pretense of liberating slaves. He gained the confidence of the local inhabitants by telling them that he was from Maryland and that the three dead abolitionists were actually members of a jayhawker gang that had murdered his older brother—all lies, for he was a native of Ohio and had no older brother. Following the outbreak of the war in Missouri, he, too, had served with Sterling Price until the general retreated back toward Arkansas, whereupon Quantrill returned to Jackson County. There he joined, then headed, a small guerrilla band in the Blue Springs area. A superb horseman and crack shot, cool and calculating, and daring yet never rash, he transformed his farm-boy followers into skilled killers whose slashing raids, murderous ambushes, and elusive tactics soon turned Jackson and adjoining counties into "Quantrill country" and made him the top bushwhacker chieftain for all of western Missouri, a status confirmed by his receiving a captain's commission in the Confederate partisan rangers.[12]

Now he was about to return to Lawrence—but not alone. With him were three hundred and fifty guerrillas and one hundred Confederate recruits whom he had invited to come with him and be "christened." On August 10 he had held a meeting of bushwhacker chieftains, Bill Anderson included, telling them, "Let's go to Lawrence . . . the great hotbed of abolitionism in Kansas. All the plunder, or the bulk of it, stolen from Missouri, will be found stowed away in Lawrence. And we can get more revenge and more money there than anywhere else."

Initially the others leaders rejected Quantrill's proposal. To be sure, he had carried out several successful forays into Kansas, bringing back loot and leaving behind corpses. But raiding Lawrence was something else. They would have to ride fifty miles into Kansas to get there, and before they did surely the alarm would be sounded, and hundreds of armed men—the town had a population of three thousand—and probably regular Union troops as well would be waiting for them. No, it was too risky.

Quantrill persisted, meeting all of their arguments with better arguments. Finally, reluctantly, they agreed. Then came word of the Kansas City prison collapse. All lingering doubts disappeared, replaced by a fierce desire to go to Lawrence and kill, even if it meant dying themselves. The lust for vengeance burned hottest in Bill Anderson. In his mind he could hear the screams of his sisters buried beneath the rubble on Grand Avenue. Only one thing would drown them out—at least for a time.

Atop the ridge overlooking Lawrence, Quantrill and his raiders waited for the scouts he had sent ahead to find out what the situation was in town. While waiting, some of the men lost their nerve. "Let's give it up," they insisted. "It's too much." Quantrill had not come this far to quit now. "You do as you please," he replied. "I'm going into Lawrence!" He then spurred his horse forward. The bushwhackers followed him, revolvers cocked and ready to fire.

They met no resistance. Lulled into a false sense of security by past alarms of guerrilla raids that came to nothing, the unprepared people of Lawrence were taken completely by surprise. Realizing this, the bushwhackers swarmed through the town, robbing, looting, burning, killing. They spared women and children; men and teenaged boys were shot down mercilessly. Bill Anderson personally slew fourteen, more than any other chieftain. He made his victims crawl at his feet in the dust, tears coursing down their faces as they clawed at his boots, begging to be spared. Around him, still clad in their nightclothes, wives, sisters, and daughters pleaded for their menfolk's lives. Anderson paid them no heed; perhaps he did not even hear them. He merely cocked his revolver and slowly placed its muzzle to each man's head. Perhaps their shrieks and cries were drowned out in his mind by the shrieks and cries of young women crushed under a pile of snapped timber and fallen bricks. . . .

Not until he shot the fourteenth man did Anderson speak: "I had two sisters arrested in Kansas City by Union men, for entertaining Southern sentiments. They were imprisoned in a dilapidated building used as a guardhouse. This building was known to be unsafe, and, besides, it was undermined. One night that building fell, and my two sisters, with three other ladies, were crushed to death."[13]

At 9:00 A.M., four hours after they entered, the bushwhackers rode out of Lawrence, leaving behind a town in flames and the bodies of close to two hundred men and boys. Before departing, Anderson told a Lawrence woman, "I'm here for revenge and I have got it."[14]

Yet it was not enough revenge. It never would be.

CHAPTER THREE

SUCH A DAMN OUTFIT

BAXTER SPRINGS, KANSAS: OCTOBER 6, 1863

On the morning of October 6, Quantrill and four hundred bushwhackers rode along the Fort Scott Road through the southeast corner of Kansas, on their way to spend the winter in Texas. Would-be historians would later say that they had left Missouri because of Order No. 11. Issued just four days after the Lawrence Massacre by Brig. Gen. Thomas Ewing Jr., it expelled all disloyal residents from three Missouri counties bordering Kansas—Jackson, Cass, and Bates—with the object of making it impossible for the guerrillas to maintain themselves in this region. Actually, though, it had no such effect. While thousands of people were forced to vacate their homes—one of them was an eleven-year-old-girl who would become the mother of President Harry S Truman—their smokehouses remained filled with hams and bacon, and stray hogs, cattle, and chickens roamed the countryside. Moreover, the swarms of Union troops who enforced the expulsion order, many of them vengeance-seeking Kansans, posed little threat to the bushwhackers, who lay low in their hideouts amid the virtually impenetrable hills and forests of the Sni-A-Bar Creek area in eastern Jackson County, emerging only at night to forage. What caused Quantrill to head south for the winter, something he had done the previous autumn, was the unusually early advent of cold weather stripping bare the foliage that provided concealment for the ambushes and surprise attacks that gave the bushwhackers their name.[1]

Toward noon a messenger from Dave Poole, who commanded the advance guard on the Fort Scott Road, brought word to Quantrill that a small Federal fort was up ahead at Baxter Springs. At once Quantrill sent reinforcements to Poole with an order to attack the fort from the south while he and his main body moved against it from the north. Perceiving an opportunity to overrun the garrison while it was outside the fort eating lunch, Poole charged before Quantrill could get into position. He drove the Federals into the fort—merely a four-foot-high log barricade open at one end—but blasts from a howitzer forced his men to fall back.

Figure 3.1 George Todd. COURTESY OF THE
STATE HISTORICAL SOCIETY OF MISSOURI.

Meanwhile, as Quantrill neared the fort, he saw eight wagons and about one hundred Union cavalry approaching. They were the headquarters train and personal escort of Maj. Gen. James G. Blunt, commander of the District of the Frontier, who was riding in a buggy accompanied by some staff officers and a demijohn of whiskey. Quantrill was too far away to identify him, but he knew an inviting target when he saw one and ordered his men to deploy for an attack. Before they could do so, however, Quantrill's chief lieutenant—the bold and brutal George Todd—yelled "Charge!" Blunt's escort, mostly raw recruits, fired a ragged volley, then fled in wild panic. Blunt, thanks to his superb horse—which he had mounted on seeing the guerrillas, thinking they were cavalry from the Baxter Springs fort because so many of them wore blue uniform jackets—managed to escape, as did a handful of other Federals. The bushwhackers slaughtered the remainder, eighty-nine in all, among them the musicians of the headquarter's band, including a twelve-year-old drummer boy. Burial parties subsequently found many of the bodies so badly mauled or in some cases burned that they no longer were recognizable as human beings, much less identifiable.

Because they were toward the rear when Todd ordered the charge, Anderson's men, some forty in number, did not participate in the massacre. Instead they ransacked the Union wagons and thus secured the lion's share of the plunder. This may have satisfied them but not their leader. He craved Yankee blood, not loot. He joined Todd in urging Quantrill to resume the assault on the fort.

"No," Quantrill answered between swigs from Blunt's demijohn, his share of the spoils. "We've done enough. Let's not take any more chances."

Anderson was disgusted. What sort of leader was Quantrill to pass up so good a chance to kill more Union soldiers? Wasn't that what it was all about? Quantrill might be content with the killing done at Lawrence and now here at Baxter Springs, but, he, Bill Anderson, was not.[2]

NORTHERN TEXAS: MARCH 1864

"If you are not a damn set of cowards, come on out in the open and fight!" Bill Anderson shouted.

"You have the most men with you—if you are not a set of damn cowards, come on in and take us out!" George Todd yelled back.

Anderson and his twenty men began shooting, and Todd and his nine followers fired back from the sheltering woods. After fifty-odd shots had been exchanged, Anderson's party rode away into the night. Todd's detachment thereupon returned to Quantrill's camp on the bank of Mineral Creek, twelve miles northwest of Sherman, Texas.[3]

Why were bushwhackers fighting bushwhackers, albeit more for show than for real? Three reasons supply the answer. First, many of Quantrill's band, including original members and top lieutenants, left him after arriving in Texas. Some were appalled by the excesses of the Lawrence massacre, others felt disgruntled by what they deemed an unfair division of spoils from Lawrence, and still more believed that with the defeats in 1863 at Gettysburg, Vicksburg, and Chattanooga, the Confederacy had "gone up the spout." Therefore, to continue the guerrilla war in Missouri would serve no purpose, not even to provide an excuse for what had increasingly degenerated into wanton plunder and murder.

The second reason took the form of Brig. Gen. Henry McCulloch, commander of the Confederate Sub-District of North Texas. The more he saw of the Missouri bushwhackers, the less he liked what he saw. Soon after they arrived, their drunken sprees, robberies, and occasional murders so terrorized the inhabitants of the region that scores fled—and many who stayed would have welcomed Union occupation. Moreover, attempts by McCulloch to have the bushwhackers perform some military service proved futile, as for instance when, having been sent to round up deserters, they shot more than they returned. By February McCulloch had concluded that the bushwhackers were "but one shade better than highwaymen," and the only thing that prevented him from disarming and arresting them was that he needed a clear-cut case and sufficient force.[4]

The first of these needs came to him as a consequence of the third reason for Todd's and Anderson's men taking potshots at one another. Early in March

Sterling Price, who acted as de facto military commander of all Missouri Confederates in the Trans-Mississippi, persuaded Quantrill to reduce his band to eighty-four men and transfer the rest to the regular service. This reorganization led Quantrill to take on the title of colonel. Todd became captain; Anderson, first lieutenant. Anderson's rank testified not only to his enhanced status but also to the change in the makeup of the guerrillas. Most of the "old men," those who formed the early bands, had left and the ones who remained tended to be wild, reckless teenagers for whom bushwhacking was an end in itself and who admired the "charge straight ahead and the devil take the hindmost" style of Anderson—and of Todd.

Becoming the number-two leader under Quantrill in no way pleased or placated Anderson. He did not like serving under him—or, for that matter, Todd—and was ready to assert his independence at the first opportunity. That came soon enough when a member of Anderson's gang named Morgan stole a bolt of cloth from one of Quantrill's Jackson County followers. Quantrill, who tried to maintain a modicum of discipline, had Morgan disarmed and escorted across the Red River into Indian Territory with a warning that if he returned to Texas, he would be shot. Unimpressed, Morgan came back, then robbed and murdered a farmer. On learning of this crime, Quantrill dispatched a squad to capture and execute Morgan.

News of Morgan's death enraged Anderson. His initial impulse was to kill Quantrill; then he calmed down. Not only was Quantrill a fast draw and dead shot, there was a better way of getting back at him. Declaring that he no longer would remain in "such a damn outfit," Anderson left the Mineral Creek camp, taking with him about twenty men, most of them from his own gang, and went to McCulloch's headquarters in Bonham. There he told the general that Quantrill was responsible for the various robberies and murders that had occurred in recent months. This was exactly what McCulloch had been waiting for. He summoned Quantrill to Bonham at once.

Quantrill came—accompanied by all of his bushwhackers except a dozen under Todd, who stayed behind to guard the camp. Arriving at noon, he dismounted and entered McCulloch's headquarters while his men waited outside. McCulloch promptly placed him under arrest and had him lay his gun belt on a bed. He then invited him to dinner, after which they would discuss matters. Quantrill refused, exclaiming, "By God! I don't give a goddamn if I never eat another bite in Texas!" With a shrug, McCulloch went off to eat, leaving Quantrill guarded by two soldiers. Presumably he thought that Quantrill's followers would not dare attempt to rescue him.

They did not have to. A few minutes after McCulloch left, Quantrill pretended to go over to a watercooler, then grabbed his revolvers, disarmed the guards, did the same to two sentinels at the outside door, and ran onto the

Figure 3.2 Bush Anderson. PRIVATE COLLECTION.

street, shouting, "Boys! The outfit is under arrest! Let's get out of here!" Seconds later he and his bushwhackers were galloping full tilt back to their camp.

Infuriated and embarrassed by Quantrill's escape, McCulloch sent a mounted regiment of Texas militia in pursuit, with orders to bring Quantrill back alive or dead. Anderson's gang joined the chase and during the afternoon exchanged harmless shots several times with Quantrill's party. At sundown the militia halted and bivouacked for the night. Quantrill, on reaching the camp, told Todd what had happened, and Todd set out with nine men on a scout. First he came upon the bivouacked militia, who fled in panic when one of the guerrilla's pistols accidentally discharged.

Satisfied that the militia represented no threat, Todd headed back to the camp, only to encounter Anderson's gang. Neither Todd nor Anderson, reckless as they were, was so rash as to make what almost surely would be a suicidal attack on the other.

In the morning Todd, with a small force, again conducted a reconnaissance. This time he met the militia approaching the camp.

"What the hell are you doing?" he asked.

"We have been sent down by General McCulloch's orders to get Quantrill," came the reply.

"Well, don't you know that you are not going to get him?" Todd sneered, advising the militia to go back to Bonham and tell McCulloch that if Quantrill was bothered any more, "he will turn his bushwhackers loose in Texas."

Todd and his men then rode away. The militia did likewise, returning to Bonham, where they delivered Todd's warning to McCulloch. Utterly disgusted, the general wrote his department commander that he could do nothing about the depredations of the "Captain Quantrill command" because his troops lacked the "physical and moral courage to arrest and disarm them."[5] Obviously they were not the bravest soldiers in the world, yet in fairness to them it should be observed that ill-trained cavalry armed with single-shot, muzzle-loading rifles were no match in an open fight with the bushwhackers and their individual arsenals of revolvers. This had been demonstrated at Baxter Springs, and it would be demonstrated again on an even bloodier scale some months later near a place in Missouri called Centralia.

Several days after their bloodless confrontations with the militia and fellow bushwhackers, Quantrill's men crossed over the Red River into Indian Territory, beyond McCulloch's jurisdiction. About April 10 they began marching north toward Missouri, where the grass was turning green and the leaves sprouting. Anderson and his followers headed back around the same time. He left behind in Sherman a woman with whom he had spent much time during the winter. She went by the interesting name of Bush Smith and "worked" at a Sherman saloon operated by Jim Crow Chiles, a transplanted Missourian. Although presumably her favors were available without that formality, Anderson married her.[6] Maybe the jilting of Mary Ellen by Baker had something to do with it; perhaps he did it as a joke or during a drunken spree—or, conceivably, he loved her. In any case, if any of his men worried that marriage would have a softening effect on him, they soon would be reassured. During the next six months Anderson did things that made what he hitherto had done look like a mere rehearsal—which in a sense it was.

JACKSON COUNTY, MISSOURI: APRIL–MAY 1864

"Lonely and weary, with continual watching," wrote Julia Lovejoy of Baldwin City, Kansas, to her family in Massachusetts on May 10, 1864, "we are looking every hour for 'Quantrill,' with his horde of fiends, to sweep through this entire region, and murder indiscriminately and burn every house, in his march of death! We are told he is VERY NEAR us and about to make another raid . . . and he says 'he will make clean work this time.' . . ."[7]

Julia Lovejoy need not have feared. Quantrill had neither the intention nor the means to carry out another Lawrence-style raid. On arriving back in his "stomping grounds" late in April, he found that although many of the people expelled by Ewing's Order No. 11 had been allowed to return by a new Union commander, the area had been so thoroughly devastated during the past fall and winter by Union troops and bands of Kansas Red Legs that it offered little in the way of sustenance. Worse, at least from a military standpoint, the Federals had stationed in Jackson County the Second Colorado Cavalry—twelve hundred "hardy mountaineer boys"—for the specific purpose of combating the bushwhackers. Consequently, Quantrill sent word to his men, who had dispersed into small squads, to reassemble in Lafayette County, where conditions were less "squally" and the prospects of profitable operations accordingly more promising.[8]

It was the last order that he ever would issue to most of them. Back in March, at about the time Quantrill reduced and reorganized his band, Thomas C. Reynolds, the Confederate claimant to the governorship of Missouri, wrote to him urging him to join the regular military service. "The history of every guerrilla chieftain," stated the highly educated Reynolds, "is the same. He either becomes the slave of his men, or if he attempts to control them, some officer or private rises up, disputes his authority, gains the men, and puts him down."[9]

Reynold's warning proved prophetic. For some time George Todd had in many respects been exercising de facto leadership, as witness his giving the order to charge at Baxter Springs and his role in scaring off McCulloch's militia. Now he decided to make it overt and total. Soon after the issuance of the order to rendezvous in Lafayette County, Todd flagrantly cheated during a card game with Quantrill. Finally Quantrill threw down his cards and declared that he would play no more unless Todd played fair. Todd then made a threatening remark, whereupon Quantrill said he was afraid of no man. Instantly, Todd yanked out a pistol and, aiming it point-blank at Quantrill, said, "You are afraid of me, aren't you, Bill?" Faced with sure death, Quantrill answered, "Yes—I'm afraid of you."

Todd lowered his revolver, Quantrill stood up, walked over to his horse, mounted, and rode away. Not one of the guerrillas present moved to back him.[10] They knew that he was no coward and that he was smarter and more clever than the crude, illiterate Todd. But they were no longer fighting for a cause—or if they were, they sensed that it was a lost cause and the war was in its last stages. What the bushwhackers wanted now was to kill as many Unionists, get as much plunder, and have a good time doing it while it still could be done. For this, what better leader than Todd? He was as fearless as he was ruthless, and so long as his men obeyed orders and fought well during a raid or fight, he did not give a damn what was done—or to whom.

Early in June, Quantrill—with his teenage mistress (or wife), Kate King, and a few still-loyal followers—headed across the Missouri and established a hideout in the rugged Perche Hills of Howard County.[11] No doubt he felt bitter and resentful; it would have been strange if he did not. In raiding Lawrence had he not conceived, planned, and executed the most brilliant exploit of its kind during the entire war up to that time? Only John Hunt Morgan's foray into Indiana and Ohio surpassed it in scale, and that had ended in disaster. Yet what had been Quantrill's reward for Lawrence and for Baxter Springs, the sole successes achieved by Southern arms in the Trans-Mississippi throughout all of 1863? Ingratitude and an attempt to arrest him by the Confederate authorities, betrayal by his own men. Well, he would lay low, bide his time, and wait. Sooner or later the traitorous George Todd would be killed, as would that son-of-a-bitch Bill Anderson—the reckless way that they fought guaranteed this—and then those who had turned against him would turn back to him. It was only a question of when.

WESTERN MISSOURI: JUNE–JULY 1864

With Quantrill no longer performing on the bloody stage of the guerrilla war in Missouri, Todd and Anderson became the prime candidates for his starring role. For a while it seemed that Todd would claim it, and in fact had it. Acting on Quantrill's plan to shift operations to Lafayette County, his band carried out a series of successful hit-and-run attacks on Federal posts and patrols, waylaid stagecoaches, cut telegraph wires, and spread destruction and death among Unionists, with the climax coming on June 13, when they ambushed and burned a wagon train near Lexington, slaying eight of the soldiers guarding it. In response, the Second Colorado launched a counteroffensive, scouring the countryside with mounted patrols and employing "foot scouts" to lie in wait for the bushwhackers, thereby "meeting them at their own game." The latter tactic proved so successful—the Second Colorado's commander claimed to have "mustered out" thirteen guerrillas by using it—that Todd ordered his men to scatter while he considered the situation.

Characteristically, his solution was to attack: If the Coloradans wanted to fight bushwhacker style, he would show them how really to do it. Declaring, "It's time to go out and bushwhack a few Feds," he assembled sixty men, then made a rapid night march deep into Jackson County, where on the morning of July 6 he set up an ambush on the Glasgow Road south of Independence. Hours passed, but apart from a stagecoach, which was duly robbed and placed out of sight, nothing occurred. Finally, late in the afternoon, having concluded that Federal fish weren't biting that day, Todd and another guerrilla rode out onto the road, intending to tell the stagecoach driver that he could continue his journey. As they did so, a twenty-six man detachment of the Second Colorado came jogging down the road. It had not been planned that way, but Todd and his companion became the bait. On seeing them, the Coloradans gave chase, expecting easy prey. Instead they suddenly found themselves beset by a horde of bushwhackers, revolvers popping. Despite being taken by surprise, the Coloradans stood and fought; even the guerrillas later conceded that they showed "sand." But along with a carbine and saber, each was armed with only one pistol—and that, an inferior model that "couldn't hit a thing." Hopelessly outnumbered and outgunned, they broke and fled when their bullet-riddled commander went down, leaving behind eight dead. Todd's men suffered only one wounded, and they had demonstrated to the Coloradans that while they and other Union troops might hold the larger towns, the rest of the country belonged to the bushwhackers any time they desired it.[12]

Shortly after this encounter, the Second Colorado moved across the Missouri River into Platte County, where Confederate partisans had captured Platte City and were terrorizing Unionists. Taking advantage of the regiment's absence, Todd's band headed in the opposite direction. On the night of July 20 they occupied Arrow Rock on the bank of the Missouri in Saline County, "confiscated" forty horses and $20,000, and then retired into their favorite hideout, the impenetrable wilderness of the Sni-A-Bar. Here the band remained for most of the next two months, unmolested by the enemy and making only a few small-scale sallies.

Pressure from Federal forces had nothing to do with Todd taking a "vacation" from bushwhacking. Rather, he wished to preserve and prepare his men for an upcoming invasion of Missouri by Sterling Price's army out of Arkansas. There, during the spring, the Confederates had driven back the Union army into its fortifications around Little Rock, opening the way for yet another attempt by Price to "liberate" Missouri, an event pro-Confederates eagerly anticipated. To quote from the official report of Maj. Gen. William S. Rosecrans, the new Federal commander in Missouri, all summer, "traitors of every hue and stripe . . . swarmed into life at the approach of the great invasion. Women's fingers were busy making clothes for rebel soldiers out of goods plundered by the guerrillas, women's tongues were busy telling Union neighbors 'their time was coming.'" If Price succeeded in taking St. Louis or at least occupying the state capital at Jefferson City while in the east the Confederate armies held onto Richmond and Atlanta, Southern independence still might be won. In any event, his coming was the last chance for the Confederate cause in Missouri, and everyone knew it.[13]

With Todd taking it easy, nothing stood in the way of Anderson moving to the forefront of the guerrilla war—and so he did. During the next four months he would preside over a bloody bacchanalia that far surpassed in ferocity all that had gone before it. William Quantrill, George Todd, and other bushwhacker chieftains were merciless killers, but only Bill Anderson became what one Missourian wrote of him: "Like the rider of the 'pale horse' in the Book of Revelation, death and hell literally followed in his train."[14]

CHAPTER FOUR

LET THE BLOOD FLOW

WESTERN AND NORTHERN MISSOURI: SUMMER 1864

Early July found Bill Anderson in a jolly mood—for him. Since returning to Missouri in May, bushwhacking had been good. Thus on June 12, near Kingsville in Johnson County—Archie Clements's home territory—Anderson's and Yager's bands, some eighty strong and all attired in Yankee uniforms, had been able to ride up in a "friendly manner" to within point-blank pistol range of fourteen unsuspecting Federal troopers and kill twelve of them and shoot another so badly that he was unlikely to live. They then stripped the bodies and scalped one of them. Hitherto, the bushwhackers had rarely engaged in scalping, but in 1864 they would make it a common practice—none more so than Anderson's men who, with Little Archie Clements taking the lead, made it their trademark.[1]

Following the Kingsville massacre, Anderson proceeded north into Lafayette County, where on June 14, twelve miles south of Lexington, his band routed a thirty-five-man Union detachment escorting a wagon train, killing nine and destroying the wagons.[2] His men then dispersed into small groups, with the main one under Anderson himself heading westward to the Missouri River village of Wellington. There, on June 24, Anderson took the postmaster and two other Unionists hostage, then sent a message to Brig. Gen. Egbert Brown, Federal commander of the District of Central Missouri with headquarters at Warrensburg, declaring that he would shoot the three captives if Brown executed a prisoner named Erwin. Brown countermanded the execution but at the same time ordered the arrest and "close confinement in irons" of six "prominent rebels or rebel sympathizers in the vicinity of Wellington." They would, he notified Anderson, be put to death "if our friends [the hostages] are not returned to safety."[3]

Satisfied with having, at least for the time being, saved Erwin from the hangman's noose, Anderson released the hostages and, reversing course, headed east along the river until he reached Waverly. Here, on the morning of July 4, he and his followers, which an eyewitness described as numbering fifteen or sixteen—"all stout, able-bodied looking men"—each armed with one to four revolvers and a carbine, attempted to seize a docked steamboat taking on freight. The crew, realizing its peril in time, cut the mooring cable, and the craft escaped despite having its pilothouse splintered with 150 to 200 bullets, one of which wounded the watch in the arm. The bushwhackers thereupon "quietly repaired" to Waverly, a strongly pro-Southern village and home of Confederate general Jo Shelby, and celebrated the Fourth by having their photographs taken, getting drunk, and firing on another steamer as it passed by.[4]

Two days later Anderson, with a force that the Federals estimated to be one hundred but probably consisted of less than half that strength, showed up on the outskirts of Lexington. Its garrison, believing itself outnumbered and fearing a repeat of the June 16 fiasco, dared not venture forth from its fortifications. On the other hand, some of the many Confederate sympathizers who lived in and around the town visited the bushwhacker's camp, bringing with them copies of the latest issues of Lexington's two newspapers. Anderson read them and disliked what he read—in particular, editorials urging citizens to resist the guerrillas and the reports of Col. James McFerran, commander of the garrison, and Cap. Milton Burris, who had been in charge of the wagon train escort. Anderson decided to make his displeasure known—and provoke the Federals in Lexington to come out and fight. On July 7 he dictated or supervised the writing of a long letter that combined threats with taunts and was addressed "To the editors of the two newspapers in Lexington, to the citizens and community at large, General Brown, and Colonel McFerran and his petty hirelings, such as Captain Burris, the friend of Anderson":

Mr. Editors:

In reading both of your papers I see you urge the policy of the citizens taking up arms to defend their persons and property. You are only asking them to sign their death warrants. Do you not know, sirs, that you have some of Missouri's proudest, best, and noblest sons to cope with? . . . But listen to me, fellow-citizens; do not obey this last order. Do not take up arms if you value your lives and property. It is not in my power to save your lives if you do. If you proclaim to be in arms against the guerrillas I will kill you. I will hunt you down like wolves and murder you. You cannot escape. . . . I commenced at the first of this war to fight for my country, not to steal from it. I have chosen guerrilla warfare to revenge myself for wrongs that I could not honorably avenge otherwise. I lived in Kansas when this war commenced. Because I would not fight the people of Missouri, my native State, the Yankees sought my life, but failed to get me. Revenged themselves by murdering my father, destroying all my property, and have since that time murdered one of my sisters and kept the other two in jail twelve months. But I have fully glutted by vengeance. I have killed many. I am a guerrilla. I have never belonged to the Confederate Army, nor do my men. A good many of them are from Kansas. I have tried to war with the Federals honorably, but for retaliation I have done things, and am fearful will have to do that I would shrink from if possible to avoid. . . . Young men, leave your mothers and fight for your principles. Let the Federals know that Missouri's sons will not be trampled on. I have no time to say anything more to you. Be careful how you act, for my eyes are upon you.

Colonel McFerran:

I have seen your official report to General Brown of two fights that have taken place in Johnson and La Fayette Counties with your men. You have been wrongfully informed, or you have willfully misrepresented the matter to your superior officer. I had the honor, sir, of being in command at both of those engagements. To enlighten you on the subject and to warn you against making future exaggerations, I will say to you in the future let me know in time, and when I fight your men I will make the report. . . . [McFerran's troops] are such poor shots it is strange you don't have them practice more. Send them out and I will train them for you.

To Burris:

Burris, I love you; come and see me. Good-by, boy; don't get discouraged. I glory in your spunk, but damn your judgment.

General Brown:

General: I have not the honor of being acquainted with you, but from what I have heard of you I would take you to be a man of too much honor as to stoop so low as to incarcerate women for the deeds of men, but I see that you have done so in some cases. I do not like the idea of warring with women and children, but if you do not release all the women you have arrested in La Fayette County, I will hold the Union ladies in the county as hostages for them. I will tie them by the neck in the brush and starve them until they are released, if you do not release them. . . . General, do not think I am jesting with you. I will have to resort to abusing your ladies if you do not quit imprisoning ours. As to the prisoner Ervin [*sic*] you have in Lexington I have never seen nor heard of him until I learned that such a man was sentenced to be shot.

I suppose he is a Southern man or such a sentence would not have been passed. I hold the citizens of Lexington responsible for his life. The troops in Lexington are no protection to the town, only in the square. If he is killed, I will kill twenty times his number in Lexington. I am perfectly able to do so at any time.

Yours, respectfully,

W. Anderson
Commanding Kansas First Guerrillas

(Editors will please publish this and other papers copy.)

Presumably by the same means that he received the newspapers, Anderson had the letter conveyed into Lexington, where it came into the possession of Colonel McFerran, who sent it to General Brown at Warrensburg. Brown in turn passed it on to departmental commander Rosecrans in St. Louis "as a curiosity and specimen of a guerrilla chief's correspondence."[5] As a result, twenty-odd years later it finally was published—in the *Official Records of the Union and Confederate Armies,* probably the sole document of its kind in that mammoth 128-volume compilation of reports and correspondence. It tells us that Anderson wanted to be perceived as an invincible warrior fighting to avenge unforgivable personal wrongs suffered at the hands of dastardly foes, and it also reveals that he was not without a sense of humor—at least of sorts.

Anderson lurked for several days more around Lexington, waiting for a response to his letter either by word or act. With none coming, and knowing that it was dangerous for guerrillas to linger in one place too long, he and twenty-one followers, late on the afternoon of July 11, used a skiff to cross the Missouri River into Carroll County, where they promptly went on a rampage, murdering nine civilians in less than four hours. One victim, on being told that he was going to be shot because he was a Unionist, cursed Anderson, whereupon Little Archie knocked him down with a pistol butt, then cut his throat from ear to ear with a bowie knife. Another unfortunate, a young German farmer named Solomon Baum, suffered in some ways an even worse fate. Thinking that the bushwhackers were militia because they all wore Federal uniform jackets, he declared himself to be a loyal Unionist although in fact pro-Confederate (a rare thing for a "Dutchman" to be in Missouri). Not until a rope was being placed around his neck did he realize his mistake, whereupon he fervently proclaimed his true sentiments and his reason for concealing them—to no avail. Anderson merely said, "Oh, string him up. God damn his little soul, he's a Dutchman anyway."

The bushwhackers' blue coats brought on a similar fate, but in a different way, for their next victim. Riding on, they came to the farm of Cyrus Lyons, who was digging a well with the aid of a neighbor while another friend watched. Anderson called Lyons to the fence and asked:

"Why ain't you in the service?"

"I do belong to the militia," Lyons answered, thinking that Anderson was a Union officer.

"Well, why in hell ain't you out trying to drive out the bushwhackers? Didn't you know they were in the country?"

"No—nobody's told me that. But I belong to Captain Calvert's company of Moberly's regiment, and while in service, I always try to do my duty and am ready to do it again."

"Well, I guess you have done enough. *I am Bill Anderson, by God!*" And so saying, Anderson shot Lyons dead.

Several other guerrillas then leaped their horses over the fence and did the same to Lyon's two companions. Resuming their march, the gang halted only to rob a family, threatening to kill both the husband and his wife, and at nightfall crossed the Grand River into Chariton County.[6]

Such was Anderson's first unforgettable visit to Carroll County. And it would not be the last.

After a short rest, the band continued eastward through Chariton into Randolph County. There, just as night began to give way to light on the morning of July 15, the raiders entered Huntsville by way of the Keytesville Road. Because the horsemen in advance wore blue uniforms, the few townspeople who were up and about at first paid them little heed—until the sound of shattering glass and splintering wood filled the air. While some of the bushwhackers kicked in doors and looted the stores, others roused merchants and clerks to open the safes. Since there were no soldiers in or near the town, the bushwhackers went about their work methodically

Old acquaintances scarcely recognized Bill Anderson—eight years or more had passed since he had left the family farm near Huntsville with his mother, brothers, and sisters to go to Kansas. Most remembered him as a rather shy, slow student in school, a quiet boy who much preferred spending his time outside playing with bows and arrows to reading and writing indoors. Now, sitting astride a big charger and clad in a gold-trimmed black hunting shirt, the old schoolmate had obviously changed. For a while, as Jim and he chatted with friends, their homecoming resembled a "social gathering."

Like nearly everyone in Huntsville, George Damon was sound asleep when the guerrillas rode into town. Up from St. Louis on business, Damon's first hint of trouble came when men outside his hotel door pounded for him to open it. Doing so, the salesman found himself staring into the bores of several big pistols.

The men holding the guns took Damon's money, allowed him to dress, then led him down to the street, where he joined other prisoners. Nearby, some bushwhackers using hammers and crowbars struggled to open a safe they had wrestled to the sidewalk. Suddenly one of them spotted Damon's military belt buckle inscribed with "U.S." Cursing, the bushwhacker ordered Damon to remove the buckle and declared that he intended to shoot him. Nervous fellow captives whispered to the trembling salesman to stay calm and do nothing rash.

Bill Anderson overheard the curses and threats. Glancing over at Damon, he, too, saw the buckle with the big "U.S." stamped on it.

"Come here," he growled.

The pressure was too much for Damon. Panic-stricken, he sprang from the crowd and ran up the street.

"Damn you," the bushwhackers yelled as they followed, "stand when we tell you!" The salesman kept running. Just as he rounded a corner, a volley of shots rang out. He went down but an instant later was up, and amid the whoops and shouts of his pursuers, he raced among some houses.

Setting spurs to his mount, Anderson himself gave chase. As the terrified salesman began climbing the fence at the rear of the hotel, the chieftain rode up, aimed, and fired. Damon pitched over into the yard. With blood pouring from his numerous wounds the dying man dragged himself toward the hotel, crying for water. When the innkeeper started forward to help, Anderson pointed his pistol. "If you don't go away and let that man alone," he warned, "I'll shoot you." The innkeeper backed away.

Anderson watched as the victim painfully inched his way into the hotel. Finally he motioned to two of his men: "Go and finish him!" he ordered.

The two bushwhackers stomped into the dining room, where they met the hotel owner's wife. Sobbing, she pleaded with them not to shoot, only to be told, "We would shoot Jesus Christ or God Almighty if he ran from us." Then, laughing, they bent down to listen for Damon's heartbeat. Hearing none, they holstered their revolvers and turned to leave. Spotting Damon's ring, one of them paused long enough to pluck it from the dead man's finger and place it on his own.

At sunup, with fresh horses and nearly $50,000 in cash, the bushwhackers left Huntsville. Jim Anderson, with a small band, headed one way; Bill and the rest, another. Soon afterward, a Federal patrol came stealing up behind Bill's company south of the town. For the next several miles a running battle took place along a road littered with abandoned plunder—but not the greenback-stuffed valise carried by Bill. Eventually the guerrillas' horses pulled away, and the pursuit ceased. Bill Anderson's return to Huntsville did not begin to compare with Quantrill's return to Lawrence. Even so, the people there would remember him for the rest of their lives.[7]

For most of the ensuing week Anderson operated along the Missouri River, occupying the village of Rocheport and firing at steamboats. Then on the morning of July 23 his gang struck the North Missouri Railroad at Renick, where it looted stores, tore down the telegraph wires, and set fire to the depot before moving northward on to Allen (present-day Moberly), with the object of seizing a train due to arrive there at noon. This scheme was frustrated, however, by the unexpected presence at Allen of a forty-man Union detachment sent from Glasgow to collect a shipment of arms and ammunition. Although taken by surprise while eating lunch, the Federals quickly converted the station house into a fort by barricading the windows with salt barrels and bales of hay. They held their assailants at bay until a troop-filled train that had been summoned by telegraph from Macon compelled the guerrillas to ride away. Neither side suffered any casualties, but before departing, the guerrillas shot twenty horses tethered outside a tobacco warehouse.[8]

Twenty-seven soldiers and twelve civilian volunteers gave pursuit. They killed two of the raiders and wounded several more but could not overtake the main body, which scattered into the brush. The following day the soldiers, who belonged to the Seventeenth Illinois Cavalry, headed back to their base at Glasgow via the Fayette Road. Having chased and dispersed the supposedly fearsome Anderson gang as if it were a pack of cowardly dogs, they saw no need to take any special precautions and so did not. This proved to be a mistake. Suddenly, near Huntsville, a horde of bushwhackers attacked from an ambush, revolvers blazing. The soldiers tried to fight back, found that they couldn't, and fled, leaving behind two dead. Dismounting his big horse, Little Archie rolled up his sleeves, drew a sharp knife, and went to work on the corpses. First he scalped them; then he cut a circle of skin the size of a "Spanish dollar" from the forehead of one and a strip of skin from the forehead of the other. When he finished, Anderson scrawled a note on a piece of paper and pinned it on the coat collar of one of the bodies. It read:

YOU COME TO HUNT BUSH WHACKERS. NOW YOU ARE SKELPT.
CLEMYENT SKEPT YOU. WM. ANDERSON.[9]

From the Huntsville area Anderson struck off in a northeasterly direction. On the morning of July 27, the raiders burst into the quiet square of Shelbina on the Hannibal & St. Joseph Railroad. After lining up and robbing the male inhabitants, they looted the stores, pillaged several houses, and burned the depot and two railroad cars. During the holdup Anderson singled out a nattily dressed young man wearing a stovepipe hat. But on being ordered to "shell out," the young man handed over only a dollar coin.

"That's all you have?"

"Yes."

Contemptuously, Anderson tossed the coin back. "A man dressed as fine as you are and with only a dollar in his pocket needs money worse than I do."

The bushwhackers next rode east five miles and torched the depot at Lakenan. A few miles farther brought them to the bank of the Salt River. Here they set ablaze the 150-foot-long railroad bridge and destroyed a house, the water tank, and an abandoned blockhouse built earlier in the war to protect the span. They then headed south, having stopped through traffic on the Hannibal & St. Joseph, the only railroad to traverse the entire breadth of Missouri. Not since 1861 had any Confederate force, regular or irregular, accomplished such a feat.[10]

Three days later, after being rejoined by brother Jim and his followers, Bill Anderson again approached Huntsville. From friendly civilians he learned that the town now had a garrison and that the father of the officer in charge resided on a farm two miles south. At once Anderson and the band went to the farm and demanded that the father, a seventy-two-year-old former judge, tell where he kept his money. The old man refused. The bushwhackers then slipped a noose around his neck and suspended him from the crossbeam of a gateway. When he began to lose consciousness they let him down, only to jerk him back up after he still refused to tell. One of the raiders, finding a heavy whip, began flogging him "unmercifully." A screaming and sobbing little girl ran into the yard and begged the guerrillas to stop hurting her grandpa. They dropped him to the ground, but after shoving the girl back into the house, they once more pulled him up and resumed whipping him.

Meanwhile, a black servant of the judge ran to Huntsville with word of what was happening on the farm. Men had to grab and hold the garrison commander to prevent him from rushing to the rescue of his father—and to a sure and terrible death in what was an obvious trap.

Back at the farm, the old man's body stopped twitching. Thinking he was dead, the bushwhackers gave him some parting lashes, then remounted and rode rapidly west. Incredibly, though, the judge still lived. And even more incredibly, on regaining consciousness he half staggered, half crawled all the way to Huntsville, the noose still around his neck.[11]

The bushwhackers now split into two parties. One, numbering eleven and led by Bill Anderson, rode due west. The other, commanded by Jim Anderson, headed northwest. On the morning of Sunday, July 31, the second group came to a schoolhouse, where thirty-two young men and boys were holding a religious service. Jim's band took them prisoner and marched them northward to a church in Macon County. Here Jim asked those men who would fight for the

South—if they would fight at all—to step forward. Twenty-four did so, where-upon they were released. The bushwhackers then subjected the eight recalci-trants, to quote a subsequent account in the *Huntsville Randolph Citizen,* "to all sorts of indignities, such as being stripped of their clothing," whipping two of them while shaving the heads of four more, and forcing two others to "kneel in prayer under threats of immediate execution." Having thus amused themselves on the Sabbath, the band then allowed the eight to go free and proceeded west into Chariton County.

The next morning, August 1, Bill Anderson's party forded the Grand River and entered "the Gourd," an area in southeast Carroll County between the Grand and Missouri, obviously so called with but a glance at a map. Now in what was largely unfamiliar territory, Anderson compelled the first civilian he met to come along as a guide and did the same with a second. Toward evening he stopped at a farmhouse, where he ordered the four women present to provide supper for him and his men. After eating, some of the bushwhackers stretched out in the yard and fell asleep while others played tunes on a fiddle or flirted with the women. Anderson did not bother to post a picket or sentinel—a cardinal mistake for guerrillas, one that would cost Quantrill his life a year hence in Kentucky.

It could have cost Anderson his life then and there. A dozen home guards-men had been following the bushwhackers' trail, and it led them to the farm-house. Leaving one man behind to hold their horses, the guardsmen crept cautiously through a cornfield until within easy range, then opened fire with rifles and shotguns. Bullets and pellets poured through the house's open door and windows, slightly wounding two of the women and a baby but striking none of the bushwhackers who, although caught by surprise and in several cases literally napping, reacted quickly, scrambling for cover and firing back with their revolvers.

Terrified by the gunfire, one of the women ran screaming from the house out into the yard. Anderson yelled at her to stop, then dropped her with a bul-let in the shoulder when she continued running. One of the captive guides, tak-ing advantage of the turmoil, managed to slip away. The other bolted toward the cornfield. Several guerrillas fired at him but all missed, and it seemed that he, too, would escape. Then one of the home guardsmen, mistaking him for a bushwhacker, shot him dead.

He was the only man that these amateur soldiers managed to kill, whereas just one bushwhacker suffered a wound—and it a mere scratch. Worse, some of the guardsmen's horses, unused to the roar of gunshots, broke loose. Seeing this, and by now realizing that they were outmatched when it came to firepower, the attackers scurried back through the cornfield. The bushwhackers sprang out of the house, leaped into their saddles, and thundered off on the hunt. Some of the guardsmen managed to mount their horses; the rest fled on foot into the brush. Several were wounded but all escaped except one rider, a man named John Kirker. His horse stumbled, throwing him to the ground. A bushwhacker named John Maupin galloped up, shot Kirker, then jumped from his mount. Drawing a knife, he first sliced off Kirker's scalp. Then he plunged the blade deep into the neck and sawed away until the head fell off. Still not content, Maupin stabbed and slashed the body before finally standing up, his hands dripping blood and his clothes splattered with it. Maupin was a recent recruit. Obviously Anderson's band now had another member who enjoyed using a knife as much as Little Archie.

Maupin's grisly deed did not bother the bushwhackers—it would be a salutary warning to other civilians who had the temerity to attack them—but some of them asked Anderson why he had shot the woman. Wasn't that going a bit far? With a shrug, he answered, "Well, it has to come to that before long, anyway." In fact, for him, with Josephine's death and Mary Ellen's mangling, it had already come.[11]

Having thus disposed of the guardsmen, Anderson's party resumed its march, stopping along the way to pillage and burn two houses, loot a third, and take several men prisoners to serve as guides. Two militia companies gave pursuit, but it soon became dark, they lost the raider's trail, and so stopped to rest for the night. Anderson pushed on until midnight, then camped at a farm near the Ray County line.

In the morning he crossed into Ray County near a settlement named Russellville. Here, he and his men, all dressed in Federal uniforms as usual, met Russell himself and his son, a Union officer on leave. For a while Anderson talked in a pleasant manner to the unsuspecting pair; then he suddenly pulled out a revolver and shot the officer dead while another guerrilla, probably Clements, did the same to the father. Other bushwhackers stripped and robbed the corpses, after which they all rode away with, in the words of a local chronicler, "the wailings of the murdered men's family in their ears."

A few miles farther they met a young man riding toward them on a mule. Anderson ordered him to halt and, when he did so, asked him what had now become the most-asked question in all of Missouri: "What are you?" Meaning: Are you Union or Confederate?

Assuming from their uniforms that the bushwhackers were a Federal patrol, the young man promptly replied: "I am a Union man."

"Can you kill bushwhackers?" asked Anderson.

"Yes, I can."

Normally the crack of a revolver shot would have followed these words and be the last thing to be heard by the unlucky young man. But Anderson decided that shooting him would result in too easy a death. Instead, he had his followers strip the man naked and whip him with switches until he was barely alive, his body scored with bleeding lacerations. They then tied the reins of the mule around his neck, attached the saddle to the mule's tail, and turned the animal loose in the expectation that it would dash off, dragging its owner to death. Much to their frustration, the mule went only a few feet, then stopped. They then yelled at and pushed the mule, but to no avail—it did not budge, much less run. The guerrillas thereupon remounted their horses and rode away, probably assuming that their victim would die in any case. If so, they were mistaken. He survived to tell the tale of how his mule had saved his life by remaining faithful to the stubborn traditions of its breed.

Although Carroll County militiamen sighted the bushwhackers several times, and although they numbered 124 as opposed to a mere dozen, they stayed far behind and were quite happy to turn over the chase to a contingent of Ray County militia. As a Carroll County historian later admitted, "It is but the truth to say that, while among the militia there were many men of undoubted great personal courage, the most of them did not court an encounter with the ferocious guerrillas, of whose fighting qualities they had heard such wonderful accounts, and whose horrible work some of them had seen."[12]

Anderson continued through Ray County into Clay County from where, after teaming up with a gang headed by Fletch Taylor and being rejoined by brother Jim's outfit, he swept into Platte County, looting, burning, and killing, sometimes with a bullet, other times with a blade, and occasionally with both. Once he personally tortured a victim "in all manner of ways," to quote the *St. Joseph Herald,* then cut off his ears and nose before putting him out of his agony with .36-caliber lead slugs.[13]

Perhaps this atrocity temporarily sated Anderson. Possibly, too, even he now felt a need for a vacation from murder and mayhem. In any event, he returned to Clay County and spent most of the second week of August in a camp ten miles north of Liberty. For the time being his march of death ceased.[14]

There never had been anything like it—over three hundred miles, across the breadth of Missouri, a railroad had been broken, telegraph lines cut, depots destroyed, towns captured and sacked, steamboats attacked, troops routed and slaughtered, civilians robbed and shot down, perhaps a million dollars in property gone up in flames—and all by a handful of bushwhackers. Worse, they had made it look easy. For years Union officers had argued that the main reason they were unable to stamp out the guerrillas was because the cowards lurked in their inaccessible hideouts and rarely risked their skins in a fight unless they held all the advantages. But now a tiny band of them had ridden with impunity by daylight through the very heart of Missouri. And emboldened by their success, they and other bushwhackers were sure to go forth and do the same again.

But there was more to this Bill Anderson than his spectacular success. With him, something new had entered the picture, something that reached out with an iron fist and grabbed one's throat. It was savagery—sheer, terrifying savagery. His killings were accompanied by acts so monstrous, so vicious, so depraved, it was hard to believe that he was human.

So what was he? "Bandit" and "desperado" were utterly inadequate. "Monster" or "fiend" came closer to the mark but not close enough. Finally the editor of the *St. Joseph Herald* found the words that best conveyed what Anderson was to Missouri Unionists. Writing in the August 10 issue of his paper, the editor declared Anderson to be

> the most heartless, cold-blooded bushwhacking scoundrel that has operated in Missouri since the outbreak of the war. . . . His acts are characterized by a fiendishness and diabolism of the devil incarnate. Quantrell [*sic*], Todd . . . and others we might name have written their names high upon the pages of infamy, but Bill Anderson overtops them all in crime. His appearance in North Missouri is of a recent date, but in the few weeks since he commenced operation he has been guilty of more outrages than all others. Indiscriminate plunder and murder seem to be his mission, and as we trace his career it is impossible to find where he has exhibited the least trait of humanity.[15]

At the outset of July, Anderson had still been so little known that the Federals in their reports referred to him as "one Anderson" or "the guerrilla Anderson." Now he had become "the devil incarnate," the most ferocious and feared bushwhacker of all—and for Federal troops, the one they wished most and tried hardest to kill. Scarcely a day passed without the commander of the Union District of North Missouri, Brig. Gen. Clinton B. Fisk, telegraphing one or more of his officers to "exterminate" Anderson. But his soldiers rarely so much as engaged him, or if they did, usually it was they, not he, who got the worst of it.

To begin with, they had trouble locating him. He knew where he was going; they didn't. He had plenty of sympathetic civilians willing to shelter and feed his men and provide information about the "bluebellies"—where and how many. The Federals had their sources of aid and intelligence also, but not as many or as reliable. Consequently, in this particular chase the fox enjoyed an advantage over the hounds.[16]

And this fox, if brought to bay, turned into a wolf—with deadlier fangs. Most of the Federals were militiamen, ill-trained, ill-mounted (if mounted at all), and worst of all ill-equipped. Maj. Lucius Matlock, commanding the garrison at Glasgow, spoke for the majority of militia officers when on July 31 he pointed out to General Fisk that "our muskets"—single-shot muzzle loaders—were "poor arms to fight bushwhackers," who typically possessed four revolvers, whereas his men were "without one revolver." Could "we not," he plaintively asked Fisk, "be better armed?"[17]

Last, but not at all least, some of the militia consisted of "Paw Paws," Southern sympathizers who had been pressed into military service, and others who simply were afraid of the bushwhackers—above all, Anderson's—because of what they did to any living, or for that matter dead, soldier who fell into their hands. As a consequence, whole companies of militia occasionally surrendered to guerrillas without firing a shot or else fled in wild panic at their approach—or what was thought to be their approach. In one case, a single Union officer put to flight fifty militiamen who mistook him for a bushwhacker![18]

Because Missouri had been stripped of troops during 1863 to bolster Ulysses S. Grant's campaign against Vicksburg, only four regiments of regular Union cavalry operated in what the bushwhackers called their stomping grounds. Of these, the Second Colorado and First Iowa achieved at least some limited success, even though they, too, were handicapped by inferior weapons. The other two, the Seventeenth Illinois and the Fifteenth Kansas, were virtually worthless, if not worse. Their men, especially the Kansans, tended to consider all Missourians rebels and acted accordingly, plundering whenever and wherever they had the opportunity. On one occasion, for example, a company of the Fifteenth Kansas, whose commander was the notorious jayhawker Charles Jennison, ignored the thrice-repeated warning of the pickets of the Missouri militia garrisoning Harrisonville to halt and identify itself, and when told that he had barely escaped being fired on, the company commander answered that if that had happened, his men would have burned the town and killed every person in it. Such units and their conduct lent credibility to the bushwhackers' claim that they were protecting and retaliating against Union depredations and so engendered civilian support that they might have otherwise not received.[19]

Little wonder, then, that Bill Anderson and his gang felt utter contempt for their Federal foes and believed that they could whip them in any "fair fight"—defined as one in which the Federals did not enjoy the advantage of fortifications or overwhelming numbers. Up to a point, this attitude was an asset in that it gave the bushwhackers a sense of superiority, even invincibility, making them all the more formidable in battle. Beyond that point, however, it could turn into a liability by causing them to become overconfident and thus careless and reckless, as witness Anderson's failure to be on guard against the assault by the Carroll County home guardsmen. Furthermore, most of the militiamen were staunch Unionists, they often had personal scores to settle, they were learning experientially how best to fight guerrillas, and a growing number of them were obtaining better weapons—specifically, revolvers. The time was coming when victory over their better units would not come easily or, if it came at all, tend to be so costly as to be hardly worth it.

But that time had not come yet. For now, Anderson was the king of the bushwhacking hill, and, attracted by his reputation, dozens of recruits flocked to his camp north of Liberty. Among them was Alexander Franklin James, a lanky, blond, twenty-one-year-old who went by the name of Frank and who had followed Quantrill to Lawrence. With him came his sixteen-year-old brother, Jesse. The James boys, as they would be known to millions someday, lived with their family on a farm near the Clay County town of Kearney, so they did not have to travel far to join Anderson. Frank had served in Sterling Price's army in 1861 and turned guerrilla the following year. Jesse no doubt would have followed his example in any case, but having been lashed by the whips of Union militiamen when they "visited" the James farm in 1863 gave him an extra incentive.[20]

Anderson's band, which hitherto had never numbered more than fifty, quickly increased to more than a hundred men. Most of the newcomers were, like Frank James, veterans of other bushwhacker gangs, notably that of Yager, who had been killed in July during a fight at Arrow Rock. But whatever their background, Anderson wanted and took only those whom he believed could be relied on to kill Unionists, Yankees, and Kansans—especially the ones in blue uniforms—with utter ruthlessness and who were willing to risk death themselves while killing. Thus, when a man described as a "desperado" asked to join up, Anderson turned him down, saying that he had heard the man was "a coward" and so didn't want anything to do with him.

"Try me, Captain," the man pleaded.

"It is no use," Anderson replied.

But the man persisted. Finally, losing patience, Anderson spit in his face. A second later "Bloody Bill," as some had started calling him, lay sprawled on the ground, knocked there by a blow to his face.

He stood up, but instead of reaching for a revolver, he rubbed his jaw and said, "Swear him in boys; any man that will knock down Bill Anderson surrounded by his men will do as a member of our band."[21]

All of the recruits knew full well what kind of war Anderson waged—which was another reason why they joined him. As one of them, Jim Cummins, later explained, "Having looked the situation over I determined to join the worst devil in the bunch [and] so I decided it was Anderson for me as I wanted to see the blood flow."[22]

And flow it did. Sending out word that the time had come to go on the warpath again, Anderson and his enlarged guerrilla gang headed east into Ray County. There, on the night of August 12, he routed a militia company at Fredericksburg, killing its captain and four soldiers. The next day Fisk, in his customary style, telegraphed the post commander at Chillicothe to "form an Anderson extermination party" and "follow him until he is dead," adding in a

Figure 4.1 Frank James. COURTESY OF
THE NATIONAL PORTRAIT GALLERY.

second message that "Anderson is the worst of all, and he must be killed, or he will cause the death of every Union man he can find."[23]

The following day 150 mounted militia picked up Anderson's trail in Ray County. They had no trouble following it. South of Knoxville in Carroll County they came upon the corpses of two soldiers. One had been trampled to mush by horses' hooves, the other had been scalped after having his throat cut. Further on they found a man sprawled dead in a wagon. There could be no doubt that Anderson was up ahead.

At midmorning on August 14, the pursuers reached the Wakenda River. Here the advance, about fifty men, paused to water their horses and wait for the rest of the column to close up. Suddenly, like a bolt from the blue, bushwhackers charged into the shallow stream, their revolvers spewing a hail of lead. Several soldiers tumbled from their saddles, the remainder scurried back up onto the west bank—only to be greeted with a shower of bullets from the main body of the militia, who mistook them for bushwhackers. The actual bushwhackers followed close behind, still firing. Some of the militiamen fought back, but on seeing most of their comrades fleeing, they had no choice if they wanted to live but do the same. Fisk's "extermination party" lost at least eight and perhaps as many as fifteen, killed outright or mortally wounded.

In contrast, only one guerrilla died in the clash, and although a large number suffered wounds, including Clements and Anderson himself, the sole seriously wounded raider was Jesse James, shot by a pistol through the right chest.

Figure 4.2 Jesse James. COURTESY OF THE
STATE HISTORICAL SOCIETY OF MISSOURI.

His slightly wounded brother, Frank, left him with the family of a Confederate soldier to be sheltered and nursed back to health.[24]

Anderson pushed on eastward and crossed the Grand River that night. The next day he veered south and led his band through Chariton into Howard County. During the ensuing two weeks he operated in this general region, swinging northward to the vicinity of Huntsville and swooping south to around Columbia and Rocheport, leaving mutilated corpses and plundered farms in his wake. As before, Federal detachments scoured the countryside attempting to intercept or catch him. As before, they rarely succeeded; even when successful, the results were minimal, if not discouraging. Thus, in an August 21 (anniversary of the Lawrence massacre) dispatch to Fisk, a civilian scout reported: "The Seventeenth Illinois . . . yesterday had a fight in the Perche Hills with Anderson. . . . There were several wounded on both sides. The rebels scattered in every direction in such small numbers they could not be pursued by our forces. They go home to the old sympathizers, where they are quietly fed and protected until it suits for them to turn out again."[25]

To be sure, Major Matlock at Glasgow notified Fisk the following day that during the preceding week his troops had killed and wounded thirty-five guerrillas belonging to Anderson's and two other bands. But two days later he in effect belied this claim by reporting that a steamboat laden with supplies for Fort Leavenworth in Kansas had been stopped from proceeding beyond Glasgow on the Missouri River because of a bushwhacker attack. He also renewed his pleas for better firearms, specifically carbines and pistols: "With our muskets we can well defend, but pursuit and attack is another thing." He also stated that "Anderson used our signals on August 20 when approaching our men [in the Perche Hills encounter]; that spoils them for [our] use."[26]

Further evidence of the ineffectiveness of the Federal counterguerrilla campaign comes from two other documents, both also of Union origin. The first is a letter dated August 25, 1864, to Rosecrans from the "Committee of Safety for Montgomery County." The key passage appears at the beginning:

> The murders, robberies, and other outrages committed by guerrillas are fast making the county untenable for Union men. Not a day passes but some Union man is robbed of almost all he is worth, and if he offers any opposition to the robbery he is at once shot. Of course the greatest consternation prevails. Something must be done and done at once, or loyal men must leave this county.[27]

Making this letter all the more significant is that Montgomery County is located in eastern Missouri, only about seventy-five miles from St. Louis itself. It was not a major center of guerrilla activity, and none of the main bushwhacker gangs operated there. If conditions for Unionists there were as described in the letter, one can only conclude that they must have been far worse in what had now become Anderson's stomping grounds in central Missouri.

The other document, also dated August 25, consists of a "Statement" made by George Williams, a Union spy who, disguised as a bushwhacker, spent a week with members of Anderson's and other guerrilla bands in Randolph County. He "talked with them all," and "[t]heir conversation seemed to be all about the same; they were 'going to make [Randolph] county hotter than hell,' and intend, they say, 'to hold it, by God, to a certainty.'" Moreover, added Williams, "They also say part of Quantrill's men are now crossing the Missouri. . . . They are going to have Huntsville" and "burn everything and kill all the people in it," and Anderson was endeavoring to induce the local guerrillas to join him for the raid on Huntsville.[28]

Clearly the bushwhackers—in particular, Anderson's gang—believed that they held the upper hand, a belief that could only have been strengthened by an encounter that took place near Rocheport on August 28. On that day a large mounted patrol of the Fourth Missouri State Militia clattered from the ferry opposite Boonville and set off on a scout in quest of guerrillas. They soon found them. As the Federals rode north along the Fayette Road, they spotted two horsemen up ahead and immediately gave pursuit. Not until they heard the shrill yells and crack of revolver fire in the woods behind them did they realize too late that they had galloped into a trap. Panicked by the onslaught and unable to turn in the narrow road, they broke in wild rout. Most of the bushwhackers continued to chase the fleeing foe, killing and wounding a dozen or more. Others swarmed over seven wounded soldiers lying on the ground. First they stripped off their uniforms. Then, as the soldiers watched in helpless horror, the raiders pulled out large, sharp knives and stabbed some of the victims in the heart, cut the throats of others, and either castrated or scalped or did both to all of them. As a final touch, they looped a rope around the neck of a militiaman who had been "skinned" and left his body dangling from a tree branch. That way it would be obvious to all who had performed these deeds: Anderson's bushwhackers.[29]

Following the ambush, Anderson ordered his men to scatter among the nearby Perche Hills; again, strong Union forces were concentrating against them. With a group of about twenty-eight, Anderson went to Rocheport, a village perched beneath high bluffs overlooking one of the main crossings along the Missouri River. The staunchly "secesh" inhabitants welcomed the bushwhackers, who in turn refrained from their usual depredations. In effect, Anderson took another vacation from the war and killing—his last one, as it turned out.

Anderson remained at Rocheport, which he dubbed "my capital," for two weeks. He and his followers devoted most of their time to getting drunk and staying that way. When not drinking, they occasionally sallied forth to the riverbank and fired on passing steamboats, forcing them to turn back. They allowed one boat, a tug, to dock, then captured it, killing a crew member in the process. Soon traffic on the Missouri between Jefferson City and Boonville ceased entirely.[30]

"Anderson," complained the editor of the *Jefferson City State Times,* "with his thieving, murdering, misbegotten, God-forsaken, hell-deserving followers have [sic] at last established themselves in and about Rocheport . . . and they are having things entirely their own way."[31]

As befitted a ruler, Anderson also sent forth some of his "most trusted men" to collect a "contributory tax" from civilians in the area for the "support and maintenance" of his company. According to the subsequent account of a member of that company, Hamp Watts, "The tax was not manditory [sic], but altogether voluntary."[32] In other words, a man need not pay it if he did not mind being shot or at the very least pistol-whipped; women likewise were exempt if they were willing to have their houses ransacked and perhaps burned.

All went well for Anderson's tax collectors until the morning of September 12. When a steady rain began falling, five of Anderson's men took shelter in a barn owned by a widow named Turner. Deeming themselves safe from the enemy because of the weather, they unsaddled their horses, spread out their blankets to dry, and began cleaning and oiling their revolvers. While they were so engaged, a twenty-five-man mounted militia patrol, which had picked up their trail in the muddy road, entered the farmyard and asked a black servant—

slavery had been abolished by now in Missouri by act of a Radical Republican–controlled state constitutional convention—if he had "seen any bushwhackers 'round here." The servant merely pointed toward the barn. As he did so, two guerrillas, having spotted the Federals, rushed out of the barn, a pistol in each hand. First one, then the other, went down, ripped by militia bullets. The remaining three fled through a cornfield into a brush-filled forest. For a time it seemed that they would escape, but their pursuers eventually overtook and killed them. The militiamen, who belonged to the Ninth Missouri State Cavalry stationed in Fayette, also captured seven horses, several of which wore bridles bedecked with scalps. Their sole disappointment came when they examined the corpse of the first guerrilla they had slain; it was not, as they had thought, Bill Anderson. But, sooner or later somebody would get him. It was just a matter of time.[33]

Word of the tax collectors' fate reached Rocheport later that day. The bushwhackers took it hard, none more so than Anderson. He was, Hamp Watts later wrote, "pitiable to behold. Great tears coursed down his cheeks, his breast heaved, and his body shook with vehement agitation." Then he became "morose, sullen, and gloomy." As with the deaths of his father and sister, there could be but one response: It was time to start killing again.[34]

The next day he rode out of Rocheport, heading north toward Fayette. Most of his men followed him; the rest galloped off into the Perche Hills to summon the other portions of the command.

On the evening of September 23, some seven miles northeast of Rocheport, a train of eighteen wagons, carrying supplies of all kinds and escorted by eighty members of the Third Missouri Militia, creaked along the road between Columbia and Fayette. Suddenly scores of bushwhackers charged out of the woods and brush lining the road, their shrill yells shattering the air. Surprised and terrified, the militiamen fled. Most escaped, an unknown number were killed or wounded, and twelve simply threw up their hands in surrender. Their captors ordered them to remove their uniforms. When they did so, each was shot through the head, as were three black teamsters. The bushwhackers then plundered and burned all the wagons except, for some reason, those carrying food and ammunition. They then rode away, dividing and subdividing into small groups to baffle pursuit.

It worked. But a detachment of the Ninth Missouri, patrolling out of Fayette, picked up the trail of one bushwhacker party, followed it, and overtook seven "prairie wolves." It killed and then scalped six but took prisoner the seventh, Cave Wyatt, who had been wounded and was "sergeant" in Anderson's band.[35] Unless the militiamen hoped to extract useful information from Wyatt, their sparing him is inexplicable; almost certainly pity had nothing to do with it. Whatever the motive, it would have remarkable consequences for another sergeant, a Union one, who on this particular day was in Nashville, Tennessee, on his way to home and family in a little place called Hawleyville, Iowa.

Ambushing the wagon train and murdering twelve of its escort—the teamsters, being "niggers," did not count in the tally—had been Anderson's retaliation for the slaying of his tax collectors. Now he had something else to avenge, and he resolved to do it in a big way. In both instances the bluebellies who had killed his men belonged to the Ninth Missouri stationed in Fayette. He would go to that town and "clean it out," thereby teaching the Ninth—for that matter, all Union troops in Missouri—that they could not kill and scalp his men with impunity, and they were not safe from his wrath even in a fortified town.

Early the next morning Anderson and his men, who had regrouped, left their bivouac beside Bonne Femme Creek and marched toward Fayette, six miles due north. As they neared the town, they saw something they had not expected to see: a large force, perhaps two hundred or more, of fellow bushwhackers. It turned out to be George Todd's band, accompanied by the gangs of Dave Poole, John Thrailkill, and a band of six or seven guerrillas headed by none other than Quantrill. What, they wondered, were they doing here?

They soon found out. On September 8, a Confederate officer had delivered to Todd a message from Sterling Price, stating that his invasion of Missouri was about to begin and asking Todd and all other guerrillas to help prepare the way by disrupting Union defenses and supply lines. Todd thereupon reassembled his band and crossed over to the north side of the Missouri, where he was joined by Thrailkill, Poole, Si Gordon, Tom Todd (no relation), Cliff Holtzclaw, and finally by Quantrill, who said that while he would not serve under his former lieutenant, he would cooperate with him. Not since Lawrence and Baxter Springs had so many bushwhackers been assembled at one time and place. Altogether they numbered more than four hundred, counting several score Confederate recruits accompanying Thrailkill.

Tacitly putting aside their past animosity, Anderson and Todd held a conference in which all of the chieftains, including Quantrill, participated. Anderson urged an immediate attack on Fayette. Most of its garrison was away, searching for him. He had intended to go into the town with just his own men. Now, with Todd's and the other bands, taking Fayette would be a walkover.

Todd promptly agreed. Just four days earlier he and Thrailkill had ridden into Keytesville, seat of Chariton County and Price's hometown, and secured the surrender of its Paw Paw garrison without firing a shot or losing a man. Should the militiamen in Fayette try to stave off the enemy, they would not stand long against so many of the fiercest bushwhackers in Missouri.

Quantrill objected. Unless taken by surprise, the Federals in Fayette would literally fight for their lives rather than meekly lay down their arms like the Keytesville garrison. They were not Paw Paws. More important, they would be protected by the brick walls of the courthouse and probably other brick and stone buildings as well, against which revolver fire would be virtually useless. No, an attack on Fayette was too risky, and even if successful it would cost too many casualties to "make it pay."

Todd jeered, "We are going into Fayette no matter what! If you want to come along, all right. If not then you can go back into the woods with the rest of the cowards!"

Unfazed, Quantrill rode away from the conference, which continued without him.

Again asserting that it would be easy to take Fayette, Anderson offered to enter the town first with his men, who, wearing Federal uniforms, would surprise and dispose of the garrison. All Anderson wanted was revenge against the Ninth Missouri. After that Todd's and the other bands could have the place all to themselves.

Todd accepted Anderson's proposal. It promised little fighting and a lot of loot for his boys. That Quantrill opposed attacking Fayette merely made Todd more determined to do it. He already had shown himself to be a better man than Quantrill. Now he would prove that he was a better leader.[35]

It didn't turn out that way. Because one of Anderson's men was trigger-happy—the one who shot the Yankee uniform-attired black man standing on the sidewalk—the ruse for taking the garrison by surprise failed just as it was about to succeed. Instead of easy pickings in a defenseless town, Todd's followers found themselves doing most of the fighting and suffering most of the losses against the Federals holed up in the log cabins. As the bushwhackers retreated from Fayette along the Glasgow Road, they had to have thought that while Anderson and Todd were utterly fearless, Quantrill was a damn sight smarter.

That night, after leaving their wounded with friendly farmers, the guerrilla bands camped near Glasgow. It had been a bad day, the worst most of them had ever experienced. Anderson's men in particular felt frustrated and angry. Not only had they failed to avenge their dead, scalped comrades, they now had a humiliating defeat to redeem. They resolved to do this the first chance they got. And the sooner that chance came, the better.[36]

CHAPTER FIVE

THERE ARE GUERRILLAS THERE

CENTRAL KENTUCKY: NIGHT, SEPTEMBER 25, 1864

All was quiet in the train's coach except for the steady chugging of the engine up ahead, the clanking of iron on iron below, and the snoring of men asleep on the hard, wooden benches. Half of the passengers were soldiers, veterans who could sleep anywhere, anytime. They came from Gen. William Tecumseh Sherman's army down in Georgia. Exactly three weeks and three days earlier, that army had captured Atlanta, thereby ending four months of hard, bloody, incessant campaigning. Also ended was the South's last chance of winning by holding on until the North lost its will to continue the war. That will had started to erode when the summer gave way to fall, and Gen. Ulysses S. Grant, despite hideous losses, remained stalemated in Virginia while Sherman seemed stymied in Georgia. Then Atlanta fell, and most Northerners decided that the war *could* be won—in fact, it *would* be won. It was just a matter of time.

But what mattered most to the soldiers on the train was that they had survived—survived the rain of lead at Resaca, the corpse-strewn slopes of Kennesaw Mountain, the fierce Rebel onslaughts at Peachtree Creek, Bald Hill, and Ezra Church, and the final fighting at Jonesboro. They had survived, too, the cold rain and torrid sun, the clinging mud and choking dust, and the endless marching and trench digging that had put more men in hospitals and graves than all the battles combined. And because they had survived, they were going home. Some, whose enlistments had expired or who had received medical discharges, could stay home and never have to return to the army. Others, the vast majority, had thirty-day furloughs and were delighted to have them. It meant that for a few weeks at least they could live like human beings instead of beasts, killing and being killed. Besides, maybe by the time they were to rejoin their units, Grant would have taken Richmond, and Sherman would have finished off the Rebels in Georgia. If so, the war would be as good as over. In any event, at least for a short while it was over for them.

One of the furloughed veterans in the car was Thomas Morton Goodman of the First Missouri Engineers.[1] Six feet tall and beefy, he looked like what he was—a sergeant. Beneath his blue army blouse were the powerful shoulders and arms of the blacksmith he had been before joining up in October 1862. That was the reason why—along with his having served in the Mexican War and being, at thirty-five, much older than most of his fellow soldiers—he wore three large V-shaped gold stripes on his sleeves. A blacksmith was an asset to any unit, especially in an engineer outfit where there were many things he could do besides shoe horses.

Belonging to the First Missouri Engineers also greatly enhanced Goodman's chances of remaining a survivor. During most of the Atlanta campaign his regiment had come nowhere near the front. Instead it had been in Tennessee, laying track and building and repairing blockhouses along Sherman's railroad supply line. Not until toward the end of August had it joined the fighting army, and then it had remained well to the rear while the final clashes took place at Jonesboro and Lovejoy's Station.[2] And since his regiment would continue to perform noncombat service, Goodman could be reasonably confident that he still would be alive and well when his enlistment ended in 1865—supposing, that is, the war lasted that long.

Now he was going home, back to Hawleyville, a little town in Page County, Iowa, near the Missouri line. Home to his wife, Mary, their three children, and his younger brother.[3] He yearned to see them, to be with them, to hug them. Almost two years had passed since he had done those things. That was a long, long time.

Goodman's journey back home began in Atlanta on September 22, when he and other furloughed members of the First Missouri Engineers boarded a train destined for Nashville by way of Chattanooga. About an hour out of Atlanta, at a place with the unpoetic name of Big Shanty, the train came to a grinding halt: Up ahead, Rebel raiders had wrecked about a quarter-mile of track. To Goodman and his fellow engineers this was merely an annoying nuisance. They had had plenty of experience patching railroads, and Sherman kept stockpiles of rails all along the twin bands of iron that constituted the lifeline of his army. Within five hours they had the break repaired, and the train resumed its northward progress.

At every station the local loafers—whom the soldiers called "half-and-halfs" because they suspected that their professions of loyalty to the Union derived more from convenience than conviction—sought to amuse themselves by declaring that Joe Wheeler's Confederate cavalry were on the loose in northern Georgia and soon would strike the railroad below Chattanooga in huge force. Goodman and his comrades laughed at these "yarns." They knew that back in August, Wheeler had tried to compel Sherman to retreat by destroying the railroad

Figure 5.1 Thomas Morton Goodman. COURTESY OF THE BETTY PIERCE COLLECTION.

between Chattanooga and Atlanta but had failed miserably, and they doubted that he would try it again now that Atlanta had fallen. Maybe a few mangy guerrillas were prowling about, but all they ever did was take pot shots at trains and occasionally derail one. They would not dare attack a train, especially one packed with soldiers and in the daytime. They were too cowardly for that.

The train reached Chattanooga without incident or accident, then proceeded on to Nashville, arriving the following day. Here the soldiers had a long layover, and they made the most of it. That meant starting out with restaurants, where one could eat real food instead of army rations, and ending up, if one was so inclined, on Spring, Front, and other streets lined solidly with saloons, brothels, and similar places that combined the two, as most did.[4]

> In eighteen hundred and sixty-four
> Hurrah! Hurrah!
> We'll all go home and fight no more,
> Hurrah! Hurrah!
> In eighteen hundred and sixty-four,
> We'll all go home and fight no more,
> And we'll all drink stone blind.
> Johnny come fill the bowl.

If there was one place and one time in their lives to celebrate and "drink stone blind," it was here and now. And celebrate they did, exploding in a single moment all the emotional black powder pent up from months of hardship and toil. When their train pulled away from the Nashville depot, every man somehow succeeded in getting aboard bodily—but not so much as a spark of their former spirit and enthusiasm remained. Half asleep and half awake, Jim Hilly, Ed Pace, Cass Rose, giant Valentine Peters, and the other members of the First Missouri Engineers lay scattered about the coach. Reaching their homes in Missouri and Iowa was the one and only thing on their minds. Each hour on the train was an hour less sitting around the supper table, an hour less horsing with the boys, an hour less sparking with their girls. Lost in their own worlds of clacking wheels, memories, and passing night-time landscapes, one by one those in the train car quietly dropped away until all were mantled in sleep. All, that is, save Sgt. Tom Goodman.

The big man pulled himself up and walked to a window. There was worry on his otherwise calm face, lines where normally none existed. What was it that he was feeling? What did it mean? Why couldn't he shake it? Was it the whiskey? Was it that hollow "high lonesome" one suffers after a losing bout with liquor? Or was it simply human nature—the cautious, doubting side of man which raises its guard against anything that seems too good and beautiful to quite be true—such as, in his case, returning home? Whatever it was, whatever it meant, he had never felt it before. . . .

He lowered the window of the stuffy coach and sucked in the cool night air. Up ahead the lantern on the big engine burned through the blackness. The train now was far north into Kentucky. Perhaps at this very moment it was passing through Hardin County, where he had been born on February 22, 1829, almost exactly twenty years after another, far more prominent native of that county. If so, then in a sense he had already come home.

But no, his real home was Hawleyville, Iowa. There were his friends, his neighbors, his little ones, and their mother, his wife, Mary, sweet Mary. He would think of her. That would drive the shadows from his mind that would not let him sleep.

Mary. He could almost see her smiling face, could almost hear her soft voice, feel her warm, loving arms. She was a good woman, a kind woman, always looking on the bright side and never turning her back on those in need. The year before their marriage in 1849, he had taken over the rearing of his five-year-old brother after their mother had died. And although little more than a child herself at sixteen, Mary had accepted the boy and raised him as her own. Several years later they had their own children, Willie and Jim, followed by the little one, Danny. Soon after Danny's birth in 1862, Tom Goodman had gone off to the war, determined to do his part to preserve the Union.

The two years since had passed quickly, yet it all seemed so very long ago, almost in a different lifetime. Now, he was on his way back home. In a few more days he would be there.

The dark feeling in his mind now gone, Goodman went back to his seat and soon fell asleep.[5]

PARIS, MISSOURI: 10:00 P.M., SEPTEMBER 26, 1864

The column of Federal troops cleared the village, a little place with the grandiose name of Paris, and rode into the darkness. A pale crescent moon shone dimly over the shadowed prairie. The only sound came from the soldier's slow-moving mounts and the creaking wheels of a couple wagons following in the rear. Earlier that evening, guerrillas—reportedly about eighty in number—had passed to the south of Paris. Now Companies A, G, and H of the Thirty-ninth Missouri were setting forth to track them down and, pursuant to Gen. Clinton Fisk's oft-repeated exhortations, "exterminate" them. The hunt was on.

The Thirty-ninth Missouri was a new regiment—so new that it still was being organized. Most of its men were recruits so raw that they barely knew how to aim, fire, and reload their Enfield single-shot rifles, and when they drilled, any veterans who happened to be around laughed at their clumsy revolutions. But with Sterling Price's army coming up out of Arkansas and the guerrillas running rampant through central Missouri, every available unit had to be put in the field, ready for battle or not. Companies A, G, and H totaled only about 160 men, little more than half of their authorized strength, but soldiers were needed now. Later might be too late.

Officially the Thirty-ninth was an infantry outfit, which is why it had the Enfields plus bayonets. Yet, except for a dozen or so men trudging along on foot beside the wagons, all the soldiers were riding as they marched out of Paris. To be sure, most of their mounts were mules, brood mares, and plow horses and thus no match for the fast steeds of the bushwhackers. But they at least gave them a chance to catch up with those thieving, murdering prairie wolves. And if they did catch up with them, they would give them a good thrashing. That is, if the raiders didn't run away like the band encountered on the way to Paris. As everyone knew, bushwhackers fought only when they could attack by surprise from ambush and in overwhelming force. They never took on a stronger or equal foe, especially out in the open where they could not get in close with their revolvers. Since the Enfield had an effective killing range of three hundred yards, there was little chance of guerrillas being able to use their pistols against the soldiers of Companies A, G, and H of the Thirty-ninth Missouri. If they tried, they would be slaughtered.[6]

ST. CHARLES, MISSOURI: PRE-DAWN, SEPTEMBER 27, 1864

Except for the puffing of the big engine as it built up steam, the train sat silently by the depot. Thick morning fog rising from the Missouri River closed in from all sides, and the station workers moved through the gray vapors like phantoms. A group of Iowa soldiers, Tom Goodman among them, stood by a coach, waiting to board. Yesterday afternoon they had arrived in St. Louis, just two more train rides from their homes, families, and friends. Many of their Missouri comrades, loath to waste any more precious leave time, promptly crossed the Missouri by ferry to St. Charles and took an evening train on the North Missouri Railroad, which connected with the Hannibal & St. Joseph at Macon City. The Iowans, on the other hand, saw no point in pushing it and so decided to remain in St. Louis and get a fresh start in the morning.

While they were at the North Missouri Railroad ticket office in St. Louis, a worried-looking man had approached the soldiers and said that he had just come down from Macon City and that at every stop he had heard reports of guerrillas lurking about Sturgeon, Centralia, and other villages along the line. The government, he declared, was wrong to allow mail and passenger trains to travel the line without guards. So, too, were the directors of the North Missouri, who ignored warnings of danger.

The soldiers noted the man's tone of voice and studied his eyes. He was, they concluded, sincere, not merely an idle wag trying to put a scare into them. To be sure, what he said was hearsay—nothing really solid. Yet, rumor or not, conditions along the North Missouri were obviously unsettled. Indeed, earlier that day a report had circulated through St. Louis that guerrillas had captured one hundred troops at a place on that line called Centralia. Although this had soon proved false, it was nevertheless worrisome, and along with what the traveler from Macon City had related, it confirmed for Tom Goodman the belief that he and his fellow Iowans were doing the right thing by waiting for the morning train. If there were bushwhackers prowling the prairies to the northwest of St. Charles and they did attack a passenger train, in all probability they would do so at night rather than in the daytime.

To catch the 4:15 in the morning meant Goodman needed rest, so despite the attractions of the big city, he headed for a hotel. After four long nights on railroad cars and weeks and months of sleeping most of the time in tents with nothing but a rubber ground sheet beneath him, how marvelous, how wonderful, it would be to sleep in a real bed!

But he didn't sleep. The words of the stranger kept echoing through his mind. Why hadn't the Missourians waited just one more night? By light of day, all could have traveled home in safety. Of course, all the talk about guerrillas might be and probably was just that—talk. And yet. . . .

The same dark presence he had felt two nights before stirred in the depths of his soul once again. It had not gone away after all. Goodman finally slept, but only for a few fitful hours during which his dreams were filled with such frightful scenes that he could not help but wonder, after awakening, if they portended the future.

To Goodman's surprise, in St. Charles, on the coach assigned to soldiers, he found Josh Comer, Jim Robinson, big Val Peters, and all the other Missourians who had gone ahead. On reaching St. Charles the evening before, the same rumors about guerrillas on the railroad that circulated through St. Louis had caused them to wait for the greater safety that daylight and added numbers would bring. They greeted the newcomers warmly, and, Goodman noted, everybody felt better and braver.

Overhearing the soldiers and sensing their change of mood, some of the Irish station hands could not resist having a little sport. The guerrillas, they taunted, would have the last laugh. By sundown the scalp of every man aboard would be hanging from a bridle. As they had five days before in north Georgia, the veterans responded with jibes and jeers of their own, accompanying them with contemptuous comments about bushwhackers being too cowardly to take on real soldiers.

"Ye are brave now ain't you?" shouted back one worker. "Begorra and ye need to be, for the guerrillas will be after ye, sure!"

The soldiers merely laughed. When the train pulled out of the station, it seemed to Goodman that during the entire trip they had never been in higher spirits. Yet at the same time he saw on their faces the same anxious expression as that of troops about to go into battle—the expression of men who hoped to live but who knew that they might soon die.[7]

YOUNG'S CREEK: DAWN, SEPTEMBER 27, 1864

As sunlight began filtering through the leaves of the trees along Young's Creek, some three miles southeast of the village of Centralia, Bill Anderson's men—and boys—began awakening from their slumber or, in many cases, drunken stupors. If anything, they were in a fouler mood than they had been right after the Fayette fiasco, for since then affairs had continued to go badly. First, on September 25, they and the other guerrilla bands, Todd's included, had swung northward from the Glasgow area to the outskirts of Huntsville. There Anderson proposed paying his hometown another visit. To that end, he had sent a farmer into the town with a message stating that unless the garrison surrendered, it would be wiped out. He could not have picked a worse place to make such a threat. The Union commander in Huntsville was still Lieutenant Colonel Denny—whose father Anderson's men had tortured by hanging back in August. Denny's reply had been quick and to the point, instructing the farmer: "Tell them that if they want us to come in and get us." Hearing this, Anderson still wanted to attack. Not so Todd. He and his followers had no desire to repeat what they had experienced at Fayette. Consequently, the bushwhackers had resumed their march, heading east to the North Missouri Railroad, where they vented some of their frustration by tearing down several miles of telegraph wire between Allen and Renick. That night they had bivouacked near Middle Grove in Monroe County.

The next day they had continued northeastward in the direction of Paris. But on learning that it, too, contained a large Federal force, they had abandoned any notion of raiding it and swerved off to the south until they reached their present camp along Young's Creek.[8] After three days, the largest guerrilla force assembled since Lawrence had accomplished nothing except to yank down some telegraph wire and kill some poor devil of a sentry while suffering at least twenty casualties, a large portion of whom either were dead or likely to die. Still unavenged were the six members of Anderson's band shot and scalped on the twenty-third and the five comrades whose bodies had been left behind to be trampled into the dirt at Fayette. It seemed that every town worth taking had a strong garrison in it and that Union detachments swarmed all about, hunting them—they who were accustomed to being the hunters. They had assembled their full strength and moved into this region so as to prepare the way for Sterling Price. But was he coming? And if so, where and when could he be expected to arrive?

After the men had breakfasted and taken care of their horses, Todd went to Anderson and asked him—he could not order him—to go to Centralia and obtain what news he could of Price. Anderson promptly agreed.[9] He did not particularly care about Price—his was a different war both in purpose and kind—but Centralia had stores, and those stores had money, plunder, and whiskey. Also, Centralia was a stop on the North Missouri Railroad, and maybe a train would come along. A freight train would be best but a passenger train would do since there would be plenty of people aboard with jewelry, greenbacks, and real money in the form of gold and silver. In any case, a visit to Centralia could prove profitable as well as enjoyable. And it would help make up for what had happened at Fayette and had not happened at Huntsville and Paris.

THE PRAIRIE, TEN MILES SOUTH OF PARIS, MISSOURI: DAWN, SEPTEMBER 27, 1864

Maj. Andrew Vern Emen Johnston, commanding Companies A, G, and H of the Thirty-ninth Missouri Infantry, slowly adjusted his field glasses. Sunshine sliced through the morning mist, casting long, blue shadows over the prairie. At a distance of two miles the view was dim and uncertain. Johnston carefully adjusted the glasses, making the sighting as good as it ever would be—and it was enough. Though difficult to discern through the vapor, he was now sure it was the bushwhackers. Their horses, tiny specks in the distance, moved about in various directions, obviously grazing. The raiders numbered between fifty and eighty, certainly not more than a hundred. That was the size of the force that had passed south of Paris the evening before. Now it was in sight. The bushwhackers had been found!

Throughout the night the three companies had moved slowly in the dark, hindered by the unfamiliar terrain as much as by lagging foot soldiers. In the end, however, the pace had proved a godsend. Had the march been pressed, they might have passed the fresh tracks they stumbled on at dawn. Those men without mounts had been promptly sent back to Paris, and the pace of the excited column increased. By sunup, with both men and beasts hungry, the troop had halted to rest and eat. That was when the scouts had come racing back with word that those making the tracks were just ahead—the soldiers had located their quarry. The Thirty-ninth was in luck.[10]

Major Johnston continued to gaze through his glasses, scanning the southern horizon. At last he lowered them and ordered pickets posted to the south. He would allow the men to finish their breakfasts and, as some were doing, take a short snooze. Before the day was over they would need all of their energy and endurance. He then raised his field glasses and resumed the watch.

Standing in the crisp early-morning air, the brass buttons on his uniform aglow in the golden sun, the major presented a striking figure: tall and erect in his bold blue coat, a long saber dangling in its scabbard by his side, rich, full beard framing a rugged, handsome face that was at once youthful yet mature, strong yet sensitive. He looked as a military leader should.

This was, in fact, paradoxical, for prior to the war he had been a teacher and sometime preacher in Ralls County near Hannibal, where he was known and respected as a kind and courteous "Christian gentleman" who never drank, swore, or whored. Furthermore, he had followed a strange and, in the eyes of some, suspicious route to become a Union Army officer. In the summer of 1861 he had been a lieutenant in the Missouri State Guard, whose commander was Sterling Price and which would provide the nucleus for that general's army when he went over to the Confederacy. Johnston, though, had remained loyal to the Union, which he proved by joining the pro-Federal state militia in September 1861. During the ensuing three years he had risen to the rank he now held and gained the praise of a fellow officer who served under him as being a leader who "follows the bushwhackers to fight them on their own ground"—something he had done with notable success in the Hannibal area. How fortunate they were, his young, neophyte soldiers, to have such a capable and experienced commander.[11]

Like most other Missouri Unionists, Johnston was no abolitionist. When Lincoln issued his Emancipation Proclamation the major had denounced it as unconstitutional and declared he would no longer "follow Old Abe." But he had soon realized, like most other Missouri Unionists, that slavery was doomed no matter what, and nothing could be done to change that fact. Besides, the main thing was to put down the rebellion, which in Missouri meant putting down the bushwhackers. They were the worst kind of Rebels, and Johnston had come to despise them. They boasted about how tough, brave, and skilled they were, but in truth they were nothing but skulking scum good only at murdering defenseless men and stealing from helpless women. Whenever faced with a real fight against real soldiers, and without the advantage of surprise and overwhelming numbers, they always ran like the cowards they were. All Johnston asked was a chance to get at them in a regular, straight-out battle. Then he, Andrew Vern Emen "Ave" Johnston, would teach them a lesson they never would forget—that is, those who survived, which he hoped would be few, very few.

Continuing to peer through his field glasses, Johnston saw the guerrillas begin to move southward. At once he called in the pickets and ordered his men to mount up. After taking one more look through the glasses, he stowed them away in their case and climbed into the saddle of his beautiful gray. Ahead was a sight few Federals in Missouri had been privileged to see: bushwhackers out in the open, outnumbered, and obviously unaware that they were being trailed.[12]

Of course his soldiers, on their farm animals, could not hope to overtake them if it came to a chase. But the trail was hot, the scent strong, and maybe, just maybe, they would get close enough to pour into these men hot lead in the form of .577-caliber Enfield slugs that ripped guts to pieces and shattered arm and leg bones so badly that as a rule only amputation could prevent a wounded man from becoming a dead man. All they needed was for their luck to hold.

Ave Johnston waved his arm and gave the command. Companies A, G, and H, each lined up in a column of twos, resumed their march across the prairie.

What Johnston did not and could not know was that the guerrillas he had observed through his field glasses were not the same ones who had menaced Paris the evening before. Those raiders were camped southeast of Centralia and so far beyond the range of Johnston's glasses that he

Figure 5.2 Major "Ave" Johnston. COURTESY OF THE STATE HISTORICAL SOCIETY OF MISSOURI.

could not have seen them even if they had not been concealed by the woods along Young's Creek. In all probability, what Johnston saw was a bushwhacker band and/or some Confederate recruits seeking to join up with Anderson, Todd, and the rest. But whoever they were, by being where and when they were, they performed a key role in transforming that glorious autumn day into the most horrible one in Missouri's entire bloodsoaked history of the Civil War.[13]

CENTRALIA, MISSOURI: 10:00–11:00 A.M., SEPTEMBER 27, 1864

Two stores, as many hotels, and a score of squat houses huddled around the large, new depot. Such was Centralia, one among dozens of little whistle-stops that had sprung up along the North Missouri Railroad. So far the great Civil War had hardly touched the hamlet. In 1861 some local secessionist zealots had wrecked railroad culverts in the vicinity, and only three weeks earlier guerrillas had surprised a freight train at the water tank and took some horses and soldiers off of it. But otherwise the war had left Centralia alone. There was simply nothing in or around the place worth fighting for. Even so, at 10:00 A.M. on September 27, 1864, Bill Anderson and his men rode in and helped themselves to what Centralia had to offer.[14]

Some of the bushwhackers drifted into homes demanding breakfast. More looted the tiny stores of their pathetic stock—cloth, candy, ribbons and other notions. What they did not want, they tossed out onto the street, where their horses soon trampled the items into the dirt. Snooping about the railroad tracks, others enjoyed better luck. Although the six boxcars on the siding proved empty, inside the depot they discovered crates of much-needed boots and shoes and—glory be!—a large barrel of whiskey. A pistol butt quickly stove in its top, and with shouts of glee everyone began dipping madly with their cups. In short order most of the men became wildly drunk, and a dull morning turned into a joyous revel.[15]

Few drank deeper than Anderson himself as he sat, wearing a Federal uniform jacket, in the lobby of the Eldorado House hotel. Whiskey had become more than just a good drunk; it was a warm friend. It deadened his brain and blurred his memories. The liquid fire roaring down his throat soothed his soul and melted away the hard ache within. But what he thirsted for more than whiskey was blood—the blood of Union soldiers. Only that would wipe from his mind the image of his six good men shot, scalped, and left to rot on the ground.

Toward 11:00 A.M. the guerrillas saw a dust cloud approaching Centralia on the road to the south—the Columbia stage. Several raiders raced for their horses to be first in line to rob it. As the men galloped away, Anderson drank his whiskey and listened to the wild laughter and shouting of the men who remained behind. Let them have their fun. There was no danger of an attack. A Federal column would be spotted long before it reached the village. The broad treeless prairie offered an unobstructed view in all directions. Only to the east, where the land dipped briefly to the strip of timber along Young's Creek, was the flat plain disturbed. Beyond that shallow valley, five miles from Centralia, the twin iron bands of the North Missouri Railroad made a bend. According to the schedule posted in the depot, a westbound passenger train was due to reach the village at 11:35 and so would be rounding that bend before long. Anderson had men posted in the woods along Young's Creek to give warning should there be a strong guard aboard that train. That was unlikely, though. The Federals were obviously employing every soldier they could to guard the main towns and hunt down guerrillas, his band in particular. Besides, why would they put troops on a passenger train? They no doubt figured that since bushwhackers had never stopped and robbed one of them, there was no risk of that happening. If that was their reasoning, they were about to learn that there was a first time for everything. . . .

Meanwhile, the pack of Anderson's men, wild-eyed and more or less drunk, who had ridden off after the stagecoach caught up to it and surrounded it. "Out with your pocket books!" they shouted as the passengers stepped out of the stage. With revolvers pressed against their chests, they all promptly complied. One of them, however, protested: "We are Southern men and Confederate sympathizers. You ought not rob us."

"What do we care?" came the reply. "Hell's full of all such Southern men. Why ain't you in the army or out fighting?"

One of the passengers had a lot more to worry about than losing his money. James Sidney Rollins happened to be a member of the U.S. House of Representatives, not to mention a two-time candidate (unsuccessful) of the Whig Party for the governorship of Missouri. If the guerrillas found out who he was, they would either kill him on the spot or—more probable—hold him prisoner until they obtained a large ransom and then put a bullet into him, if not worse. Although a conservative who had opposed immediate and universal emancipation of slaves and the Radical Republicans who espoused it, Rollins also was a staunch Unionist and well-known to be such. In Confederate eyes he was a traitor.

So when one of the bushwhackers asked him his name, he answered, "The Reverend Mr. Johnson, minister of the Methodist Church, South," emphasizing the last word. This seemed to satisfy his questioner, and Rollins relaxed a little. Then the robbers began searching the pockets of their prisoners and going through their luggage. Rollins carried letters and other papers bearing his real name, and the clothes in his bag had been inscribed with the initials JSR. They surely would learn his true identity. And then. . . .[16]

MEXICO, MISSOURI: 11:05 A.M., SEPTEMBER 27, 1864

The shrill whistle sounded, and with a screech of brakes and clank of iron, the train jolted to a halt. A warm sun bathed the depot, just beyond which lay the pretty town of Mexico. A number of well-dressed passengers stepped from the cars and onto the platform. Most of them were delegates to a convention of Missouri's Conservative Party, the convention to which Rollins had been traveling until he was abruptly stopped on the outskirts of Centralia.

Tom Goodman and his fellow soldiers sat staring out the windows. Nearby, a construction train loaded with men and gravel sat on a siding, steam up, waiting for the coaches to pass that it might follow. The ride up from St. Charles had proved to be nothing like the suspenseful trip imagined by the soldiers. Wentzville . . . Wright City . . . Warrenton . . . Wellsville . . . Jefftown . . . a monotonous succession of tiny towns dropped down on land as flat as a griddle. Far from being charged with rumors and alarms, the hamlets along the line were as quiet and drowsy as Iowa on the Sabbath. The noise at St. Charles about guerrillas had been, like that in north Georgia about Wheeler's cavalry, just another humbug.

Then, to their surprise, Goodman and his companions noticed a commotion around the station. Men paced the platform, pausing from time to time to cast quick, nervous glances up the track. Others—their faces long and serious—stood in small clusters, for the most part silent. From what little those in the coach could glean, something was occurring not far ahead up the line. The stir around the station spread rapidly through the train until a buzz of excitement swept the cars.[17]

Richard Overall, the train's conductor, left the depot and started across the platform. Several excited men followed, urging him to remain in Mexico. It would be madness, they argued, to proceed farther. The train should not leave the station without a proper guard.

While he listened to these pleas, Overall pondered what he had been told earlier that morning at Jefftown by an eastbound conductor: Guerrillas had been spotted around Centralia. But it was only twenty miles west from Mexico to Sturgeon, with its blockhouse and garrison, and broad, flat prairie all the way—that is, except at Young's Creek just east of Centralia. There, three weeks ago, by a water tank at which trains normally stopped so that the steam locomotives could replenish their thirsting boilers, a band of bushwhackers had dashed out of a belt of timber and captured a freight train. Not only had they seized four carloads of good horses, they had also led away a half-dozen soldiers to be held as hostages for a captured comrade. Since then, however, no guerrilla attacks on trains had occurred, and traffic continued to run normally.

Overall made his decision. As conductor he had a schedule to keep—which the presence of the superintendent of the North Missouri Railroad on his train made him all the more resolved to do. Besides, if trains stopped for every report or rumor of guerrillas along the line that had buzzed about like a swarm of bees during the past few weeks, the road might as well shut down for good. When all was said and done, these alarms had been nothing more than whiffs of smoke, and each sighting of guerrillas had turned out to be merely some farmers on horseback going to town. As for guards, blue uniforms already filled one car, and even now seven troopers of the First Iowa Cavalry were boarding it, several with sidearms. No, the train would continue as scheduled, and that would be the end of it.

Overall climbed aboard the lead coach and glanced up and down the train: engine, tender, express car, baggage car, and four coaches containing 125 passengers, one-fifth of them uniformed soldiers. He then checked his pocket watch; it read 11:05. He closed up the watch and waved the signal. The locomotive's whistle answered, and with a mighty heave, the train pulled away from the station.[18]

ON THE PRAIRIE SOUTH OF LONG BRANCH CREEK: ABOUT 11:10 A.M.

Throughout the morning Johnston's men had continued southward, but ever so slowly. Their plow horses and mules, most of them poor specimens even of their kind, simply could not move fast, and it was necessary to rest them periodically to keep them moving at all. Worse, the bushwhackers' trail had soon become lost, resulting in a long halt while scouts tried to find it again.

Finally they did. It swerved off to the southwest, in the general direction of Centralia and Sturgeon. Johnston decided to head for the first of those towns, some ten miles distant. His march resumed.[19]

NORTH MISSOURI RAILROAD BETWEEN MEXICO AND YOUNG'S CREEK: 11:15–11:30 A.M.

James Clark knew every inch of the North Missouri Railroad. From the hilly banks of the Missouri at St. Charles to the flat plains around Macon City, every bridge, culvert, switch, crossing, grade, bump, twist, and turn on the route was known intimately by the twenty-five-year-old engineer. Since 1860 the young English immigrant had been hauling freight and passengers over the two-hundred-mile ribbon of iron until he had come to know the moods and currents of the surrounding countryside as well as he knew the valves and gauges of the great fire-consuming monster he operated. Although the risks seemed remote, in Clark's mind if there was any truth to this latest rash of rumors, the most likely spot would be at the tank, just before Centralia. In all that flat and treeless plain from Mexico to Sturgeon, the brush along Young's Creek was the only possible place where a large group of men could lay in wait unseen.

When the conductor had given the go-ahead back at Mexico, Clark ordered his fireman to lay on the wood with a will. They were blowing her through, he said, all the way to Centralia, fourteen miles ahead. The engineer also took the precaution of making sure there was plenty of water in the boiler. There would be no stop at the tank this trip. James Clark had already suffered one close shave on this line—or so it had appeared—and it was more than enough to last a lifetime.

Back early in the war, Clark had been in his cab at some quiet village depot, getting set to take her out. Suddenly a wide-eyed telegraph operator burst from the station, screaming that the guerrillas were coming. In his scramble to leave the station, Clark had jerked the throttle back so hard that the lurch almost "ditched" the train—tender, cars, and all. Although he had soon learned that the cry had been a false alarm—just a few locals celebrating word of a victory somewhere—the shaken engineer, on reaching the nearest military post, announced that without a large guard for his train he'd not go one tie farther. When the officer balked, Clark had made good his vow.

Things had quieted down somewhat since, and over the years Clark had mellowed and learned to abide surprises on the North Missouri. But the memory of that one terrifying moment was a thing not soon forgotten, and he would do whatever it took to avoid a repetition.[20]

Back in one of the coaches, Tom Goodman became aware of the train's acceleration. It had pulled out of the Mexico station as usual. But then it began moving faster and faster, and now it rattled along at an almost frightening pace. And as the speed increased, so did the passengers' concern. Obviously the engineer thought that there might be trouble up ahead. Perhaps the rumors about guerrillas were true after all. . . .

Goodman sat tensely in his seat, eyes fixed on the sun-washed prairie flying past the window. To the west, a long strip of trees appeared on the horizon.[21]

Nine miles out from Mexico, the locomotive swung around the final bend before the water tank. Beyond, Centralia came into view. With a full head of steam the train thundered down the slope into the valley of Young's Creek, clattered across the short bridge, and roared past the tank. James Clark gave a sigh of relief. There would be no trouble that day.[22]

Someone glanced out and spotted several horsemen watching the train from the edge of the woods. Other passengers saw the same and yelled for the conductor. Richard Overall went to a window and stared out for a moment. He then turned around and announced that there was nothing to worry about. The horsemen were just farmers—or perhaps hunters.[23]

The engine cleared the valley and leveled out again. James Clark had a straight shot into Centralia, less than a mile away. As he drew nearer, he beheld a large group of blue-clad horsemen lined up along the south side of the track across from the depot. He prayed that they were soldiers, but he knew that the guerrillas, too, often wore Federal uniform jackets.

"We may strike the wrong gang this time," he yelled to the fireman. "If we do, look out for yourself."

Then he saw men around the station piling ties onto the track. That settled it. They were bushwhackers. He briefly thought of reversing the train, but to do that, he would first have to stop it, and before he could get it going backward the bushwhackers would be swarming all around. And even if he somehow managed to get away, there was the danger of colliding with the gravel-filled work train following behind his own.

So he decided to jerk open the throttle and throw himself onto the deck of the engine house. Maybe traveling at full tilt as it was, the train could smash through the obstructions on the track without derailing. If so, it could go on to Sturgeon and safety. Not even the guerrillas' fastest horses matched the speed of an iron horse.[24]

Leaning from a window, someone in Goodman's car shouted that there were riders around the Centralia station. Another passenger looked out and declared that they were militia on drill. An Iowa trooper sitting beside Goodman jumped to the window to see for himself; he knew guerrillas when he saw them, for he had seen them many times and could tell them from militia no matter what they wore. He peered intently up the line.

When he turned around, his face drained of color, he muttered: "There are guerrillas there, sure!"

No one seemed to notice the brakeman scurrying down the aisle, doing what a brakeman is supposed to do: setting the brakes, located at the rear of each car, when approaching a station. The train began slowing. It was stopping. The shrill whistle blew and from below came the awful screech of grinding brakes.

Goodman listened to these sounds. He listened to the shouts of the blue-uniformed men riding around outside the train. And, rising above the groan of spinning wheels and grinding brakes, he listened to the sobs and screams of the women and children inside the train.[25]

Now he could understand the uneasiness he had felt while passing through Kentucky and why he had trouble sleeping the last night before in St. Louis. He had been experiencing a presentiment of what was about to happen to him: death.

He would not be going home. He never would see and hold his wife and children again, nor they him. Not in this world.

CHAPTER SIX

YOU ALL ARE TO BE KILLED

CENTRALIA: HIGH NOON, SEPTEMBER 27, 1864

"The train! The train! Yonder comes the train!"

To the east a black plume of smoke appeared above the bend, growing larger as it moved toward Centralia. Wild excitement swept the drunken bushwhackers gathered around the depot. Some grabbed rails and ties to throw on the track, most ran to their horses. Among the latter were the men who had held up the stagecoach. Why bother looking through luggage when there were whole carloads of people who could be robbed? Realizing that he had gotten a reprieve, if only temporary, Congressman James Rollins sought what he hoped would be a good hiding place. Thanks to Thomas Sneed, proprietor of the Boone House, one of Centralia's two hotels, he found it in the maid's room on the second floor.[1]

The train rumbled down the far grade, then dipped into the valley of Young's Creek. It came at full speed, as if intending to race through Centralia. Bushwhackers piled more rails and ties on the track. Then the train began slowing . . . slowing . . . slowing. Finally, although the drive wheels of the engine still revolved, iron screeching against iron, the train stopped. It was beside the depot but short of the obstructions across the track.

Goodman saw them through the window: long-haired, wild-looking young men in uniforms identical to his own, astride horses and waving revolvers. Suddenly they opened fire on the cars. Glass shards and wood splinters rained down on the passengers who huddled in terror on the floor. The screams of women and children provided a shrill counterpoint to the roar of gunfire.[2]

Lying on the floor on the engine cab, James Clark regretted that his attempt to run through Centralia had failed. Reaching up, he closed the throttle; the groaning wheels grew silent. Clark then found himself staring into the muzzles of a half-dozen big revolvers.

"For God's sake, don't shoot!" cried the fireman, who lay on the floor next to Clark.

"Get down from there!" commanded one of the gunmen.

Clark and the fireman obeyed. Practiced hands quickly relieved them of their money and timepieces. Either by intent or accident, one of the bushwhackers shot the fireman in the chest, inflicting a nasty, but as it turned out, not serious, wound.

Money and watches, though, were not all the guerrillas wanted. "Take down those flags, you son of a bitch," they growled at Clark, waving their pistols at the two United States flags attached to poles on each side of the locomotive's headlamp.

Clark climbed up the engine front and tore away the flags. Although he moved as fast as he could, it seemed to him that his feet were caught in quicksand, and he expected to be shot when he completed the task. Instead, much to his relief, the bushwhackers holstered their revolvers and headed for the express car. Before leaving, one of them tossed the reins of his mount to the fireman. "If you let my horse get away," he warned, "I'll blow your damn head off."[3]

Once the wheels of the engine stopped turning, and having met no resistance, the guerrillas ceased firing, dismounted, and boarded the train. In the express car, the agent, faced with enough pistols literally to blow him apart, promptly surrendered the key to the safe. Anderson himself opened it and pulled out $3,000, which he pocketed. In the baggage car Frank James and Peyton Long found a valise. "Good God! Here's thousands of greenbacks!" James yelled. "Run here, quick!" Seconds later, more than a dozen men crammed the baggage car, tearing frenziedly at luggage, trunks, and boxes.

Other bushwhackers led by Archie Clements entered the passenger cars, where they promptly relieved men, women, and even children of money, jewelry, watches, and anything else that struck their fancy. Noting that the raiders refrained from searching the clothes of females, some of the male passengers hastily slipped money and rings to women standing next to them. All the while the guerrillas fired bullets into the ceilings of the coaches and shouted obscenities, eliciting in turn sobs and screams from terrified women and children.[4]

"Are there soldiers on the train?" a voice, probably Clements's, demanded. Passengers answered that they were, adding that the soldiers were not armed. Seconds later the door to the coach carrying Tom Goodman burst open, and the bushwhackers rushed in, revolvers in hand, shouting "Surrender! Surrender!" Then, seeing the soldiers grouped and standing in the aisle as if prepared to resist, they hesitated and one of them said: "Surrender quietly and you shall be treated as prisoners of war."

"We can only surrender," a soldier replied, "as we are totally unarmed."

At once the guerrillas' caution gave way to angry growls and threats as they stuck pistols into the soldiers' faces and proceeded to rob them. In addition to money, three troopers of the First Iowa handed over their revolvers. They had not attempted to use them, knowing that it would be useless and only lead to terrible retaliation.[5]

Anderson, now mounted, rode alongside the train, telling his men to leave the women alone. Some of the bushwhackers, drunk as they were, had "taken liberties." He then ordered all passengers out of the train and onto the platform—except, that is, the soldiers; they were to go to the other side. Goodman and his comrades felt that there was something ominous about being separated from the civilians. As they stepped down into a waiting circle of guerrillas, terror clutched their hearts. Never had they seen such faces: young, cruel, scornful, and full of hate.

"Take off your uniforms! Strip!" cursed the bushwhackers. The soldiers began unbuttoning their jackets, removing shoes or boots, pulling off pants. Someone had to help Bill Barnum—a member of the Twenty-third Iowa Infantry and like Goodman from Page County, Iowa—because of his crutches.

On the other side of the train, Anderson watched the civilians filing out of the coaches. With a wave of his pistol, he motioned the men to one side. The bushwhackers then did a more thorough and systematic job of robbing them than had been possible amidst the noise and confusion on the train. A wealthy sutler surrendered $1,600 in currency and a $400 gold watch. Another man, whose attire suggested affluence, turned over only a few dollars. Disappointed and suspicious, his robber asked his if that was all he had. The man replied that it was. Staring into his eyes, Anderson warned him that he would be searched, and if anything was found hidden. . . . The man quickly tugged off a boot and pulled out $100. A sharp explosion shattered the air, and in a blue cloud of smoke the victim tumbled to the track. His mother, with whom he had been traveling, screamed, then broke into sobs. Many of the other women also began wailing and screaming, as did their children.

One of the guerrillas spotted a man who had once testified against him and almost got him hung. The bushwhacker raised his revolver and fired. The bullet missed and the man ducked into the crowd. Other guerrillas pulled him out, and the next bullets hit their target, dropping him by the track, where he lay moaning and writhing in agony.

Anderson next ordered that the depot, a warehouse, and some boxcars sitting on a siding be set afire. That done, he rode away; he had other business to attend to.[6]

Tom Goodman and his companions stood helpless under the bright sun, clad only in their underwear or in some instances nothing at all. Altogether they numbered twenty-four. One of them, though, was actually a civilian who had been wearing a blue blouse. He tried to explain that he was not a soldier, but he also was a German whose English was so poor that he could not make himself understood. It would have made no difference if he had; the bushwhackers hated "Dutchmen" only slightly less than they did Federal troops and Kansas jayhawkers.

Anderson rode up and ordered the soldiers to form a line across the street next to the store. They now realized that they were going to be killed. Some accepted their fate stoically, and if they prayed, they did so silently. Others sobbed and begged for mercy, only to be cursed by the guerrillas, who herded them over to the store with shoves and vicious kicks. Barnum hobbled along on his crutches. Two soldiers hung back and called on the others to do the same. Anderson immediately shot them. Their corpses tumbled between two of the cars.

Once the line was formed, Little Archie Clements turned to Anderson and asked, "What are we going to do with these fellows?"

"*Parole* them, of course."

"I thought so," Little Archie laughed. "You might pick out two or three, though, and exchange them for Cave." He referred to Cave Wyatt, the bushwhacker "sergeant" who had been wounded and captured by a detachment of the Ninth Missouri Militia four days earlier.

Anderson pondered the matter. The odds against being able to arrange a prisoner exchange were great. But it was worth a try.

"One will be enough," he said as he rode over to where the soldiers stood. For a while he sat in his saddle, silently staring at them. Finally he spoke:

"Boys, have you a sergeant in your ranks?"

A cold shiver ran through Goodman. *Why?* he asked himself. *For what purpose?*

"Have you a sergeant in your ranks?" Anderson repeated in a louder voice. "If there be one, let him step aside."

Goodman remained frozen in the line. He dared not move. A sergeant was being selected for some terrible fate, he was sure, and to step forward was to commit suicide. Then, to his horror, he saw the bushwhacker who had taken his jacket with its sergeant chevrons approach Anderson. In fact, there were several sergeants among the prisoners, but he would be the one picked. It would be better to. . . . Suddenly he found himself standing alone in front of the line.

Anderson, his eyes and face expressionless, gazed at the stalwart man in his underwear for a moment. Then he ordered two of his followers to take the prisoner away and keep a close watch over him. As he marched off with his guards, Goodman wondered what fate Anderson had in store for him. Whatever it was, it would be something special. And awful.

Anderson turned once more to the line of soldiers.

"You Federals have just killed six of my soldiers, scalped them, and left them on the prairie. I am too honorable a man to permit any man to be scalped, but I will show you that I can kill men with as much skill and rapidity as anybody. From this time forward I ask no quarter and give none. Every Federal soldier on whom I put my finger shall die like a dog. If I get into your clutches, I expect death. You all are to be killed and sent to hell. That is the way every damned soldier shall be served who falls into my hands."

Some of the soldiers begged for mercy, declaring that they were from Sherman's army in Georgia and had nothing to do with killing and scalping Anderson's men.

"I treat you all as one!" Anderson shouted back. "You are Federals, and Federals scalped my men and carry their scalps at their saddle bows."

He then raised his revolvers, cocking them. The other bushwhackers did the same. Some of the soldiers turned away, their eyes closed, waiting for the cruel jolt of pain to come. Others fell to their knees, crying, "No! No!" and, "O God, have mercy!" Those who looked into the faces of their executioners saw only hatred staring back.

The roar of revolver fire shattered the air, followed by wild yells from the guerrillas and moans and cries from their victims. Most of the soldiers lay on the ground, dead or dying. A few still staggered about in the swirling gun smoke but soon went down as more bullets tore into them. All except Val Peters. His giant, naked body streaming blood, he rushed toward his assailants, knocked down several of them with his fists, then ducked under the train and slid beneath the platform.

The bushwhackers gave chase and quickly surrounded the depot, waiting for the flames that engulfed it to force the big Yankee out into the open. They did not have to wait long. Bolting from the rear of the station and brandishing a piece of firewood, Peters again charged his attackers, clubbing down two of them and forcing others to back off. But the bullets kept coming. Struck again and again, he finally teetered for a moment and then, like a great oak chopped off at the base, crashed to the ground. With his last remnant of strength, he raised himself with an elbow and lifted a huge fist to heaven.

"My Lord . . .," he cried out.

Riddled by twenty bullets, Valentine Peters at last dropped to earth.[7]

Back in front of the store, the bushwhackers strode among the bodies, sometimes kicking them. If there a groan was emitted, a shot in the head would follow. One victim lay unconscious with a bullet above the eye, another in the face, and a third in the chest. Even so, his heel continued to dig at the ground, back and forth. Watching him, Clements remarked, with characteristic humor, "He's marking time." The guerrillas finished off two other soldiers by crushing their skills with rifle butts and another by stabbing him in the throat. Anderson's words to the contrary, two soldiers had their scalps hacked off.[8]

From his hiding place in the hotel Rollins watched all of this with mounting horror. Now all he could do was hope and pray that no one in Centralia had recognized him and told the guerrillas about him. But someone had—and told Anderson, who resolved to hunt Rollins down. That should be easy enough in a hamlet of no more than a couple dozen buildings. Moreover, a congressman would make a far better hostage than a mere sergeant. But then Anderson changed his mind. Maybe he decided that it wasn't worth the bother. Or maybe it was the whiskey. For whatever reason, instead of conducting a search for Rollins, he sent several bushwhackers to find the train's engineer, tell him what he was to do, and make sure he did it.[9]

When they reached the locomotive, they found the wounded fireman, still holding the horse, but not James Clark. "Where's your boss?" they asked.

Pointing, the fireman answered, "There he is, getting over the fence."

The guerrillas caught Clark straddling the fence and brought him back to his train. Once he was in the cab, they ordered him to tie the whistle down, open the throttle, and then jump out when they gave the signal.

Meanwhile, other bushwhackers set fire to the express and baggage cars. On seeing this, Thomas Sneed, who had provided Rollins with a hiding place in his hotel, ran frantically through the coaches, searching for anyone still in them—and still alive. He discovered a mother and her three children cringing beneath a seat and paralyzed with fear. Only by repeatedly telling them that they would burn to death if they remained did he persuade them to leave.

Other townsmen, on orders from the guerrillas, cleared away the pile of rails and ties on the track. Clark then set the locomotive in motion. With riders on both sides yelling "Give 'er hell!" he took the train from the blazing station out onto the prairie. Satisfied that the engine was on its own, the bushwhackers shouted at Clark to jump, which he did. The flaming train, its whistle screaming, went hurtling up the track toward Sturgeon.

Anderson felt pleased, and with good cause. He had come to Centralia to obtain word about Price, which he had done from newspapers found on the train. But he had done a hell of a lot more than that. He had revenged four times over his murdered and scalped men. Plus, he and his followers had acquired plenty of money, jewelry, and sundry other loot, not to mention burning a depot and a warehouse and torching the train—now hurtling toward destruction. Only Lawrence and, in its way, Baxter Springs topped what had been done there in Centralia that day.

But now it was time to leave. At Anderson's command, the guerrillas mounted up and formed into a column. While they did so, Anderson rode over to the passengers, assessed the trembling group for a moment, then asked,

"Anyone care for a drink?" A nervous man stepped forward—he realized that he was as likely to receive a bullet as a drink—and Anderson handed him a bottle. He took a quick swig and handed it back. After warning that the bodies of the soldiers were not to be moved or any fires extinguished, Anderson started to turn his horse around.

"Can we go on with our trip?" a woman asked.

"Go on to hell, for all I care," Anderson answered.[10]

Seconds later he led his band, some of whom had whiskey-filled boots hanging from both sides of their saddles, south out of Centralia. With them, still clad in his underwear and riding atop a mule, was Tom Goodman. From the stable where his two guards had taken him, he had watched the butchery of his fellow soldiers and Val Peters's titanic struggle to escape death. He himself had come close to suffering the same fate. Drunken bushwhackers had surrounded him, taunting and threatening him: "Hellfire is too good for you, you son of a bitch!" "Kill the damn yankee!" Several attempted to do just that, pointing their pistols at him. Only the efforts of his guards and their threat to call Anderson saved him from being shot, if not torn to shreds. He owed his life to them, yet knew that at a mere nod from Anderson they would deprive him of it. Why was he being spared? Was it for some slow, special torture? If so, he wished he was already dead.[11]

Hardly had the bushwhackers left Centralia than they heard a familiar sound. Looking off to the east, they saw a construction train approaching the village. Anderson and the main body continued on toward their camp, but a large group broke away from the column. It halted the train just short of the burning depot—why its engineer had not stopped and reversed on spotting the flames and smoke is beyond fathoming—and proceeded to rob the crew and workmen. That done, the guerrillas placed a soldier's corpse across the track, then ordered the engineer to move the train up to the station. Horrified, he protested and pleaded, only to be greeted with howls of laughter and the brandishing of pistols. Easing back on the throttle, the engineer inched his train forward until, with a sickening crunch, the locomotive rolled over the body and sheared off the legs at the knees. The bump caused the front wheels to jump the track, thereby preventing more such acts and also demonstrating that in all probability Clark's attempt to ram through the obstructions on the track would have ended in disaster had there been enough speed to try. After setting fire to the tender and caboose, the bushwhackers rode off to rejoin the main body while the crew and workers began trudging back toward Mexico.[12]

Many of the passengers also set out for Mexico, some walking, others in buggies and wagons, and a few on a handcar. Most of them, though, followed Clark as he set out on foot toward Sturgeon. Three miles along they came upon the smoldering remains of the train's cars. Climbing into the cab of the still intact locomotive, Clark carefully fed wood from the tender, which also was little damaged, into the firebox until he raised a head of steam. Then, with dozens of people clinging to its sides, the engine started rolling westward.

Meanwhile, large numbers of Centralia's residents fled the village, most heading in any direction except south. Among them was James Rollins. He would be late for the convention at Mexico but did not mind in the least. That was better than being dead—or for that matter alive and a prisoner of the bushwhackers.[13]

CHAPTER SEVEN

THE LORD HAVE MERCY

THE GUERRILLA CAMP, YOUNG'S CREEK: 2:00–3:00 P.M.

"I say, Bill, I wonder how in the hell Anderson has permitted this damn Yankee to live so long?"

"Dunno, can't say, lest like 'twas a Providence, for taint like Old Bill, is it?"

No, thought Tom Goodman, who overhead his two guards talking, *it is not like Anderson at all.* The big sergeant lay on the ground. Around him, most of the bushwhackers were sleeping off the whiskey they had guzzled. He, too, had tried to sleep but in vain. He simply could not stop wondering what Anderson intended to do with him—or, rather, to him.

He looked about and observed the guerrilla chieftain sitting with George Todd, John Thrailkill, and other leaders, apparently discussing future operations. *Can,* he thought, *yon pale, sad looking man be this fiend in human shape?* Anderson's face, when passive as it now was, did not look like that of a man to be feared. Even his cold and expressionless eyes revealed nothing; they were "unfathomable." So what had made him what he so terribly was? The best that Goodman could think of was a scrap of poetry remembered from school days: "Man's inhumanity to man/Makes countless thousands weep."

Suddenly a rider came racing full speed across the prairie toward the camp. At the same time another horseman, coming from the north, rode up to Anderson, who along with everyone else sprang to his feet. Goodman could not hear what the second rider said to the chieftain, but within minutes the guerrillas had mounted their horses and formed into squads of ten or twenty. While they were doing so, the first rider reached Anderson, who asked him a couple questions, after which a bushwhacker came over to Goodman and spoke to his guards: "Have your prisoner saddle yon gray horse, and mount him quick—and mark me, if he attempts to escape in the battle, kill him instantly!"

As he saddled and mounted the designated horse, a wave of hope surged through Goodman. There was going to be a battle! Forgetting the threat of death hanging over him, he could think only of the battle. He longed to see a line of Federal blue dealing retribution, like avenging angels of God, to the murderers of his comrades.[1]

Should this happen, perhaps he would be rescued and so live to see his wife and children again after all. . . .

CENTRALIA: 3:00–3:30 P.M.

Major Johnston and his men rode into Centralia from the east, having headed straight for the place on seeing columns of smoke rising from its vicinity.[2] Nothing they had ever encountered or imagined matched the dreadful scene they now beheld. The few people of the village who had not fled or remained cowering in their homes stood around as if transformed into statues, mute, pale, and with vacant eyes staring from frozen faces. Debris from the looted stores littered the streets. Alongside the railroad track lay heaps of smoking ashes. Far worse were the bodies which seemed to be everywhere. One sprawled near the burned depot was a black and almost shapeless mass. Behind the station was a huge, nude form literally shot to pieces. Next to the track were two chalk-white legs and close by a dismembered trunk. And on the south side of the track, lying in pools of reeking blood and covered by swarms of blowflies, was a long row of twisted, bullet-torn corpses, most of them attired in underwear but some stark naked.

Some of Johnston's young soldiers, most of whom were still teenagers, struggled not to vomit. The eyes of others blazed with anger, and still others shuddered as if suddenly chilled despite the warm September sun. They had heard what bushwhackers did to captured soldiers. Now they saw it for themselves.

Johnston asked several villagers about the size of the guerrilla force and what direction it had taken on leaving. All answered that it numbered no more than eighty and that it had headed south. Then, led by Dr. A. F. Sneed, Thomas Sneed's brother, Johnston went to the Boone House Hotel and climbed up to the attic. Through his field glasses he scanned the prairie to the south and sighted a group of horsemen riding toward Centralia from the belt of timber along Young's Creek.

"There they are now!" he cried, then raced down the stairs. Dr. Sneed followed and asked him if he intended to attack the bushwhackers.

"I do," snapped the major, who then asked: "How many are there are of these fellows?"

"I do not know exactly, but they are said to number about four hundred. They outnumber you."

"But you told me a little while ago there were only eighty of them in town this morning."

"Yes, but the remainder of them are in camp. Besides, they all have revolvers and they are better mounted than your men."

"They may have the advantage of me in numbers, but I will have the advantage of them in arms. My guns are of long range and I can fight them from a distance."

"It's folly to fight them," pleaded Sneed—who, ironically, was a Southern sympathizer. "They are well-trained and desperate men."

For a moment Johnston said nothing. All around him were the wreckage, the burned building, and the bodies—most of all, the bodies. Finally he spoke: "I will fight them, anyhow."

He mounted his horse and rejoined his command. First he sent a courier speeding back to Sturgeon with a request for reinforcements. Next he instructed Capt. Adam Theiss, commander of Company H, to remain in Centralia with thirty-three of his men and two teamsters to guard the wagons. Then, with the remainder of his troops, about 115 in number, he set forth on the Columbia road to engage the enemy.[3]

SOUTHEAST OF CENTRALIA: 3:30–4:15 P.M.

Once beyond Centralia, the major sent forward an advance guard of twenty-five skirmishers at a trot to flush out any guerrillas who might be lurking in ambush. After about a mile they saw ten or so of them two hundred yards up ahead. The bushwhackers at once retreated southward, passing through a previously made opening in a rail fence. The advance guard pursued, followed by Johnston with the main body, now moving at a "brisk walk." Once, then again, the bushwhackers halted to fire a flurry of revolver shots, then resumed their flight. "Wait for us, you damned cowards!" Johnston yelled.

Two miles from Centralia the guerrillas swerved off to the east and disappeared over a ridge. Some of the excited soldiers raised a cheer and galloped ahead. Cursing, their officers ordered them back into line. A little farther on anxious troops again broke away and again had to be shouted back. Intent on holding formation, Johnston and his officers failed to note the small but ever-deepening ravines on either side of them and the increasing amount of brush and weeds that grew there.

The soldiers reached the top of the ridge. Spread out before them lay a broad, open plain sloping gently a quarter of a mile to a belt of trees along Young's Creek. From the trees, their horses moving at a slow walk, emerged lines of bushwhackers. They were not running after all—they were coming out to fight. At a glance Johnston could see that there were only around eighty of them. He could whip that many, He *would* whip them. . . .

A short distance from the trees the advancing bushwhackers suddenly halted and dismounted. This puzzled Johnston. "They will fight on foot," he muttered to an officer nearby. "What does that mean?"

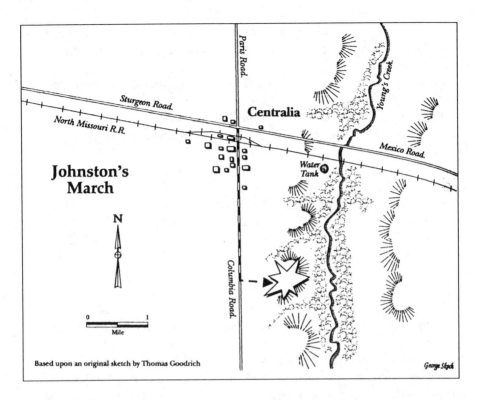

Johnston's March

N

0   1
          Mile

Based upon an original sketch by Thomas Goodrich

George Skoch

He quickly had an answer. The bushwhackers flung off their Union blue jackets, tied them to the back of their saddles, rolled up their shirtsleeves, tightened saddle girths and adjusted bridles, and then checked their revolvers, spinning cylinders and making sure that the caps were solidly in place. Satisfied, they remounted their horses and reformed their line into a single rank in front of which, slightly overlapping it on the left, was the squad that the Federal skirmishers had been chasing. Dave Poole led it, and he had perfectly performed his mission: lure the enemy to where he now was.

Realizing the obvious—that the guerrillas intended to make a mounted charge—Johnston ordered all of his troops to dismount except for twenty-three whom he sent to the rear with the horses. He then deployed his remaining ninety-odd soldiers in a double row about 150 yards long and told them to fix bayonets.

"My God, the Lord have mercy on them!" exclaimed one of the bushwhackers. "They are dismounting to fight!"[4]

An eerie calm reigned over the ridge and the plain below. Not a whisper of wind stirred the tree leaves, now beginning to turn yellow. From a clear blue sky the golden rays of an early-autumn sun slanted down. For several minutes the opposing forces merely gazed at each other.

Johnston grew impatient. Weren't the bastards going to attack, after all? He rode forward, a big Colt revolver grasped in his right hand, and yelled angrily, "We are ready, come on!"

The bushwhackers remained motionless.

Seconds later a horseman, attired entirely in black, rode along behind the bushwhacker line. It was Bill Anderson. As he passed, he repeatedly said, "Boys, when we charge, break through the line and keep straight on for their horses. Keep straight on for their horses."

He then rode out slightly in front of his men, lifted his hat in the air, and gave it a twirl. Up and down the line came the sharp click of revolvers being cocked. Anderson then raised and lowered his hat three times, after which he placed it back on his head, pulled a pistol from his belt, and started forward at a slow walk. His men followed at the same pace.

Johnston watched the guerrillas advancing. Good. It was what he wanted, hoped for, longed for. Now let them get within effective killing range, say three hundred yards, and—

His blood froze. From out of the woods emerged a second line of raiders, a huge one more than double the size of the first. At the same time, from out of the brush-filled ravines on either side of the Federals came still more bushwhackers, with those on the south being headed by George Todd and Si Gordon and those on the north by John Thrailkill and Tom Todd. Johnston had marched his men into a trap from which there could be no escape and in which there could be only one outcome.

Johnston must have realized this. And now he would pay for his blunder. Dismounting, he cocked his revolver, unsheathed his sword, and turned to face his fate.

His eyes riveted on the ridge above, Anderson pushed his steed into a faster walk. His men followed suit. So, too, did the second line. From more than a thousand rapidly pounding hooves a vast cloud of dust rose in the attackers' wake.

Ahead, Anderson saw the enemy begin to waver as soldiers threw down their muskets and broke to the rear. The time had come.

"Charge!" he screamed, digging spurs into the flanks of his horse.

His followers raised a bloodcurdling shriek that ripped the air apart. The soldiers fired a ragged, feeble volley. Many, paralyzed by fear, did not fire at all. Of those who did pull triggers, most fired too high. Only two or three guerrilla toppled from their saddles. The rest kept coming in a veritable avalanche of death. Forty yards from the crest they opened up with their revolvers. Seconds later they swept through and over the soldiers, some of whom were frantically trying to reload their Enfields. Obeying Anderson's instructions, they headed straight for the horse holders, who already were in panic-stricken flight. One by one the raiders overtook and shot them until none were left.

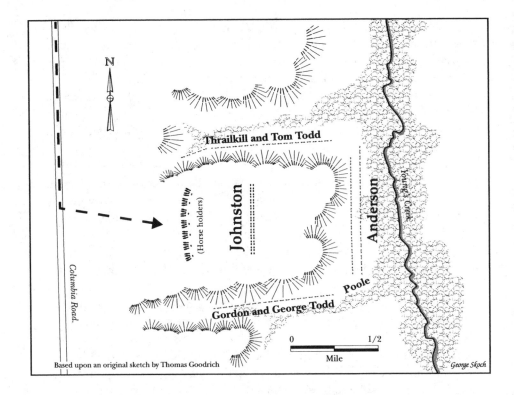

Based upon an original sketch by Thomas Goodrich

George Skoch

On the ridge, the guerrillas emerging from the ravines surrounded and gunned down the surviving soldiers, all the while yelling, "Surrender! Surrender!" A few of the bluecoats fought back with the bayonets; incredibly, they wounded a couple of assailants. Most of them, though, threw down their muskets and raised their arms or else sank to their knees, sobbing and begging for mercy. An exception was Ave Johnston. Standing beside his dead horse, he fired away with his revolver until felled by a bullet. A rider dashed over, leaned down, and shot him in the head. Just to make sure.

The firing ceased. For a moment the bushwhackers sat on their horses, looking at their helpless captives. Their eyes, hitherto filled with the fire and fury of battle, took on a frightening gleam. Then they holstered their pistols and dismounted. Several picked up officer's swords from the ground. More grabbed rifles with their eighteen-inch-long bayonets. Most pulled out great, sharp knives. The prisoners stared at the cold steel in stunned disbelief, then they looked into the faces of the men approaching them.

"I always spare prisoners!" cried a Yankee captain.

"I am a Mason!" pleaded another soldier.

The bushwhackers grinned and continued approaching. . . .[5]

CENTRALIA: APPROXIMATELY 4:15–5:00 P.M.

Dr. A. F. Sneed and Lt. J. E. Stafford of Company H stood together by the attic window, gazing intently southward. They had followed the course of Johnston's column as it pursued the guerrillas. Then mysteriously it had swerved off to the east, halted atop a ridge, dismounted, and formed a thin blue line. Several minutes passed, and then on both sides of the soldiers the brush seemed to be moving. Moments later everything along the ridge disappeared in a cloud of smoke and dust, and a sound came rolling up that reminded Sneed of a "heavy hailstorm beating on glass roofs."

For about three minutes the two men watched and listened in breathless anticipation. Then, almost as quickly as it had begun, the roar of battle ceased. Soon afterward they saw a soldier madly lashing his horse toward Centralia on the Columbia road. A string of riderless horses followed him. Lieutenant Stafford scrambled down the stairs and reached the street just as the horseman entered the village. At once Stafford recognized him: Lt. Thomas Jaynes, commander of Company G.

"Get out of here! Get out of here!" Jaynes shouted as he sped by. "Every one of you will be killed if you don't!"

Terror-stricken, most of the soldiers Johnston had left behind in Centralia leaped on their mounts and whipped them either north up the road to Paris or west toward Sturgeon. Others, however, ran around wildly, seeking places to hide.

Anderson's and Poole's men smashed into the village like a tornado, shooting left and right at the fleeing Federals. Most of them, including Archie Clements and Frank James, never broke stride and with wild whoops gave chase along the road to Sturgeon. The rest pulled up and began searching houses and other buildings for more victims.

One soldier ran into a woman's home and dived under a table. Moments later two bushwhackers burst through the door. Assuring the woman that they "wouldn't kill a dog in a lady's house," they dragged their victim outside and killed him there—proving that they were men who kept their word.

Another fugitive, caught in the open, sought refuge in a privy. Unfortunately for him, several guerrillas saw him enter this convenient, but also highly vulnerable, place of concealment. "Come out!" they demanded. Receiving no reply, they shouted that all of his comrades had been taken prisoner, and he would be treated the same as them. So assured, he opened the door and, beholding friendly faces, smiled with relief. Shots then rang out and he dropped dead. These guerrillas, too, had spoken truly.

Tired and thirsty, a raider rode up to a house and asked for a glass of water. As he started to reach for it he noticed a soldier break from cover and leap a fence. Wheeling his horse around, he gave chase. Soon the sharp crack of a pistol shot came from beyond the fence. Then the guerrilla reappeared and rode back to the house.

"I'll take that drink now," he said blandly.

Another bushwhacker, apparently looking for somebody else to kill, found several women and a driver, a young express agent, sitting in a wagon behind a barn. They all were endeavoring to escape the hell that Centralia had become. One of the women, possibly assuming that she could act with impunity because of her sex, said something that angered the bushwhacker, who responded by striking her with the barrel of his pistol. Outraged, the driver grabbed the barrel, and the two men briefly struggled. The bushwhacker jerked his weapon free and, as the women screamed, shot their would-be protector to death. He then rode away, having found what he had been looking for.

Elsewhere, a group of drunken raiders—whiskey as well as blood was again flowing in Centralia—smashed their way into a house. One of them made an insulting remark to a woman, whereupon she slapped him. Instantly, he knocked her to the floor—but that was all. The taboo against raping or killing women still held.[6]

SOUTHEAST OF CENTRALIA: APPROXIMATELY 5:00 P.M.
Dave Poole returned to the battlefield—or, rather, slaughter ground—where he demonstrated a new way to count enemy dead: hop from body to body. It was

Figure 7.1 Dave Poole. COURTESY OF THE STATE HISTORICAL SOCIETY OF MISSOURI.

easy to do because they lay so closely massed. Guerrilla chieftain Thomas Todd, who was a Baptist preacher, protested that this was "inhuman." Poole merely laughed. "If they are dead I can't hurt them. I cannot count them good without stepping on them. When I got my foot on one this way I know I've got him."[7]

But there were far worse things here than a drunken murderer dancing on corpses.

Some of the dead soldiers, almost all of whom had been stripped naked, lay twisted and crooked in their death agony, pinned down like bugs by bayonets.

A dozen or so, including Ave Johnston, had been scalped. Still more were eyeless, earless, or had dark, oozing holes where their noses had been.

Many lay with heads flattened into mush or smashed open like melons.

Then there were those who had no heads. These had been cut off, stuck on rifle barrels, tied to saddles, or placed atop fence posts and tree stumps like jack-o'-lanterns. If a corpse had a head, it was likely someone else's.

Here and there were bodies lacking hands and feet or arms and legs.

Worst of all, though, was the naked body of a soldier whose genitals had been sawed off and then stuffed into his mouth. His contorted face testified that this had been done to him while still alive.

Altogether, more than a hundred corpses, most horribly mutilated, carpeted the ridge and the field behind it. Bushwhacker casualties totaled two killed outright, one mortally wounded (he died of lockjaw), and ten wounded. The Civil War produced many slaughters and many of them had much higher butcher bills. But few of them were as one-sided as this one three miles southeast of Centralia, Missouri, and none equalled it in gruesome, obscene viciousness. It was the war's epitome of savagery.[8]

Presiding over the slaughter had been Bill Anderson. Some claim that George Todd and John Thrailkill conceived and directed the entire operation.[9] Much more likely is that all of the bushwhacker chieftains present conferred and agreed on the plan, which was merely a standard guerrilla tactic. In any case, Anderson had the leading role and performed it perfectly. More than that, it was his name that became linked to what happened in and near Centralia on September 27, 1864, with the result that he achieved a reputation that rivaled, and in some respects surpassed, that of Quantrill, as witness this editorial that appeared in the *Leavenworth Daily Bulletin* of October 7, 1864:

As Anderson is taking the place of Quantrel [*sic*] in the management of cutthroats in Missouri, the question is often asked, "Who is this Anderson, who is more bloodthirsty than Quantrell!" He is more of a fiend, if possible, than Quantrell. . . .

Henceforth he would be known, and remain known, as Bloody Bill—Bloody Bill Anderson of Centralia.

STURGEON: LATE AFTERNOON

James Clark was doing all he could to get out of Sturgeon. When a southbound train arrived, he told its crew of what had happened in Centralia and at once obtained permission to hook his locomotive onto its cars and head north to Macon City with his passengers. Then two survivors of Johnston's command dashed through the town, yelling that the guerrillas were right behind them. Clark promptly climbed into his cab, yanked open the throttle, and steamed from the station.

But not far. Almost too late he discovered that he had no fuel and so pulled up at a woodshed north of Sturgeon. As he did so, the passengers in the cars began screaming—a horde of horsemen was approaching across the prairie. Clark called for help to load wood onto the tender. Soon there was more than enough, and once again he sent the train racing north. Nearing Renick, he saw blue-clad riders around the depot. With the throttle wide open, the train rumbled on through the village, much to the astonishment of the waiting Federal troopers. Glancing out and recognizing an officer—Lieutenant Draper of the Ninth Missouri—Clark slowed just long enough to shout out to him the news about Centralia and Johnston. Then the train resumed hurtling up the track to Macon City and safety.[10]

CENTRALIA: LATE AFTERNOON TO EVENING

Bushwhackers drifted in and out of Centralia. Many rode back from the chase to Sturgeon joking and laughing with one another, as if returning from some great fox hunt. One bragged that while riding at full gallop, he shot two Federals from their saddles at fifty yards; when he inspected his handiwork, each man had a hole neatly drilled through the head. During the eight-mile dash to Sturgeon, those guerrillas on the fleetest horses sometimes halted to borrow loaded weapons from slower comrades. Archie Clements, whose gun and knife had wreaked the most havoc, had had the satisfaction of killing his final victim within sight of the drawn-up garrison at Sturgeon.

The last rays of the sun reddened the western horizon, and whiskey continued to flow like a river in Centralia as the bushwhackers celebrated what they all hailed as an "extra occasion"—which indeed it had been. Counting those taken from the train, they had killed at least 146 soldiers plus three civilians.[11] This surpassed Baxter Springs and in some ways Lawrence, where all the victims had been unarmed and there had been no resistance, and it avenged the fiasco at Fayette with compound interest. Furthermore, they had demonstrated—and this no doubt gave special satisfaction to Anderson and Todd—that they got along quite well, thank you, without Quantrill leading them. Finally, by capturing and destroying a passenger train, they would surely cause the Federals to shut down the North Missouri Railroad and perhaps the Hannibal & St. Joseph, as well, or else have to employ thousands of troops to ride the rails and guard the towns along them. Sterling Price had asked them to "raise hell" north of the Missouri River, and by God they had!

When it started turning dark, Anderson ordered his men to return to the camp on Young's Creek. Soon they straggled out of Centralia, many so drunk that they could barely stay in their saddles. They left behind, in addition to the corpses of the murdered soldiers and civilians, the bodies of the two comrades killed in the charge. Unlike the other dead, these two lay buried in the village cemetery, encased in wooden coffins that Anderson had had a local carpenter construct. They also left behind images of ghastly horror that would linger in the memories of the people of Centralia for as long as they lived.[12]

ANDERSON'S CAMP BESIDE YOUNG'S CREEK:
NIGHT, SEPTEMBER 27, 1864

Tom Goodman, still clad only in his underwear and without a blanket, lay on the bare ground. On either side of him, his two guards slept, as did all the other bushwhackers, except for a few pickets posted around the camp. Anderson had told them that they could have three hours of shut-eye prior to moving on. Given what they had done during the day, hundreds if not thousands of vengeance-seeking Federals would be heading for the Centralia area, and it was best to get a good start on them. Already Todd and Thrailkill had marched off to a separate bivouac several miles away.

Goodman wanted to sleep and tried to sleep. But again he couldn't. In his mind he kept seeing the bushwhackers bursting into the passenger car, his comrades being mowed down, and Val Peters's desperate death struggle. For a brief while, as Goodman had ridden with his guards as the guerrillas advanced to attack the blue-clad troops on the ridge, the hope that he somehow might escape had grown brighter and brighter—only to dissolve into the darkness of despair when the bushwhackers literally swarmed over their hopelessly outmatched opponents. Far worse, though, was what had followed: the torture and murder of the still-living soldiers, the mutilation and mockery of the dead ones. It had been a scene out of Hell—or, rather, *in* Hell, for that was where he was now, surrounded by demons.

Later, back in Centralia, he had watched those demons hunt down and slay still more victims. They had wanted to kill him, too, and being aware of Anderson's order that he be spared, some of them sought to evade it by handling their weapons in a deliberately careless fashion so as to make shooting him seem like an accident. Several times his guards saved him from death by knocking up the barrel of a revolver or carbine as it spewed out a bullet intended for him.

Now he lay on the hard, cold ground in the bushwhackers' camp. Abandoning any attempt to sleep, he opened his eyes and gazed at the silent stars, thinking once more of all that had happened this bloody day of September 27, 1864.

And then he wept.[13]

CHAPTER EIGHT

RESERVED

BOONE AND HOWARD COUNTIES, MISSOURI:
SEPTEMBER 28–OCTOBER 8, 1864

It was the dying time. The chill of autumn hung heavy on the night air. The old season fell prey to the death and decay of the new. Above, black clouds spread a somber shroud across the land. So still, so impenetrably dark, was this world that it might have been the silent, black void of a tomb. No life stirred in this strange realm; no currents rippled its deathlike calm.

Then came a sound—a faint hissing in the darkness. Suddenly, like the dawn of creation, the world exploded in a blinding flash. A bright ball of flame cast an eerie blue glow over the prairie. Like phantoms frozen in ice, the long column of horsemen stood stark and motionless in the road. The fire soared through the sky, slowed, hung for a moment or two, and then finally fell sputtering to earth.

"Signal men!" cracked a sharp voice at the head of the column. "Advance!"

Three mounted figures galloped forward from different points. Another rocket shot up over the land, briefly throwing its lurid glare down on the riders before the world returned to blackness. Several minutes passed. Suddenly two fiery comets, one red and the other white, soared up from the head of the column, arced through the sky, and disappeared. Again all became dark, the sole sound the haunting hoot of an owl. Then, off to the right, hoofbeats approached the head of the column, ceasing when they reached it.

The column resumed moving. At first low murmuring drifted up from it, but after a while fatigue set in, and only the clop of hooves, the creak of wagon wheels, and the jingle of spurs disturbed the night. Many of the riders dozed or even slept while they jogged along, an ability acquired through much experience with nocturnal marches.

As the sun began rising, the column descended into brush-covered bottoms along a creek. Here, at the edge of a clearing, it halted. Anderson rode forward a short distance to survey the ground. Like a bird of prey, his eyes scanned the scene with quick, darting glances. No movement in the trees. No sound on the hill. No smoke in the valley. Brush on three sides, a farm on the fourth. Stacks of oats and hay (the horses would eat), water in the creek (the horses and men would drink). . . . It would do. He waved his hand and pickets went out. The rest of the guerrillas rode into the clearing, spread out, and dismounted for a short rest.

Among them was Tom Goodman.[1] Yet in a sense he had ceased to be Tom Goodman and instead had become a thing, a mere object. When his captors looked at him, he saw in their eyes nothing but hatred and loathing. When they spoke of him, he heard them say such things as, "I would like to kill the damn Yankee." And if they spoke to him, the mildest thing they said was "Hellfire is too good for you, you son of a bitch!"

They would kill him, of that he was sure. The only question was when and how. All he could do was pray that when death came, it would be quick. If there was a God Almighty above, it would be quick.

At midmorning the bushwhackers resumed their march. For the next several hours they moved steadily south, holding to the back roads and lanes, availing themselves of the concealment provided by brush as much as possible. Around noon they halted to await darkness. When it came, they pushed on into more open country, traveling swiftly and silently, for during the afternoon a scout had brought word that large numbers of Federals had been spotted the day before, quite likely in quest of Anderson.

They were. After describing the Centralia massacres, a correspondent of the *St. Louis Republican* in its September 30 edition declared that "Bill Anderson roams over the prairies and forests of northern Missouri as free almost as the air he breathes." Now every available Union soldier, militiaman, and home guard in central Missouri had been assembled to hunt him down and put an end to his breathing—and his killing.[2]

Toward midnight, by which time they had reentered woodlands, the bushwhackers stopped to camp. Using their saddles for pillows, they quickly fell asleep. Not so Goodman. He lay on the bare ground shivering with cold, hungry from having nothing to eat since leaving St. Louis, and weak from the terrible stress. His restless mind would not allow him to sleep, as it constantly churned away at thoughts of escape—thoughts that included fantasies of bribing his captors with gold made alchemy-like from the soil around him. Finally, mercifully, sheer exhaustion brought him sleep and with it temporary rescue from the nightmare in which he now existed.

The sun rose, and strong hands shook him awake. His two guards took him to where Anderson's horse was feeding and told him to curry and saddle it. Although he was loath to do so, he set to work with a will; indeed, he gave the horse such a thorough grooming that the animal would remember it, he thought, "as long as he is a horse."

The grooming pleased Anderson. An hour or two later, while on the march, he reined up beside Goodman and asked: "Well, my old fellow, how do you get along?"

"Very well, sir," Goodman replied.

"You, my man," Anderson continued, a flicker in his steely eyes, "are the first being whose life I ever spared who was caught in federal blue!"

"That's so, Colonel!" some nearby guerrilla shouted in confirmation.

They addressed Anderson, it should be noted, by a title that hitherto had been accorded solely to William Clarke Quantrill among Missouri partisans. Anderson surely knew this and just as surely derived great satisfaction from it. Not George Todd, Quantrill's supplanter, but he, Bill Anderson, who had been humiliated by Quantrill back in 1861 and insulted by him in Texas, was now the de facto king of the bushwhackers.[3]

Shortly after Goodman's brief conversation with Anderson, a tall, handsome man attired in a gray uniform, and evidently a Confederate officer, joined the column. Observing Goodman, the officer rode up to his guards and asked, "Who is this man?"

"A prisoner," the guards answered simultaneously, saluting as they spoke. "Taken, sir," one of them added, "at Centralia."

"I thought you took *no* prisoners, my man."

"This *one,* Colonel, by orders, you see."

"Whose orders?"

"Anderson's—no, only *reserved* by his orders."

"Aha, I understand. Anderson was right."

The officer then rode on, leaving behind a puzzled and worried Goodman. "*Reserved,*" he thought—but for what purpose? Presumably it was something special. He saw in his mind again the soldiers on the ridge south of Centralia and how they had first begged to be allowed to live and then pleaded to be permitted to die. He shuddered inwardly and resolved to try to escape the first good chance he had.

The march continued until about noon, whereupon the bushwhackers halted within the shelter of a large grove of trees near a cultivated field. They dismounted, fed their horses, and sent out a foraging party to procure food for themselves. A bare twenty minutes later the foragers galloped back, yelling, "The Yankees are coming! The Yankees are coming! Ride as though hell was after you!"

The guerrillas leaped into their saddles, formed in a column of twos, and rode rapidly out of the woods and back onto the road, Anderson in the lead and Goodman with his guards not far behind. Then they heard a *boom,* and something invisible shrieked overhead and exploded in some timber a hundred yards to the right. A six-pound shell, judged Goodman. Anderson held up his hand as a signal to halt. Even as he did so, another *boom* reverberated through the air, and a second shell crashed near the same place.

Visibly frightened—artillery was something new for most of them—the bushwhackers returned to the woods, swung through them in a half-circle, and emerged on the other side where they beheld, to their joy, a broad, open prairie. Pleased at having escaped what they believed to have been a trap, they shouted out words of derision for the Federals and their cannons as they galloped toward a lone, high hill.

When they reached its crest, the shouts abruptly ceased. On every side, for miles around, blue-clad cavalry dotted the brown plain. Instead of evading a trap, the raiders had entered one. The shelling had successfully flushed them, like quails, from their cover.

Wheeling his horse around, Anderson screamed a strange cry, whereupon his followers broke into groups of five to eight, then scattered in all directions down the hill. Anderson himself, though, remained. Accompanied by eight men, he rode over to Goodman and his guards.

For what seemed like an eternity, Anderson gazed at the bedraggled sergeant; his eyes, as always, revealed nothing. Was this the end? Goodman wondered. Was he about to be killed? When he saw the Union troops all around, hope of being rescued surged through him. Now all he asked for was that Anderson shoot him and be done with it—and not use a knife. . . .

Finally Anderson spoke, and what he said was not what Goodman expected to hear:

"Prisoner, you must now ride for your life! Boys, we all must!"

For his life! He still lived, but in a world turned upside down. To win was to lose, to lose was to win, his saviors were his destroyers; his destroyers, his saviors. Goodman raced down the hill with the others; to dash away and perhaps escape a bullet in the back would be to ride toward the blue pursuers and receive a bullet in the front. The entire world was after him, thirsting for his blood, keeping him alive only to prolong the terrible torture. There was no choice. He must ride like a madman and pray that he and his future murderers escaped.

Galloping far in front, Anderson steered his men into an opening between the oncoming columns. Only by the swiftness of their mounts did they elude the first wave of Federals, and only through the strong nerves and sharp instincts of the man leading them did they avoid several ambuscades. The rattle of revolver and rifle fire in the distance announced that others were less fortunate.

Hour after hour the game of hide and seek continued: over brown prairies, along brushy ravines, among rolling hills, from one stand of timber to the next. Once Anderson rode off alone after instructing his band to stay on their southward course. An hour later, as they were about to enter a thicket, he swooped back from nowhere and stopped them in their tracks. A Federal outpost, he said, was just beyond the trees. They turned and headed north.

Finally, late in the afternoon, they made their way into woodland and, after riding about twenty-five minutes, came upon a camp inhabited by twenty or so of Todd's men, two of whom were badly wounded. They were now in the Perche Hills, and there they were safe. Federals rarely ventured into those dense forests and labyrinthine ravines, and when they did, they even more rarely found any guerrillas—unless the guerrillas chose to find them.

More and more raiders arrived, singly and in groups. To Goodman's astonishment, many were drunk, including George Todd, who seemed to be in a bad humor. The camp itself was obviously a regular place of refuge, for it contained crude shelters of poles covered with bark and boughs, as well as large caches of food and whiskey.

That night the latter flowed freely and copiously. Before long almost all of the bushwhackers were drunk—so drunk that they acted like madmen, whooping, running, jumping, and yelling. Never had Goodman beheld such a spectacle or heard such profanity. He felt as if he were in Hell itself.

Suddenly Anderson leaped onto a horse and galloped through the camp, screaming hideously, firing his revolvers in wild abandon, his face glowing red in the light of the campfires.

Goodman trembled in terror. Not only was he in Hell, but his life was in the hands of its reigning devil.

Eventually, one by one, the guerrillas sunk to the ground in sodden slumber, oblivious to the falling rain. Although Goodman now wore a cast-off shirt along with pants that had been given him during the morning, he again could not sleep. It occurred to him that it would be both easy and safe to simply get up and walk away—walk away to freedom and life. And he would have done it had it not been for his two guards. *They never drank!* Often they had saved his life. Now, thanks to their sobriety, they prevented his escape. His world remained upside down.

Morning finally came and the rain ceased. The men moved about in the mud, sorting equipment, drying blankets, and currying their horses. Anderson, Todd, Thrailkill, and Poole discussed the future. Clearly, they would have to split up. Their plan to draw thousands of Federals north of the river and keep them there had worked, if anything, too well. As their narrow escape yesterday had shown, it was too risky to remain together. So they agreed to scatter into squads and "bush-range" for a week, then rejoin near the river and cross it together. The wounded would remain behind until they were able to ride, and the wagons filled with rifles captured at Centralia would be cached until the day Price required them for the recruits he expected to gather. With everyone in accord, the council broke up and the various squads departed. At length, Anderson and Todd, along with a score of men, all dressed in blue, saddled and struck off as well.

Goodman accompanied this group. Although he was hungry and gaunt, he no longer was starving, having been given some "grub" the night before. In addition to shirt and pants, he now wore a black coat received from Anderson himself when the chieftain changed to a Federal officer's jacket. Goodman attributed his better treatment to Anderson's appreciation of his good job of horse currying. Furthermore, following his conversation with Anderson, his two guards, Hiram Litton and Richard Ellington, had become friendlier, and the guerrillas in general had stopped glaring at him with murderous eyes. In fact, they increasingly paid little or no attention to him at all. That suited the sergeant fine. The less they noticed him, the better his chance of escape.

All day their party traveled at a rapid pace, slipping up back roads, dodging down lanes, skirting villages and farms. Near sunset, and not far from Columbia, it halted beside a large white church. Here Anderson ordered Goodman's guards to lead him down the road a short distance, and once more the sergeant feared his time had come. But after a wait of a half hour Anderson reappeared, and the column continued on as before. The church, Goodman surmised, probably served as a hiding place for plunder.

Just before dark the column halted again, and Anderson directed his men to take supper at the farms in the area. As luck would have it, Goodman's group went to a house occupied by one of the few Unionists left in that region. Learning that Goodman was a Federal soldier, the owner, a woman, did everything in her power to make sure that he got his fill. After supper the bushwhackers bivouacked nearby, and that night, for the first time in what seemed like eternity, Goodman lay down both warm and fed. Instantly, like a great, soothing wave, merciful, healing sleep rolled over him. For some hours he found peace.

At sunup the march resumed, passing close to Rocheport. A short distance from that village Anderson paused at a farmhouse and spoke with two women. Apparently learning something of importance, he summoned Todd and conversed with him for a while. Then Todd sent a man to fetch a handsome mare from the adjoining pasture, and when it was saddled and bridled, Anderson mounted it and rode off, leaving behind his own horse in exchange.

The march continued at a leisurely pace until noon, when it halted at yet another farmhouse. A woman and an old man came out to meet the riders. The worried expressions on their faces immediately changed to ones of relief and joy when they discovered that the blue-clad horsemen were bushwhackers, not Federals. The old man quickly went back to the house and after a few minutes reappeared with a Confederate officer who had hidden himself at the approach of what he too thought was a Union cavalry patrol. Anderson and the officer—a Texan who was a recruiter for Price's army—moved off a short distance and talked at length, after which the officer mounted up and joined the guerrilla party to return to Texas; his recruiting efforts in Missouri had evidently not proved fruitful. Before departing, Anderson pulled two beautiful shawls from a saddlebag and presented one each to the girls of the family.

During the afternoon the bushwhackers circled slowly back in the direction they had come from until dusk found them on the bluffs overlooking Rocheport. That night Anderson had a front-row seat for watching the destruction of his "capital." On September 26 Gen. Clinton B. Fisk had, with special reference to Rocheport, instructed the Federal commander at Macon City to "let the rebels in that region to understand that there is something besides Bill Anderson power in North Missouri," whereupon troops had occupied the village and levied crushing fines on its inhabitants for harboring guerrillas. Now, prior to evacuating it, the troops set it afire. Plainly visible in the light of their torches, they moved from house to house and building to building, obeying their orders with ruthless precision. When they rode away, flames engulfed all of Rocheport. The fire, reported Fisk on October 3, was "accidental."[4]

The next morning the bushwhackers struck west over the river bluffs. Throughout the day they maintained a tortuous up-and-down march, holding to forest trails and back paths. In the evening they camped near a run-down cabin deep in the timber. Here a strange, solitary figure—an evil-looking man, thought Goodman—tended a herd of fine horses, providing further proof that the vast woodlands of central Missouri were in effect guerrilla territory. Indeed, the bushwhackers seemed to be at home in these great, brooding forests where the sun seldom shone and the wind never blew. As he ranged through them, Goodman saw sights and heard sounds he had never dreamed existed. By day the partisans "spoke" to one another with strange hand signals and waves; at night they uttered uncanny, lifelike cries of the crow, owl, and wild denizens of the dark. Sometimes they baffled would-be pursuers by spreading blankets over roads and small clearings, then crossing them without leaving a hoofprint, or else by riding along rocky creekbeds. When clouds covered the sun or the night was moonless, they determined directions via the moss growing on the north side of trees.[5] And they were adept at caring for the wounded when circumstances made that necessary. Thus shortly after Centralia, one of Anderson's men, his hand horribly swollen and crawling with maggots as a consequence of it being struck by a .577-caliber lead slug, appeared to be a sure candidate for amputation. Instead, his comrades poured oil of turpentine on the wound, and a few days later Goodman was astonished to see that the man had fully recovered. Viewing the guerrillas with the eyes of a sergeant and veteran, Goodman was also surprised to find that they possessed more in the way of military order and discipline than he had expected. To be sure, they engaged in no saluting or other "spit-and-polish" practices, and even on the march the men were free to come and go as they pleased. But if a fight was in the offing, all were expected to be on hand, and for anyone failing to show up the punishment was swift and of but one kind: death. Many, if not most, of the men, so Goodman gathered, were deserters from Price's army, former Paw Paw militia, or refugees from what they described as Unionist persecution and violence. How Anderson managed to control so wild and turbulent a bunch puzzled Goodman, for he never saw the chieftain commit an act of brutality against his followers, and (other than the drunken spree in the Perche Hills camp) he always conducted himself in a calm, quiet manner. A strange man, this Bill Anderson.

The prisoner also discovered that almost wherever he went, citizens were vehemently, indeed violently, secesh. With rare exceptions they welcomed the guerrillas with warm smiles and words, whereas on learning who and what Goodman was, they looked at him with hard faces and called him harder names. Many of the women and children were refugees from the devastated western border counties and told tales of murdered husbands, sons, and brothers, or burned homes and fields, and of wandering about hungry and cold. If half of what they said was true, it was no wonder they hated "damnyankees" (one word to them), and it also helped explain Anderson's leadership: He embodied this hatred.

After a few such encounters, Goodman realized that if he ever managed to escape, he would be doing so in enemy country. There would be no one to turn to, no one to help him. He would be on his own.

By now the appointed date for the rendezvous of the bushwhacker bands for crossing to the other side of the Missouri had drawn near. Hence, Anderson and Todd's party rode to an encampment at Maxwell's Mill in western Boone County, not far from Rocheport (or what had been Rocheport). Unlike previous forest haunts—gloomy, sinister affairs—this one was situated in a beautiful sunlit glade with a cold, sweet spring. Hundreds of guerrillas were already present, and more of them, along with recruits for Sterling Price, came in hourly. From time to time a flurry of gunshots echoed through the surrounding woods as butternut- and gray-clad arrivals mistook blue-coated bushwhackers for Federals and so engaged them in brief but, fortunately for the former, bloodless skirmishes. The camp soon took on an almost holiday air, with planters from the region visiting it to tender their thanks and wish everyone well in future operations.

It was no holiday, though, for Goodman, who once more became the center of unwelcomed attention. Young recruits and fledgling guerrillas, eager to shoot their first Yankee, took delight in aiming their weapons at the prisoner. Sometimes he found himself encircled by more than a dozen pistols pointed at various parts of his anatomy. Throughout it all—the threats, the curses, the cocking of revolvers—he remained as silent and still as a stone.

On the morning of October 5 the bushwhackers left the camp and marched south toward a place called Harker's, about four miles northeast of

Rocheport. Along the way, Anderson's party stopped at a magnificent mansion. To Goodman's surprise, Anderson and his men went inside, leaving him alone and mounted at the gate. Nothing like this had happened before, and he immediately suspected that a trap had been set. Then a well-dressed man came out of the mansion and strolled across the yard to the gate. Something about his manner put Goodman on guard.

"Do you belong to Anderson's or Todd's company, my friend?" asked the stranger.

"I am a prisoner, sir."

"What! A prisoner—and left unguarded?"

"As you see—"

"Ah!" the man interrupted. "Then *you* don't think Anderson the bloody, cruel wretch they would have us all to believe. He certainly shows that he treats his prisoners with much confidence."

"Yes, I have reason to be thankful. He has spared my life."

For a moment the man remained silent. Then he both made an assertion and posed a question: "These guerrillas, as *they call* themselves, are a careless, happy set—they are brave, too, and fight well, I suppose?"

Goodman did not answer, whereupon there was another question:

"How do you like Anderson?"

"He has treated *me* as well as I could reasonably expect. I have no fault to find."

"You would not like to join his band—you would prefer liberty? Do you know you are near to your friends; the Federals are at Fayette, and it is not far from here."

Goodman said nothing. He dared not say anything. The man's words had caused his heart to bound with hope. If he spoke, he knew that his voice would reveal his joy at learning that Union troops were in the near vicinity. That could be fatal—or at the very least ruin any chance of doing what he now was resolved to do: Attempt to escape on reaching the river.

Some of the guerrillas appeared at the door of the mansion, and the man without further ado walked away. Had he been sincere in his questions, or was he playing some sort of joke? Fifteen minutes later a guerrilla beckoned Goodman into the house, where a group of women gathered about him, laughing at and deriding his bedraggled appearance. Their conduct, which the blacksmith sergeant believed belied their claim to being "ladies," answered the question.

After awhile the march to Harker's resumed. On approaching the place, Anderson's blue-uniformed men received a volley from another guerrilla band but none were hit before they made their true identity known. Although some of the bushwhackers indisputably were crack shots, most of them, like other mortals employing a handgun, stood little chance of hitting anyone except at close range—especially when being fired at themselves.

Anderson's intention was to cross the river that night, but a fierce thunderstorm forced postponement. Yet again Goodman, blanketless and drenched, passed a sleepless night. He was determined that it would be his last such night—at least as a captive.

The guerrillas spent the morning and afternoon of October 7 at Harker's. As at the Maxwell Mill's camp, local Confederate sympathizers flocked in to express their thanks, support, and admiration, with Anderson receiving the lion's share of the last. Manifestly, to them he was a hero, their champion and avenger. They also paid considerable attention to Goodman, whom the bushwhackers pointed out as being the "sole survivor" among all of the Union troops they had captured. One youth, hardly more than a boy, pleaded to be permitted to kill "the damnyankee" and no doubt was sorely disappointed on being told that he could not, that the prisoner was "reserved."

In the evening Anderson and the majority of the guerrillas set out for the Missouri, leaving behind a force strong enough to keep the Federals in the northern part of the state fully occupied. They reached the river a mile above Rocheport, but for some reason Anderson found this to be an unsatisfactory crossing point and so ordered the march continued downstream. Passing through the burned and ghostly remains of Rocheport, the long column threaded its way through a defile in the sheer-faced cliffs and struck the river again three miles below the village.

The men immediately set to work removing saddles and preparing lead halters. Goodman dismounted. His opportunity to escape—perhaps the first and last—might come at any moment. As he stood trembling in the dark, he listened closely to the shouts and instructions. The river was low . . . the channel but twenty-five yards wide . . . thirteen skiffs . . . the horses would swim. Goodman's mind raced. He calculated that at least three trips would be needed to get everyone over. He prayed that he would not be among the first. He trained his eyes to observe what was going on around him in the darkness. He noted especially the movement of his guards, to discover if they were watching him more closely than before. They were, of course; this he knew. And the rest were watching him, too. Indeed, the entire world was watching; watching him slyly out of the corner of its eye. It was all a big trick; of that much he was sure—just as it had been back at the mansion. They were watching and waiting for him to take that first step. Once he took it, they would catch him, then kill him, and the world would have a good round of laughter.

When he heard that his group would be among the last to cross, joy and terror fought violently with one another and threatened to rip his heart out. He knew what was coming.

The first group of guerrillas, holding halter straps, boarded the boats while behind them their comrades on shore began to prod the horses into the river.

Some animals balked, then shied away. Cursing and shouting, men rushed down the bank to force the frightened beasts into the black water.

"You watch the prisoner," said one of the guards as he moved toward the shore. "I want to go and see the start."

Goodman's heart began to pound explosively. His legs weakened. His breath came in short, rapid gasps. Suddenly, there was another commotion by the river. To get a better view, the remaining guard walked off a short distance. And now Goodman was sure of the trick. Everyone was watching and waiting for him to move. And he would move. He knew it. They knew it. The world knew it. And when he did finally move he would die . . . die there in the dark. He would never see his home again . . . his children . . . his woman. . . .

His trembling body turned stiffly, and a weakened leg turned with it. A foot slowly raised, then slowly fell. Tom Goodman took his first step. The other wobbly leg dragged forward, and he took another step. And then another. And another. He walked silently into a crowd of men and horses nearby. They knew too, of course. They were part of the game. They were watching him move among them and quietly laughing. Their hands were already on their big guns, and the night was about to explode in flames, and he would fall a bleeding corpse in the weeds. But he did not care now. It did not matter. Let them shoot. Let the world kill him and have its great laugh. It was he who would have the last laugh, for he would escape now in one form or another. They would never get him back. Not now. The world would have to find a new victim to torture because Tom Goodman would be free!

He kept moving until he emerged near a tangle of driftwood and bushes. He did not pause, but quickly entered the thicket. For two hundred yards or so he walked swiftly and silently. He then stopped. He was sucking air rapidly, and his head and heart were pounding so violently that he became dizzy and felt he would faint. And yet he listened with every nerve. The moments stretched into infinity as his ears strained to catch the first shouts, the first taunts of his pursuers. He heard nothing. Perhaps the game was longer than he thought. Perhaps others were ahead, waiting to grab him.

He stepped from the trees and onto the narrow trail. Instantly he dived back again. Peering through the branches, he watched four horsemen pass by. After this heart-stopping encounter, the fugitive held hard to the woods and struggled up the steep bluffs with all of the speed and energy he possessed. At the top, across a clearing, was a house. Tied around the yard were several saddled and bridled horses, ready to ride. The thought of taking a mount flickered in his spinning brain, but fear forced him to take a long, sweeping circuit of the house instead.

Once beyond it, he breathed more easily. Perhaps his guards allowing him to leave had not been a trick after all. He heard no shouts. He heard nothing. Perhaps he *was* escaping. Perhaps he actually *was* free!

Fayette. Like the bright North Star in the heavens above that he struggled to keep in sight through the forest canopy, the very word was a beacon that drew him on. He had no idea where the town was, yet some instinct kept him moving north toward it.

All through the night he crashed through the forest, stumbling down ravines, falling over logs, wading streams, clambering up rocky hillsides. Finally he reached his limit. Slowly, painfully, he placed one foot before the other until at first light he came to a well-rutted road. He spotted a sign post and staggered over to it. Despair gripped him as he read it. Although he had traveled for hours without stopping, he discovered that for the most part he had moved in circles and was only eight miles from where he had started.

Looking around in the dawn light, he saw a rickety tobacco shed off in a nearby field. Even had he been physically able, he dared not travel by day. Making his way to the shed, he entered and saw a haystack in a corner, where he burrowed out a nest, then collapsed in a heap. Sleep came instantly and, blessedly, it remained.

Goodman slept throughout the morning and most of the afternoon. When darkness fell, he resumed his journey, plodding along slowly because of physical and psychological exhaustion. Toward daylight he saw passing along the road a man who in his time was usually called a negro when not called nigger. Surely *he* could be trusted. So he hailed him and then awaited his approach. On being asked, the black man replied that Fayette was only a mile up the road and that Federal pickets were much closer—just three or four hundred yards away. He then pointed out the location of the nearest sentinel. Goodman thanked him, then limped onward as fast as he could. His goal *he thought* was nearly won: Liberty! Friends! Home!

Suddenly he paused. He realized that attired as he was in cast-off guerrilla clothes, a bullet rather than a welcome might be awaiting him. To be killed by enemies was bad enough; to die at the hands of friends would be worse.

He went on with wary caution. As he turned the bend in the road, he heard a voice shout: "Halt, there!" Facing him, some twenty paces distant stood a cavalryman, his rifle cocked and ready to fire. Goodman promptly obeyed the command, then responded to a series of questions about his identity. Satisfied by his answers, the sentinel summoned a corporal, who reported Goodman's presence to headquarters in Fayette. A half-hour later the big but now haggard and emaciated sergeant sat in those headquarters relating his story to the garrison commander.

He had survived. He had escaped. And now he was safe. Instead of being reserved for death, he had returned to life.

CHAPTER NINE

How Do You Like That?

BOONVILLE, MISSOURI: OCTOBER 11, 1864

Sterling Price was a marble statue come to life. As he stood in the square waiting for the prisoners to assemble, he truly was a magnificent figure to gaze upon. Striking in his immaculate gray uniform and gold sash, straight as a rod at six feet two inches, robust and powerful at well over two hundred pounds, his was a presence the eye could not easily avoid. And after the first glance no one could mistake the general for anything but what he was: a true Southern gentleman. Even a brief study of his calm, handsome face, with its snowy hair and rosy complexion, clearly revealed an inner nobility as majestic and imposing as the outer. For most of his adult life other men had seen this in Sterling Price and accepted it as a mark of leadership—first in the war with Mexico, during which he attained the rank of brigadier general; then as a two-term governor of Missouri; and now as a Confederate major general in the fight for Southern independence. But beyond strength and character was also a distinct air of benevolence, something warm, even paternalistic. This more than anything else set him apart from other generals. Whatever it was, whatever it meant, his men saw it in Sterling Price and loved him for it. "Old Pap," they fondly called him. And like a loving father, Price could be strong and firm on the one hand, and on the other be patient and understanding with the failings of "his boys." For three terrible years they had followed him. Long after other soldiers had forgotten what they were fighting for and fled the colors, Missourians had held to their beloved Old Pap. As long as he led there was never a doubt. They knew. Sterling Price was faith. Sterling Price was courage. Sterling Price was the cause for which they fought. Sterling Price was Missouri.

But as he stood in the shadow of the Boonville courthouse and prepared to parole the Federals captured the previous day, this calm pillar of strength was not what he seemed. Inside his gallant old heart a quiet funeral was taking place. Hope was being buried, and at the graveside stood a sad, tired, broken old man.

Figure 9.1 Maj. Gen. Sterling Price.
COURTESY OF THE STATE HISTORICAL
SOCIETY OF MISSOURI.

For three years a vision had kept Sterling Price strong—a vision so powerful that it swept all adversity before it like dust before the storm. He had seen in his mind tens of thousands of fellow Missourians springing up from the land to join him in his crusade. He had seen them rising up from the woodlands of the south and pouring down from the prairies of the north. He had seen them rolling in from the tobacco country to the west and streaming over from the big river to the east. He had seen them coming from all directions, joining together to rally around the standard and help him hurl the Yankee vandals from the sacred soil. But the vision never quite materialized. In 1861 he had won for them a tremendous victory at Wilson's Creek in southwest Missouri. The populace had shouted and cheered his name and sang his praises to high heaven—but they did not come. He had won an even more spectacular victory a short time later at Lexington in the north. They had hugged and kissed and cried and waved their new flag furiously—but they did not come. He had issued a ringing, rousing appeal, urging them to stand up for their rights and hurry if they were coming. They had promised that they would be shortly—but they did not come, or if they did, most of them deserted when he had to retreat into Arkansas. And now he had marched with an army of twelve thousand men into the very heart of the state and stopped to wait for them. But still they did not come—not enough of them, anyway—and it was obvious to the old general as he stood in the square that his vision had been nothing but a beautiful dream. Missouri never would come. And Sterling Price was tired.

The expedition had begun full of hope and promise: His army would move up from Arkansas, capture St. Louis and the state capital at Jefferson City, attract tens of thousands of recruits eager to throw off Union domination, liberate Missouri, and then march into Kansas. It was a tall order to fill, but Sterling Price believed it could be done. His men, or at least the Missourians among them, believed it could be done. Even Missouri's Confederate governor-in-exile, Thomas Reynolds, believed it could be done and tagged along to take his seat in Jefferson City. The trauma caused in the North by the sight of a Confederacy still strong and vital and full of fight would swing thousands of votes from Abraham Lincoln and the Republicans to George McClellan and the Democrats, who had adopted a platform branding the Northern war effort a failure and calling for the restoration of the Union by means of a negotiated peace with the seceded states.

It was a grand scheme, a fine phantasm to conjure around Arkansas campfires. But Missouri dawns brought cold reality. First came the unexpected and demoralizing rebuff at Pilot Knob in southeast Missouri, where on September 27—the same day as the slaughter at Centralia—one thousand fortified Union troops commanded by Thomas Ewing Jr.—he of Order No. 11 infamy—had bloodily repulsed an assault by seven thousand of Price's soldiers, thereby putting an end to any notion of sweeping on to St. Louis. Price next experienced more frustration and humiliation on finding the defenses of Jefferson City so heavily manned (or so he mistakenly thought) that he marched away without making even an attempt to flaunt the Confederate flag from atop the capitol dome or seat Reynolds in the governor's chair.

Now, in Boonville, the most crucial part of his glorious dream, was fast fading away. Instead of a flood of recruits, only a thin trickle of unarmed youths were showing up to fill his ranks—far too few to provide him with the strength needed to remain in Missouri. Moreover, making what was bad enough worse still, some of his troops, two-thirds of whom were reluctant conscripts from Arkansas, acted more like conquerors than liberators, robbing and insulting citizens, looting stores, and drunkenly carousing day and night. Such conduct, to say the least, was not calculated to inspire a mass uprising against Unionist rule in Missouri, especially since many of the victims were pro-Confederates who had cheered Price's army when it marched into Boonville on October 10.

Thus Price's campaign to liberate Missouri and perhaps win Confederate independence had turned into nothing but a large-scale raid by a ragtag army that, except for a few units, was more adept at plundering than fighting. The most that could be achieved, Price sadly realized, was to gather as many recruits as possible while marching through western Missouri, swing into Kansas and give its people a taste of what it was like to be invaded by hostile forces, and then return to Arkansas. Although outwardly he seemed as proud and confident as always, inwardly the general was a beaten man, and beaten not by the enemy—that he could have accepted—but by what he deemed to be the cowardice and betrayal of his fellow Missourians.[1]

The process of paroling the Federal troops captured at Boonville got underway. But before it could be completed, a large group of riders approached the square on an adjacent street. An eyewitness subsequently recorded that the horsemen were all "well clad . . . in black or dark suits, and had their hats fantastically decorated with ribbons." All, too, "had at least four revolvers in their belts" and some scalps adorning the bridles of their horses, which they rode with "casual ease."[2] These were Anderson and his men, come to offer their services to Price.

Then they saw the Union prisoners. "Shoot the sons of bitches!" they yelled, drawing their pistols and swiftly surrounding the unarmed soldiers. "Shoot the sons of bitches!"

Outraged, Price rushed forward and ordered them away from the prisoners. Grumbling, they obeyed. Then Anderson, mounted on a magnificent black horse, rode up to Price and started to speak to him, only to be cut short by Governor Reynolds. Horrified and disgusted by the scalps hanging from the bushwhackers' bridles, Reynolds angrily denounced Anderson and his men for dishonoring the Confederate cause by such barbarism. Price did the same, adding that he would have nothing to do with the guerrillas until they rid themselves of their ghastly trophies.

This they did, whereupon Anderson pulled a handsome wooden box from a saddlebag and presented it to Price. Opening it, the general beheld an exquisite brace of silver-mounted revolvers. He gazed at them for several seconds, then stared deep into the steel-gray eyes of the slender, bearded bushwhacker. He knew about Centralia from Missouri newspapers picked up along the way. He knew, too, that Anderson never took prisoners, or if he did, it was only to murder them and desecrate their bodies, as witness the scalps. Should he accept this gift of pistols—probably stolen—from such a man? Should he make use of him and his band of cutthroats as he marched through Missouri?

Price answered yes to both questions. To reject the gift would offend Anderson, and clearly he was a dangerous man to offend. Also, he needed more men—fighting men—and whatever else they were or were not, Anderson's guerrillas were that, as they had so devastatingly demonstrated at Centralia. Besides, in war one cannot afford to be too choosy about the means used to wage it, especially if you are the weaker contestant and desperately endeavoring to stave off defeat. Therefore, Price thanked Anderson for the pistols and declared, "If I had fifty thousand such men, I could hold Missouri forever."[3]

Later that day Anderson received the following:

(Special Order)
Headquarters Army of Missouri
Boonville, October 11, 1864

Captain Anderson with his command will at once proceed to the north side of the Missouri River and permanently destroy the North Missouri Railroad, going as far east as practicable. He will report his operations at least every two days.

By order of Major-General Price:

McClean

Lieutenant-Colonel and Assistant Adjutant General

Price supplemented this written order by verbally instructing Anderson to "destroy the railroad bridge . . . at the end of St. Charles County." Indeed, this was to be the "main object" of his raid, for if he succeeded, the rail connection between St. Louis and the Hannibal & St. Joseph would be broken for weeks, if not months.

In addition, Price sent a message to "Colonel Quantrill," ordering him to operate against the Hannibal & St. Joseph Railroad. Evidently he knew no more about Quantrill's true status than did the various Union commanders in Missouri and Kansas, who continued to refer to him as the supreme chieftain of all the bushwhackers. But directing Anderson and Quantrill to strike the North Missouri and Hannibal & St. Joseph railways served no useful military purpose. All normal traffic had ceased on the North Missouri since the Centralia massacres, and, contrary to Price's obvious assumption, Rosecrans was using neither that line nor the Hannibal & St. Joseph to transport reinforcements from St. Louis to the Kansas City area. Instead, he had all of his available field forces—Maj. Gen. Alfred Pleasonton's cavalry division and Maj. Gen. A. J. Smith's two crack infantry divisions—pursuing Price while leaving it up to Maj. Gen. Samuel Ryan Curtis, commander of the Department of Kansas, to check his westward progress long enough for these forces to overtake and smash Old Pap.[4]

With his men, Anderson recrossed the Missouri via the Boonville ferry on October 11, carrying Price's order in a wallet where he kept other papers of special value. The order in effect bestowed on him the official sanction of the Confederacy and at least a de facto captaincy in its army. It also testified to his status as the most dreaded (by Unionists) and the most admired (by secessionists) bushwhacker chieftain in all of Missouri. He had come a long way since fleeing Kansas to escape being hanged for horse stealing.

Yet although pleased by Price's order, he had his own notions about executing it—notions that had nothing to do with wrecking a railroad or aiding the Confederate cause in Missouri. Rather, they derived from what he told Charles Strieby when, early in the war, he had tried to recruit him for bushwhacking forays into Missouri: "There is a lot of money in this business."

ST. JOSEPH, MISSOURI: OCTOBER 13, 1864

Tom Goodman stepped from the train onto the busy streets of St. Joseph. He had finally arrived at the destination he had expected to reach half a month ago.

But not only had he been "detained," to put it euphemistically, by what happened to him at Centralia, he had also encountered further delays after his escape to Fayette. Being there, it turned out, by no means assured his safety. In large part because of what he told the garrison commander about the strength of the bushwhackers and their intention to join Price's army, that officer decided to evacuate Fayette in the belief that it soon would be attacked by an overwhelming Rebel force. Thus Goodman again found himself fleeing, this time with the troopers of the Ninth Missouri as they marched from Fayette to Macon City. Moreover, not until the day before had he been able to board a train to St. Joseph, and not until now could he fully relax and feel safe. After all, if bushwhackers could waylay a passenger train on the North Missouri Railroad, they were capable of doing the same on the Hannibal & St. Joseph Railroad. And if those bushwhackers happened to be Anderson's. . . . It was too awful even to think about.

The quickest and easiest way to reach his home and family was to take a steamboat from St. Joe up the Missouri to Payne, Iowa, and then travel the nearly thirty miles to Hawleyville by stagecoach, hired horse, or if need be on foot. Accordingly, he checked at the landing and learned that the next northbound steamer did not depart until later in the day. This gave him time to go to the office of the *St. Joseph Herald and Tribune* and tell its editor the story of his capture by and escape from Anderson's bushwhackers and what he had seen and experienced between those events—a story that appeared in the paper the following morning.[5]

HAWLEYVILLE, IOWA: MORNING, OCTOBER 14, 1864

Mary Goodman had refused to believe the telegram from the army stating that her husband, Sgt. Thomas Goodman of the First Missouri Engineers, had been killed by Rebel guerrillas at Centralia, Missouri, on September 27. It was not true because it could not be true. God would not be so cruel as to let him survive unscathed two years of war deep in enemy country only to let him be murdered while traveling far behind the battlefront to his home and family. Despite what the newspapers reported, regardless of what everybody said, contrary to all reason, Mary continued to cling to her faith that he still lived and would return to her.

During the dark early morning of October 14 she had a startling dream, awoke, dismissed the dream as just that, and went back to sleep.

She dreamed the same dream.

This time on awakening she knew it had not been a dream but a foretelling, a vision. It simply was too real and vivid to be anything else.

She quickly dressed, then left the house and walked a short distance until she came to the place pictured in the vision. Here she stopped and waited. And waited and waited. But her man did not come walking up the road toward her as in the vision. Her eyes teared up, and hope slowly tumbled away like the windblown leaves at her feet.

Suddenly she saw him and he saw her. Each ran toward the other, they met, they embraced, they cried with joy, and then laughed at their tears.[6]

Tom Goodman's journey home by way of Hell had ended.

GLASGOW, MISSOURI: NIGHT, OCTOBER 21, 1864

The ticking clock on the mantel read 9:55. Another day was nearly gone. Benjamin Lewis's luck was holding. With each hour that passed the odds in the big man's favor grew. Time was his strongest ally now, and soon—perhaps any minute—Union cavalry would come and the nightmare would end.

Fifty-two years old and of Virginia birth, Benjamin Lewis was wealthy. He had been born into money, he had married into money, and above all he had made money—well over a million dollars of it. For three decades the rich aroma of tobacco rose from his warehouses on the levee, and each year he shipped tons of it down the river. He knew how to spend as well as earn, and no more sublime view in the state existed than that from Glen Eden, his parklike hilltop estate overlooking the Missouri, and his recently built mansion was one of the largest and most lavish in the entire state.

Despite having been the owner of 150 slaves, Lewis was a staunch Unionist and strong supporter of the policies of his friend President Lincoln. Thus, even though the Emancipation Proclamation did not apply to border states like Missouri, Lewis had freed all of his slaves in 1863, paid the passage of those who chose to move to Kansas, and hired on at top wages those who remained. Furthermore, he donated a church to Glasgow's blacks and had recently urged General Fisk to levy ruinous fines of $5,000 each on local secessionists, whose identities he ferreted out by spies working in his employ. As a result, Lewis was not only the richest man in Glasgow but also the one most hated by the town's Confederate adherents. Yet with a large Union garrison in Glasgow, he had little to fear from that element, much less guerrillas.[7]

His situation had changed drastically when, at dawn on October 15, the war came to Glasgow. Two brigades from Price's army surrounded the town and bombarded it with artillery. Throughout the morning the sights and sounds of battle swept from one end of town to the other. At length, with much of the business district in flames, the outnumbered and outgunned garrison surrendered, and the Confederates marched in.[8] Nevertheless, Lewis remained safe so long as he remained in his mansion. Linked to his family by marriage was a brother-in-law of Price and the mother of Brig. Gen. John B. Clark Jr., commander of one of the brigades that took Glasgow. Both of them had come to Glen Eden to provide it and Lewis with protection, and this they did while regular Confederate troops occupied the town.[9]

On the morning of October 17 those troops marched off to rejoin Price's main army as it continued moving westward along the lower bank of the Missouri River, leaving Glasgow wide open to any marauders who chose to enter it. That evening some of them chose to do exactly that. Among their number was none other than Quantrill at the head of a small band. Two of its members went directly to the home of banker W. E. Dunnica and brought him to his bank, where Quantrill had him open the safe. Quantrill extracted the contents—$21,000— then personally escorted Dunnica back to his residence to protect him from other guerrillas and Confederate stragglers who

Figure 9.2 Benjamin Lewis.
COURTESY OF THE STATE HISTORICAL SOCIETY OF MISSOURI.

were prowling the streets. That done, Quantrill and his followers rode back to their Perche Hills hideout, having obtained the richest single money haul ever made by bushwhackers. What they did not know was that Dunnica, foreseeing a robbery of his bank, had the day before removed $32,000 from the safe and buried the money in his yard.[10]

For Benjamin Lewis, Quantrill's sortie into Glasgow was a frightening event. It meant that other guerrillas might seek to emulate him and if they did, surely Lewis would be a prime, if not *the* prime, target. That was why four nights later he was in his upstairs room, watching the clock's hands move all too slowly and hoping desperately that Union troops would arrive.

Finally the clock struck ten. Soon afterward Lewis heard the faint sound of horses' hooves on the street below. The sound grew louder as it approached Glen Eden, then ceased. Moments later someone knocked, or rather pounded, on the front door. From downstairs came voices, but Lewis could not make out what was being said or by whom. He could only hope and pray that Federal soldiers at long last had come. . . .

He then heard soft footsteps ascending the long sweeping staircase and stop at the door to his room. Someone lightly tapped—a familiar tap like the one his wife, Eleanor, made. If it was she, surely Union soldiers had come. Trembling with excitement, he unlocked the door and opened it.

It *was* Eleanor!

He started to heave a huge sigh of relief, then froze. Eleanor's face was not right. It was pale, and her eyes were large and fearful.

Two heavily armed men were downstairs, she said, her voice low and qua-
vering. Mrs. Clark had let them in. After entering, one of them, apparently the
leader, forced a servant to take him to the room where Eleanor had been lying
in bed with her and Benjamin's two-year-old daughter. The man had asked her
where her husband was, and she replied that she did not know. But he had not
believed her. Instead, after pulling back the bedclothes to see if Lewis might be
hiding under them, he had told her to bring her husband downstairs or else he
would burn down the house. And he had meant what he said.

Lewis realized that he had no choice but to go. If they burned the place, he
certainly would perish. If he came down and talked with them, both the mansion and he might survive. Perhaps, too, he hoped, the presence of Mrs. Clark
and Price's brother-in-law would deter the intruders from any act of violence.

So, accompanied by his wife, Lewis went down the stairs and found what he
feared he would: two bushwhackers sitting in the elegant dining room, bolting
down leftovers and swigging away at wine bottles into which they occasionally
poured whiskey. One was Bill Anderson. The other was Ike Berry, Anderson's
orderly whom he called Weasel.[11]

Figure 9.3 Glen Eden, Benjamin Lewis's Mansion, Glasgow, Missouri.
COURTESY OF THE STATE HISTORICAL SOCIETY OF MISSOURI.

As ordered by Price, Anderson had hit the North Missouri Railroad. But it was not a destructive blow; in fact, it was scarcely a blow at all. On October 14 thirty-five of his men burned the depots at Florence and High Hill while he and the main body, eighty strong, had looted Danville—a village not even on the railroad. They had burned its stores and several houses and murdered five former Union soldiers. Ignoring Price's verbal instructions to destroy the railroad bridge in St. Charles County, Anderson had headed back west, catching up with Price's army at Waverly, where members of Cliff Holtzclaw's gang killed six militiamen who had surrendered to the Confederates at Carrolltown along with the rest of its garrison, claiming that they had committed atrocities against Southern sympathizers. Some of Anderson's men attempted to do the same to wounded prisoners from Glasgow, and only the intervention of their Confederate surgeons forestalled them.[12]

For the next two days Anderson had followed in the wake of Price's army, which on October 18 reached Lafayette County, where Todd's band joined it and proceeded to serve as advance scouts—and also murder dozens of "Dutch" farmers. Because all of the Federal troops west of Boonville and south of the Missouri River had either been captured or retreated to the Independence–Kansas City area, Anderson and his men could go wherever and do whatever they pleased. And so they did, their trail marked by plundered farmhouses and mangled corpses. Never had they had it so good, so easy, and so safe.

Then, for some reason Anderson suddenly turned around and headed for Glasgow. Possibly he had heard of Quantrill's big take there. Maybe someone had told him that the richest man in central Missouri lived there—a nigger-loving, slave-freeing Unionist to boot. Whatever the reason, Anderson now sat in the dining room of Glen Eden, drunk and getting drunker.

"Here is an old Union man," he said, looking up at Lewis. "I have heard of you, and Old Price has heard of you down in Arkansas and Texas. You have done more damage to our cause than any ten men in the state."

Mrs. Lewis tried to interrupt, but Anderson told her to shut up, as he did Lewis when the latter started to speak. Then, coming to the point, he warned Lewis that if he turned over his money, he would live; if he did not, he would die—it was as simple as that. It would do him no good, Anderson added, to lie, for he knew that there were vast sums in the house.

Lewis left the room and returned with $1,000 in silver and paper. It was all there was, he said. Without a word Anderson stood up and brought the butt of a revolver smashing down onto Lewis's head. The stunned man crumbled to the floor. As screams from terrified women filled the house, the two bushwhackers went to work. Hovering over their victim, they lashed him with the long barrels of their pistols, mixing the blows with obscenities and terrifying Indian war whoops. Once more they demanded money, a lot more. Lewis, blood streaming down his face, pleaded that he had no more. They answered with a new rain of kicks and punches. They then forced Lewis to stand on his head against a wall. A ferocious blow to the stomach doubled him up, and he fell prone on the floor. After repeatedly kicking him with their heavy boots, they jumped up and down on him as though he were a mattress.

The victim still weakly mumbled that there was no more money in the house. Anderson thereupon knelt down and stuck the barrel of a Colt revolver into Lewis's mouth. Perhaps furious memories flashed through his burning brain. It was men just like this one—big, wealthy, important, powerful—who had started it all, who had shamed his sister Mary Ellen, who had murdered his pa. . . .

He had killed Arthur Inghram Baker once. Now he would kill him again, if need be. Only this time he would be there to watch him die—and enjoy it.

He rammed the pistol barrel down Lewis's throat, plunging it up and down, up and down, ripping the throat and pumping up gushes of blood.

"How do you like that?" he screamed. "How do you like that? How do you like *that?*" After awhile he stood up, delivered some more kicks to the body, and then ordered the black house servants, who were quaking in terror in the basement, to come upstairs.

"You have been set free, have you?" he sneered. Then, looking down at the bloody heap on the floor, he added, "Yes, you damned old coon, you have set all your negroes free." A sharp blow from the pistol slammed into Lewis's head. Anderson then selected a young black girl of twelve or thirteen and led her into a bedroom for a different type of pleasure. When he finished, Ike Berry went in to take his turn.

Kicking Lewis to his feet, Anderson again demanded more money and again Lewis insisted there was none. Anderson thereupon aimed his revolver and sent a bullet through each of his victim's pant legs, scorching the fabric. Next he yanked the fallen body upright, pinned it against the wall, drew his knife, and pressed its blade against Lewis's jugular vein.

"This old fellow thinks more of his money than his life," he laughed as Berry returned from the bedroom, "and I'll cut his throat." With shrill Indian yells, he repeatedly pricked the bleeding throat. He also slashed Lewis's clothing and, along with Berry, fired a revolver so close to Lewis's face that it left powder burns. Finally tiring of these torments, Anderson dragged Lewis outside and dumped him onto the street. He then mounted his horse, a superb gray mare, and rode up to where the pathetic figure lay in the dirt.

"Paw him! Paw him!" Anderson yelled while the animal struck and stomped the victim with its sharp hooves—an unnatural act for a horse but one that Anderson had trained the mare to do. Two women, hitherto hidden, rushed up to the guerrilla and pleaded with him to stop. Lewis, answered Anderson, had been "fined" $5,000—which, probably by no coincidence, was precisely the sum Lewis had proposed levying on Glasgow's Confederate sympathizers. If this amount was not paid soon, Anderson warned, he would kill Lewis.

The women said they would try to raise the needed money and went off to do so. Anderson and Berry thereupon carried Lewis into the town, broke into a store, and placed him on a counter. Bleeding and bruised from head to foot, his throat swollen and shredded, Lewis went into convulsions. His jerking and heaving became so violent that Anderson had Berry pile chairs on top of the "old coon" to keep him from falling to the floor. He then sat down and, between swallows from a whiskey bottle, gazed at Lewis with what an observer described as "very small eyes [that] partially close when [he is] drunk and when furious, emit a peculiar gleam, which can never be mistaken."

An hour or so later one of the women, a cousin of Lewis, came with the money—$4,000 in paper, $1,000 in silver—much if not most of it contributed by banker Dunnica. Anderson counted it out. Every dollar was there. The thought of putting a bullet in Lewis's head crossed his drunken brain, but on looking at him he decided not. The high and mighty millionaire was now nothing but a battered, bloody lump of flesh. Killing him would merely be doing him a favor. It was much better to leave him alive and suffering. So, after telling the cousin that he would rather have had Lewis's life than the money but that he was a man of his word, he collected his entire band and rode from the town off into the night.

At daylight Lewis, his body racked with terrible, excruciating pain, fled Glasgow with Eleanor and their two children. It was good that they left. A group of Anderson's men showed up at Glen Eden, forced two of the black female servants to cook them breakfast, and then after eating took turns raping both of them before leaving.[13]

On February 2, 1866, Benjamin Lewis died as a consequence of his torture.[14] But for what it might have been worth to him, he had the satisfaction, before his death, of knowing that the man who had done these things to him was himself dead.

CHAPTER TEN

GOOD MORNING, CAPTAIN ANDERSON

ST. LOUIS TRI-WEEKLY MISSOURI REPUBLICAN, OCTOBER 19, 1864

Are the diabolical murders, robberies, and other outrages of the demon, Bill Anderson, never to cease in North Missouri? Is there no power in our troops or people to drive him and his gang of cutthroats from the State, or to exterminate them? Can there not be raised a volunteer force especially for this purpose?

A FARMHOUSE NEAR ALBANY, MISSOURI: DAWN, OCTOBER 27, 1864

Bill Anderson arose from his camp bed in an unusually good mood. Perhaps this was merely because he did not have, as he so often did, a morning-after hangover—but even if that was the case, he had other, more important, reasons for feeling pleased with himself. First and foremost, his decision to separate from Sterling Price's army had proved a wise one. Three days earlier, according to the latest newspaper reports, Price's army had been routed by Union forces on the outskirts of Kansas City at Westport and was now in headlong retreat southward. His campaign was an utter fiasco; far from "liberating" Missouri, Price would be lucky to escape it.

Then there was the word circulating about George Todd and his bunch. According to the rumor, on October 21 Todd had been shot and killed at Lexington while scouting for Price. The next day Price had ordered Todd's men to leave his army because they had killed some Kansas militiamen who had been taken prisoners. If all this was true—and there seemed no reason to doubt it—Anderson had another good reason to be glad he had not gotten tied up with Price. Didn't the pompous old fool understand that was what war was about: killing?

And since leaving Glasgow, Anderson's own band had done some killing. Just the day before, while passing through Carroll County, it had rid the world of six more Union men. Anderson particularly enjoyed what Little Archie had done to one of them after being given the standard instruction to "parole" an old "Dutchman" who had been pressed into service as a guide: cut off his head and place it on his chest, his hands folded around it as if holding it. Everybody had laughed at the comical sight. But the bluebellies wouldn't laugh when they saw it.

Anderson went into the farmhouse and told the woman living there to fix him breakfast. He washed his hands and face, then combed his long, thick hair. Looking at himself in the mirror, he liked what he saw and with a bow toward his reflection said: "Good morning, Captain Anderson, how are you this morning? Damn well, thank you."[1]

RICHMOND, MISSOURI: EARLY MORNING, OCTOBER 27, 1864

Acting Lt. Col. Samuel P. "Cob" Cox listened intently while the woman who had ridden to his camp outside of Richmond told him that Bill Anderson and a large number of his bushwhackers were camped near Albany. It was exactly the sort of information Cox had hoped for when, three days ago, he had accepted the mission from Brig. Gen. James Craig, commanding officer at St. Joseph, to go after Anderson. Cox had immediately ordered his troops—about three hundred men of the Thirty-third and Fifty-first Missouri Militia, all of whom were mounted—to begin marching to Albany . . . and to march fast and not stop.

In his mid-thirties, Cox was a native of Kentucky whose parents had moved to Missouri in 1839 and settled on a farm in Daviess County near Gallatin. During the Mexican War he had served as a scout in the Far West and become acquainted with such legendary frontiersmen as Kit Carson and Jim Bridger. Following that war, Cox had worked for the freighting firm of Russell, Majors, and Waddell as a wagon train master. With the outbreak of hostilities in Missouri in 1861 he became a major of militia cavalry, but in 1862 typhoid fever compelled him to go on sick leave to his home in Gallatin. He had returned to active service in the spring of 1864 and was highly successful, winning the praise of Gen. Clinton B. Fisk for routing two hundred guerrillas at Cameron on July 24. General Craig had chosen him for his special mission because he believed that Cox "would find and whip Anderson." Now he *had* found him. As for whipping him, Cox had two assets. First, although his troops were militia and, apart from several companies possessing revolvers, armed solely with single-shot, muzzle-loading infantry rifles, they had plenty of experience operating against bushwhackers and so—unlike Johnston's hapless neophytes—knew what to expect and how to cope with it. Second, and perhaps most important, Cox had studied guerrilla tactics and realized that the best way to counter them was to use them himself.[2]

Which was what he intended to do.

ALBANY, MISSOURI: MIDDAY, OCTOBER 27, 1864

About a mile from Albany, Cox's advance troop met Anderson's pickets and drove them to and then through the village, which lay on the Missouri River shore below a bluff. Cox followed with his main force until, at about noon, he reached Albany, whereupon he halted and ordered most of his men to dismount. While every fourth man held horses, he led the remainder southward four hundred yards to the edge of an open forest and deployed them in a heavy skirmish line astride a narrow, high-banked lane. At the same time he sent a mounted detachment forward with instructions to locate and engage the enemy, then fall back. After that he waited. "Everything," a Union officer afterward wrote in his diary, "seemed to stand still—not even a horse appeared to move."

Suddenly the mounted detachment came scurrying back, hotly pursued by guerrillas two to three hundred strong. The Union line opened to let the soldiers through, then closed again. The bushwhackers, "yelling like Indians," charged on. They expected another Centralia.

They did not get one. Instead, at a range of less than one hundred yards, they began receiving a steady, continuous aimed fire that toppled horses and caused men to reel in their saddles. They pressed on, shooting back with their revolvers, until within forty yards of their foes. There they wavered, then milled about, unable to advance yet unwilling to retreat.

All, that is, except two charging up the lane far ahead of the rest. The one in the lead rode an iron-gray horse, its reins clenched between his teeth, and he held a blazing revolver in each hand. Every soldier in position to do so fired at both men. Bullets showered leaves and tree limbs all around them. Yet on and on the two riders came, plunging through the Union line and continuing well beyond. It seemed as if they would escape unscathed.

But their horses slowed and started swerving to the left. First the leader and then his companion fell from their saddles to the ground. The latter scrambled to his feet and staggered off into the brush, disappearing from sight. The following day some Federals found his body in a field and identified it as Captain Rains, son of the Missouri Confederate general James S. Rains, whom Arthur Ingrham Baker had allegedly sought to join back in the fall of 1861.

The leader, though, remained where he lay, facedown. Moreover, when he fell, the other bushwhackers fled in "wild confusion." Cox ordered those companies armed with revolvers to remount and sent them pounding off in pursuit. They neither caught nor killed any of the fugitives but found "the road strewn with blood for ten miles."[3]

Several soldiers approached the body of the first bushwhacker who had burst through their line. A bullet had blown away a hunk of his skull behind the left ear and another had penetrated his left temple. In all probability he had died instantly and painlessly.

Turning the body over, the militiamen studied it. Obviously he was no ordinary bushwhacker. Beside him lay a wide-brimmed white hat with a long black plume. Under his close-fitting, dun-colored frock coat were a blue cloth vest and an elaborately embroidered black shirt. Each hand still clasped a revolver; hip holsters held another two, and the handles of two large pistols projected from holsters attached to the saddle of his magnificent gray mare, which stood nearby, a scalp dangling from its bridle.

The soldiers then went through his pockets. They found a gold and a silver watch, each with a matching chain, close to $600 in gold and paper currency, a blondish lock of woman's hair, and a striking photograph of what appeared to be the man plus another of a woman who presumably was his wife, for with the photograph was a letter signed, "your ever loving and obedient wife until death—Bush Anderson—at home Friday evening, April 20th, 1864." In it she mentioned (according to the Union officer who read it) "certain articles such as a dashing woman would fancy for dress and ornament and some toys for her babe." Enclosed with the letter and photo was "a small lock of fine dark chestnut-brown hair."

Not until they found a small Confederate flag and two folded sheets of paper did the soldiers know who the fallen bushwhacker was. The flag bore the inscription: PRESENTED TO W. L. [*sic*] ANDERSON BY HIS FRIEND, F. M. R. LET IT NOT BE CONTAMINATED BY FED. HANDS. The sheets of paper proved to be Price's October 11 order to "Captain Anderson."[4]

The dead bushwhacker was Bloody Bill Anderson—and *they* had killed him! In a way—in fact, in a lot of ways—this was a greater victory than the defeat of Sterling Price. Certainly it gave them much more personal satisfaction. They hated Anderson with every fiber of their being. Because of him they had passed the whole summer and most of the fall soldiering virtually without pay, away from their families and their farms, where corn now rotted in the fields. They had seen, too, what Anderson and his men did to Unionists, soldier or civilian, when they captured them. Some of their victims had been comrades, friends, relatives, even brothers or fathers or sons. At that very moment, in fact, one of their fellow soldiers was lying paralyzed as a result of wounds suffered in the fight just fought. Now Anderson was dead; his soul—if he had one—was surely already in hell.

On being informed of the dead guerrilla's identity and seeing the papers that proved it, Cox had the body loaded into a wagon, then ordered his troops to march back to Richmond. In a little over two days he had done what no other Union officer had been able to accomplish during the past five months: Track down and kill Bill Anderson. Cox felt proud—he had every right to. By pretending to be deceived by the bushwhacker's old trick of false flight, he had enticed the ambushers into a deadly ambush. To be sure, luck had played a

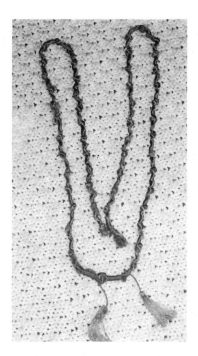

Figure 10.1 According to John N. Edward's Noted Guerrillas, *Anderson kept a tally of his killings by tying a knot for each one of them on a silken cord. If so, then this probably is that cord. It contains fifty-three knots.* PRIVATE COLLECTION.

major role in the form of the woman's tip as to Anderson's whereabouts. But luck can be as much a part of war as skill, often more so, and outside of Albany on the afternoon of Thursday, October 27, 1864, Bloody Bill's luck finally ran out.

RICHMOND, MISSOURI: OCTOBER 27–28, 1864

Dr. Robert B. Kice supplemented his income as a dentist in Richmond by taking photographs—or "ambrotypes," to give them the technical name of the time. Usually his subjects were husbands and wives, their children, a young man or woman wishing to send a "likeness" to a sweetheart, and in recent years soldiers posing self-consciously in their uniforms. This morning, however, he focused his lens on a dead man. Moreover, since the dead man was the notorious bushwhacker Bill Anderson, he anticipated a fair amount of money from the resulting pictures.

Returning to Richmond on the afternoon of October 27, Cox's soldiers had put Anderson's corpse on display in the county courthouse, where hundreds of people had filed by to view it. Now, shortly after sunup, the body sat slumped

Figure 10.2 Bill Anderson, Photo 1. COURTESY OF THE STATE
HISTORICAL SOCIETY OF MISSOURI.

in a chair, legs outstretched, its head held upright by the left hand of Adolph
Vogel, Cox's bugler, gripping the hair. Kice made at least two images of it. In
one Anderson's plumed hat is on his lap and the lifeless fingers of his right hand
are draped across the butt of a Colt revolver, the barrel slanting downward
toward the hat. The other is almost identical, except that the hat is gone and the

Figure 10.3 Bill Anderson, Photo 2. COURTESY OF THE STATE
HISTORICAL SOCIETY OF MISSOURI.

pistol barrel lies on top of Anderson's left wrist. In both pictures revolver butts
project outward from holsters on each hip, and through partially parted lips,
Anderson's teeth gleam in a macabre grin.[5]

The photographs having been taken, a detail of soldiers proceeded to
carry out Cox's order to bury the corpse in a "decent coffin." First, though,

they performed some acts that normally do not accompany a burial. Even before Kice employed his camera, one of the soldiers had, as the ambrotypes reveal, cut off the ring finger of the left hand to obtain the ring, possibly a wedding band, that adorned it. Now, after carrying the body out onto the street, the burial detail flung it unceremoniously into a wagon and drove north. At the cemetery on the edge of town the men dumped the remains into the "decent coffin," nailed it shut, shoved it into a hole, and covered it with some two feet of dirt. They then left. The monster had been buried.

That evening some militiamen visited the the cemetery to pay Anderson their last respects. They spat and urinated on the grave.[6]

Yes, it was a different war in Missouri, one that had yet to end. For some it never did end until, like Bill Anderson, they were dead and buried.

THE SPIRIT OF BILL ANDERSON YET LIVES

At first many people doubted that Bill Anderson had really been killed. His death had been reported before, and people feared, as did General Rosecrans in St. Louis, that "the news is too good to be true."[1] But once it was confirmed, a chorus of jubilation arose from Missouri Unionists. Anderson's death, declared a typical editorial, "was the breaking of the back of guerrilla war in North Missouri. . . . An avenging God has permitted bullets fired from Federal muskets to pierce his head, and the inhuman butcher of Centralia sleeps his last sleep." "It is a good thing," echoed another editor commenting on the photos of Anderson's corpse, "to know that there is one devil less in the world."[2]

For a while, however, it seemed that far from being broken by Bloody Bill's death, the back of guerrilla war in North Missouri remained as strong as ever. Little Archie Clements, described by one newspaper as Anderson's "head devil," took command of the main portion of his slain chieftain's band following the Albany fiasco and led it across Carroll County, murdering a couple of militiamen along the way, before crossing to the south side of the Missouri near Brunswick. Likewise, Jim Anderson and sixty followers, calling themselves the "Anderson Avengers," ranged through Howard and Boone Counties, pillaging, burning, and killing in their now-accustomed style. Elsewhere, other guerrilla gangs continued to do the same. By mid-November, little more than two weeks after God permitted two bullets to pierce Bill Anderson's skull, conditions in northern Missouri continued to be so bad that the *St. Louis Democrat* (which, despite its name, was the leading Republican paper in Missouri) declared despairingly:

131

They say he [Anderson] is dead. . . . Heaven be thanked if it be indeed so. Yet his spirit still lives. . . . This whole region [of North Missouri] is sprinkled with the blood of Union men, and dotted with fresh-made graves, in which they lie, and in many cases their unburied corpses furnish food for swine of the woods. Yes, the spirit of Bill Anderson yet lives. . . .[3]

In both defense and retaliation, Federal troops intensified their antiguerrilla campaign in northern Missouri. Since 1861 their policy toward bushwhackers had been, in the words of the *St. Joseph Herald,* to "shoot them and give them a trial afterwards." Now, in the wake of Centralia, they did the same to all men, teenagers included, suspected of aiding the bushwhackers, which in practice could mean anyone believed to possess Southern sympathies. Militia scouring Randolph County in late October killed fifteen civilians, one of whom they hanged, and then pinned to a tree with bayonets. They also burned and looted, usually without making any attempt to distinguish between loyal and disloyal. Why bother in an area that was, as the *Liberty Tribune* said of Clay County, "more rebel than South Carolina"?[4]

Unfortunately for Unionist civilians, as soon as the troops passed through, friends and relatives of their victims would seek vengeance in their turn. The result was a conflict that left large portions of such counties as Howard, Randolph, Carroll, Boone, and Clay more or less depopulated, with loyalists either fleeing them or seeking safety in the garrisoned towns.[5] Nowhere during the Civil War did people suffer such terror and tribulation as those unfortunate enough to reside in the guerrilla-infested regions of Missouri. Compared to what they experienced, the civilians who were in the path of Sherman's famed March to the Sea through Georgia got off lightly.

Not until November did guerrilla activity in Missouri begin to slacken, then virtually cease. As in past years the primary reason was the advent of winter—after being delayed by an unusually long and mild autumn—with its chilling winds and bare branches. Yet this time there was another and, in its implication, more fundamental cause: The failure of Sterling Price's invasion. Only the most fanatical or obstinate Confederate adherents could now fail to realize that their cause was dead in Missouri and, what with Lincoln's reelection, doomed in the South as a whole.

William Clarke Quantrill perceived this. Indeed, he possibly foresaw it as early as the spring of 1864. If so, that would explain why he did not stand up to George Todd—he was, after all, the faster draw and the keener shot—and instead took a vacation, interrupting it only to make a brief, useless appearance at Fayette and to rob the Glasgow bank.

In any case, soon after Price's debacle and the deaths of Todd and Anderson, Quantrill sent his mistress, Kate King, to St. Louis and went to the Sni Hills, where he spread word that he intended to go to Kentucky and would welcome good men to accompany him. Bushwhacking in Missouri, he declared, was "played out," whereas the Bluegrass state offered fresh fields of opportunity—meaning plunder. Moreover, should the war end—and it could not last much longer—the chances of being able to surrender without being executed as bandits afterward would be much better in Kentucky than in Missouri.

More than thirty guerrillas joined him. Most were veterans of his old band, but some, notably Peyton Long and Frank and Jesse James, had followed Anderson. In December he led them southward into Arkansas, gathering additional recruits along the way. Here six of them, including Jesse James, decided to go to Texas instead. On January 1, 1865, with the remaining forty-six, Quantrill crossed over the Mississippi to Tennessee in a flat boat, then headed into Kentucky, where he resumed his guerrilla career but without his previous success.[6]

Practically all of the other full-time, hard-core bushwhackers, among them Archie Clements and Jim Anderson, passed the winter in Texas, as did most of George Todd's men, now led by Dave Poole. Here they awaited the coming of spring and returning to Missouri. But while they waited, the Confederacy collapsed. By late April, Robert E. Lee's army had surrendered in Virginia, Joe Johnston's in North Carolina, Nathan Bedford Forrest's in Alabama, and what little was left of Edmund Kirby Smith's forces in Arkansas, Louisiana, and Texas were in the process of doing the same. Many of the guerrillas elected to remain in Texas; others, like John Thrailkill, went with Jo Shelby's brigade into Mexico to offer their services to what proved to be another lost cause, that of the Emperor Maximillian. Most of them, though, set out for Missouri, Clements, Poole, and Jim Anderson at their head. It made little or no difference to them that there no longer was a Confederacy to fight for. That had long since ceased to be their motive.

Early in May, Clements heralded his return. Soon after crossing the Osage River into Benton County, he came upon a militiaman whom he accused of having belonged to a unit that had murdered his brother and burned down his mother's house. While Jesse James, John Maupin, and another guerrilla pinned the victim's arms and legs to the ground, Little Archie sat on his chest and cut his throat, then scalped him.[7]

Continuing northward into Johnson County on the morning of Sunday, May 7, forty of Clements's men robbed the stores and killed a civilian in Holden. An hour later, more than a hundred of them rampaged through nearby Kingsville, robbing stores and citizens, torching five houses, and slaying eight men.[8] For Clements, who had grown up on a farm only a few miles from

Kingsville, this was a visit to his hometown, and he did so as Quantrill had in Lawrence and Bill Anderson in Huntsville.

Commenting on the Holden-Kingsville raid, the editor of the *Kansas City Journal* verged on despair:

> The practical question is, what should be done? Is this evil never to cease? Is there no way of reaching and exterminating these worse than fiends? It is no use to shut our eyes to the facts, and to pretend that a little thievery is at the bottom of all of this. It is a deeper and more serious evil than that.[9]

Maj. Gen. Grenville Dodge, the new Union commander in Missouri, responded to Holden-Kingsville by ordering all available troops to the region south and east of Kansas City and directing Col. Chester Harding, now in charge of the District of Central Missouri, to spare neither men nor horses in suppressing the guerrillas.[10] This sounded good; yet all of Dodge's predecessors had issued the same order and exhortation to no avail. Would it be any different this time?

At first the answer seemed to be no. From Johnson County the bushwhackers went into their favorite stronghold, the Sni Hills of western Lafayette County—and on the way they killed fifteen Unionist civilians. So much for a recent editorial in Columbia's *Missouri Statesman,* telling its readers: "Let the sight of a guerrilla be a signal to shoot him. If he comes to your home shoot him. If you meet him in the road shoot him."[11]

Poole's men remained in the Sni Hills. Here was their refuge and in a sense their home. Besides, where else would they go, and if they went there, what would they accomplish beyond adding to what a hundred-odd years later would be called a body count? The time had come to consider the future.

Archie Clements and Jim Anderson, on the other hand, sallied forth to a place that was far more familiar to them than the Sni-a-Bar country: the outskirts of Lexington. Ten months after Bloody Bill had done so, Clements sent a message to the garrison commander, who now was Maj. Berryman K. Davis, demanding that he surrender, or his troops would be massacred and the town burned: "We have the force and are determined to have it."

Davis made no reply. If Clements had actually possessed sufficient force to take Lexington, he would have attacked at once and without warning. Besides, Davis doubted that the bushwhackers had the stomach for serious fighting and the heavy casualties it would entail. In recent days he had received a number of inquiries from them as to what terms they could expect if they agreed to surrender. He believed, so he had informed Colonel Harding on May 9, that "a large portion of them are anxious to give themselves up if they can be treated as prisoners of war."[12]

His bluff called, Clements bypassed Lexington and, several days later, crossed to the north side of the Missouri, as did Jim Anderson. At about the same time Davis received a note from Dave Poole, stating that he was collecting his men for the purpose of surrendering and that he wished to meet with Davis and arrange terms. Davis promptly agreed, and on May 17, accompanied by five soldiers, he met Poole and five other bushwhackers south of Lexington on the Warrensburg Road. In accordance with instructions from Colonel Harding, he told Poole that he had been authorized by Dodge to assure all partisans that if they surrendered, gave up their weapons, and obeyed the laws, the military would take no action against them, but they would remain answerable to the civil authorities. Poole agreed to these terms and stated that he and his men would come to Lexington on May 21 and surrender.

In the Holden-Kingsville raid the bushwhackers had demonstrated that they still were formidable and ferocious. Why, then, did they decide to call it quits so soon afterward? The answer is twofold. First, once back in their stomping grounds, they realized that to continue with bushwhacking would accomplish nothing other than to prolong an agony that had lasted long enough. Most of West Missouri had been desolated and devastated. Weeds and scrub filled the untilled fields of hundreds of farms where only stark chimneys marked the site of what once had been a house. Furthermore, during the winter, Dodge, resorting to a more selective version of Order No. 11, had ordered that the families of all known bushwhackers and Confederate soldiers be sent out of the state while at the same time threatening to "punish" any civilian who "harbored" guerrillas. Obviously western Missouri required peace to prevent it from becoming what it was already close to being—a desert.[13]

Second, the bushwhackers also recognized that unless they surrendered now, it soon would be impossible for them to surrender at all. They would become both in law and fact nothing but bandits, to be hunted down and killed or, if captured alive, put in prison or hanged from a gallows. Should they desire to remain in Missouri, rejoin their families, and lead normal, peaceful lives again—and the vast majority of them so desired—their sole hope was in complying with the terms that the Federals offered them. It would be unrealistic to expect better, and it could have been worse.

Hence, early on the afternoon of May 21, Dave Poole and forty of his men rode into Lexington, dismounted, piled their revolvers and carbines into what rapidly became a huge heap, took the oath, received parole certificates, and then headed off for their homes—if they still had one. Colonel Harding, who was present for the surrender, telegraphed to Dodge: BUSHWHACKING IS STOPPED.[14]

Not quite, though. Archie Clements and Jim Anderson remained on the loose, the former in Ray County, where he clashed with militia on May 25, the latter in Carroll County.[15] But their gangs were dwindling, friends were less friendly and foes more aggressive, and for the most part they had to run and hide rather than raid and kill. Finally they, too, realized that Quantrill had been right back in December when he pronounced that bushwhacking was played out. So on June 2 they conveyed a message to the Federal commander in Glasgow, the essence of which was: On what terms may we surrender?

None, was the answer. They must surrender unconditionally. They were not ordinary guerrillas. Little Archie was Bloody Bill's "scalper," and the governor of Missouri had posted a $300 reward for his capture, dead or alive. And the Federals wanted Jim to be what his brother now was: dead and buried. For them to surrender would literally be to stick their necks into a hangman's noose.[16]

So they did not surrender. Instead, both went to Texas. Although Union troops now occupied that state, they were not fellow Missourians with blood scores to settle, and there the two men had a much better chance of avoiding the fate that had befallen Quantrill in Kentucky: A mortal wound and capture by "Federal guerrillas" specially assigned to track him down.[17] They did not intend to stay in Texas any longer than necessary, however. Once it was safe to do so, they would return to Missouri. That was where they had done most of their killing and where, given certain skills they had acquired—the only skills that they in fact possessed—they could make an easy yet exciting living.

During June most of the bushwhackers still at large either "came in," left the state, or simply returned to their homes without formally surrendering. By July bushwhacking truly had stopped in Missouri. Yet the total end of the war did not bring total peace. Far from it. The bitterness engendered by four years of bloody strife persisted and with it the vicious circle of retaliation and counter-retaliation between triumphant Unionists and unrepentant secessionists. It also provided a reason, or at least an excuse, for some of the bushwhackers to turn bandit.

At first they confined their banditry to such mundane crimes as horse stealing and stagecoach holdups. Then on the afternoon of February 13, 1866, a dozen former guerrillas robbed Clay County Savings Bank in Liberty of nearly $60,000, in the process murdering a William Jewell College student. It was the first daylight bank robbery in American history, not counting the plundering of two banks in St. Albans, Vermont, in 1864 by Confederate raiders operating out of Canada.

Among the robbers was Jim Anderson. On April 12, 1866, he and Ike Flannery, another ex-guerrilla, showed up in Rocheport, now rebuilt, and attempted to sell some bonds taken from the Liberty bank to local merchants. Finding no buyers, they left. Two miles out of the village, five men bushwhacked the two bushwhackers, killing Flannery and removing $2,000 in greenbacks and bonds from his body. Or at least so claimed Jim, who escaped unscathed. Reporting his tale, the *Kansas City Journal* hinted that it might not necessarily be the whole truth.[18]

Although the authorities did not identify him as such, some believed that another of the Liberty bank robbers was Archie Clements—indeed, that he had been their leader. In any event, during the summer of 1866, Little Archie showed up in Lafayette County, where his mother had a house, and made frequent visits to Lexington, during which he spent most of his time with Dave Poole, who now resided there. No one attempted to collect the reward on him, and he, for his part, seemed to have ample funds despite not engaging in any discernible economic activity.

Then on October 30, 1866, four revolver-wielding men entered the Alexander Mitchell and Company Bank in Lexington and extracted slightly over $2,000 from the cash drawer but failed to obtain the $100,000 they believed to be in the vault because they could not locate the key to it on the cashier's person. Thus foiled, they remounted their horses and rode from town. A posse gave pursuit but was unable to overtake the bandits, who were joined by a fifth man. Their horses, explained the leaders of the posse, were too fast. The leaders were Dave Poole and his brother John.[19]

By late 1866 crime and violence had become so rampant in the border and river counties of Missouri that the governor ordered all men of military age to enroll in the militia, at the same time declaring that anyone failing to comply would be subject to arrest. This penalty should not have made any practical difference to Clements. Nevertheless, on the morning of December 13 he, Poole, and twenty-five other former bushwhackers, all heavily armed and arrayed in military formation, rode into Lexington and signed up for militia duty. For them to do this was a joke, and no doubt they saw it that way themselves.

The Lexington garrison commander, however, was not amused. He ordered them to leave town at once. They did, but soon afterward Clements and a companion returned and went to a saloon. The commander promptly sent a squad of militiamen to arrest them. When the soldiers entered the saloon, Clements ran out the back door, mounted his horse, and galloped down the main street. Riflemen stationed in the courthouse for that purpose opened fire on him. His horse slowed to a walk, he slumped in the saddle, and then tumbled onto the dirt street, where he lay face downward, his tiny body riddled with bullets. He who had killed so many had in effect killed himself.[20]

The bank robberies continued, with former bushwhackers involved in all of them. The most sensational one occurred in Richmond, where Bill Anderson's body lay moldering in its "decent coffin." There, on May 20, 1867, twelve to fourteen men took $4,000 from the Hughes and Wasson Bank. This was a measly haul for so many robbers, and had that been all there was to it, the affair would have attracted little attention. But what it lacked in money it more than made up for in blood. Before leaving Richmond, the bandits gunned down the mayor, the town jailer, and the jailer's fifteen-year-old son, who had fired at them with a rifle from behind a tree.[21]

Neither the civil authorities nor the militia succeeded in bringing the Richmond raiders to justice, despite the fact that at least six of them, all followers of Quantrill, had been recognized. Most of them could not be found, and the few who were apprehended speedily produced affidavits from people who swore that they had been nowhere near Richmond on May 22, 1867, and so secured their release. But what the regular legal process failed to accomplish was achieved, at least in part, by other means. Frustrated and disgusted by seeing men known to be guilty of robbery and murder go free, vigilantes lynched two of them, Dick Burns and Tom Little, the latter the brother of Quantrill's closest friend, Jim Little, who had been killed in Kentucky early in 1865. Another of the Richmond robbers was found lying in a field, clubbed to death, and vigilantes shot to death yet another, Ol' Shepherd, at his father's house near Lee's Summit on April 4, 1868.[22]

Following a bloodless robbery of a bank at Independence on November 27, 1868, Missouri banks remained unmolested for more than two years, causing some to conclude that the vigilantes had put, if not the fear of the Lord, a salutary dread of the mob into the bandits.

It was a premature conclusion. On December 7, 1869, a tall, lanky young man walked into the Daviess County Bank in Gallatin, where Samuel Cox, who had been awarded the regular rank of lieutenant colonel for killing Bill Anderson, still resided. The man asked the bank's cashier, Capt. John W. Sheets, to change a hundred-dollar bill. As Sheets, who owed his military title to having served in the militia during the war, started to comply with the request, another tall and slender young man came into the bank and said, "If you will write out a receipt, I will pay you that bill." Sheets sat down at his desk to prepare the receipt, but before he could pen a single word, the newcomer suddenly snarled a curse at him, declared that he and Colonel Cox had caused the death of his brother, Bill Anderson, and that he had come to avenge it. He then whipped out a pistol and shot Sheets through the head and heart, killing him instantly.

Next, both men fired at bank clerk William McDowell as he ran out the door. Although a bullet tore into one of his arms, McDowell made it to the street, where he shouted that bandits were robbing the bank and had killed Sheets. Several townsmen opened fire on the men when they came out of the bank and mounted their horses. The one who shot Sheets was unable to mount his excited steed, which dragged him close to forty feet before he freed his left foot from the stirrup and climbed up behind his companion. They then galloped away unscathed and, for some reason, unpursued.[23]

Figure E.1 Fletch Taylor, Frank James, and Jesse James in a post-war photo. COURTESY OF THE STATE HISTORICAL SOCIETY OF MISSOURI.

Almost surely the slayer of Sheets was Jesse James. Several men in Gallatin recognized the horse that the bandits left behind as "belonging to a young man named James." Furthermore, when a posse from Gallatin finally did go after Sheets's killers, it followed their trail to the James farm near Kearney in Clay County, and as it approached the place, two horsemen suddenly dashed from out of a barn into the night, making good their escape.[24]

As for Sheets's murderer declaring himself to be the brother of Bill Anderson, which presumably would mean that he was Jim Anderson, this could only have been a ruse by Jesse to conceal his true identity and confuse the authorities. For, as he and Frank probably knew, by 1869 Jim Anderson was in no condition to avenge anybody, having been killed in Texas by either William Poole, another of Dave's brothers, in 1867, or George Shepherd, a brother of Ol' Shepherd, in 1868.[25]

Possibly, too, Jim had spent some time in prison prior to his death. The sole known photograph purporting to be of him (see p. 14) shows a handsome young man sitting beside a table with a ball and chain attached to him. But his clothes are exceptionally dapper and the expression on his face curiously jovial for a prisoner, causing one to wonder if the photo was intended to be a joke. Also, though the young man bears a strong resemblance to Bill Anderson, a life-long student of bushwhacker lore flatly denies that he is in fact Jim Anderson.[26]

Whether Frank and Jesse James participated in bank robberies previous to the one in Gallatin cannot be documented, but circumstance and logic suggest that they did. With few exceptions all of the Missouri robberies occurred within easy riding range of their home; they were close friends of Jim Anderson, Archie Clements, and others who carried out these robberies; and although the Gallatin holdup was a bungled affair that netted them a paltry $700 and nearly cost Jesse his life, their conduct of the operation indicates that they had been in banks before and not simply as customers. Finally, and conclusively, their careers and characters— first as bushwhackers, then as bandits—reveal them to have been, romantic legends to the contrary notwithstanding, rapacious thieves and ruthless killers. This was especially true of Jesse, as demonstrated by his brutal murder of Sheets.[27]

Between 1870 and 1876 the James brothers, along with ex-Quantrill rider Cole Younger and his brothers Bob and Jim, formed the nucleus of a gang that ranged from Kansas to Kentucky and from Iowa to Texas, robbing banks, holding up stages, and, most spectacular of all, stopping and sticking up trains, something that Frank had discovered at Centralia could be done with ease and considerable profit. Soon the "James boys" and the "Younger brothers" became household names throughout America. Newspapers headlined their exploits, the *Police Gazette* and similar magazines published vivid accounts, accompanied by garish drawings, of their alleged doings, and hack writers made them the heroes of highly imaginative stories appearing in countless dime novels. Only John Dillinger ever came close to matching their bandit fame.

Efforts by local law officers and Pinkerton detectives to apprehend them proved futile, sometimes absurdly so and on one occasion tragically so. On the night of January 25, 1875, a group of Pinkertons, three of whose colleagues had been gunned down by the Jameses and Youngers in recent encounters, sneaked up to the house of Frank and Jesse's mother outside of Kearney and heaved a flaming thirty-two pound iron ball filled with "Greek fire" through a window. It exploded, mangling her right arm so badly that it had to be amputated below the elbow and killing the outlaw's nine-year-old half-brother, who significantly enough bore the first name of Archie. This affair aroused much indignation in Missouri and possibly would have led to the enactment of a law pardoning all ex-bushwhackers for their wartime deeds and guaranteeing them fair trials for alleged postwar crimes had not Frank and Jesse murdered a Clay County neighbor whom they accused of aiding the Pinkertons.

The first serious setback for the James-Younger gang came in September 1876 when it attempted to rob a bank in Northfield, Minnesota. This turned into a bloody fiasco, with three members of the gang being killed outright and all three of the Younger brothers being wounded and captured. Only Frank and Jesse, by abandoning the others to their fate, escaped back to Missouri.

For the next three years they lay low. Then, presumably because they were running short of money, they went back to their idea of working on the railroad. From October 1879 to September 1881 their new gang carried out three more train robberies, one in which a conductor and passenger were murdered.

Thomas T. Crittenden, the newly installed Democratic governor of Missouri, decided to put an end to the Jameses once and for all. They were bad for Missouri, which had become known as the "outlaw state"; they were bad for business, in particular the railroads; and they were bad for Democrats, whom the Republicans accused of not really trying to catch them. Accordingly, Crittenden posted a $10,000 reward (to be paid by the railroad companies) for information leading to the capture—dead or alive—of either Frank or Jesse James.

On December 4, 1881, Bob Ford, a new member of the gang, and a veteran bandit named Dick Liddil killed Wood Hite, another outlaw and Frank and Jesse's cousin, in a quarrel over a woman. Fearing that Jesse, who knew that he and Liddil were good friends, would slay him in revenge, Ford contacted Governor Crittenden and, along with his brother Charles, offered to tip off law-enforcement officers as to the time and place of the gang's next robbery. Crittenden in turn promised the Fords immunity from punishment and a share of the reward.

Late in March 1882, Bob and Charles Ford went to the house in St. Joseph where Jesse was living with his wife and two children (he never hid out in caves) under the alias of Thomas Howard. Together with Jesse the Fords planned to hold up the bank in Platte City on April 4. But finding no opportunity to notify the authorities of the pending robbery, Bob decided to kill Jesse at the first opportunity.

That came on the morning of April 3. Jesse, complaining that he was warm, removed his coat and then his gun belt so as to avoid the chance of some passerby glancing through the window and seeing him wearing it. Noticing that a picture was hanging crookedly on the wall, he stood on a chair to straighten it. At once Bob pulled out his pistol—a revolver that Jesse had given him the previous day for use in the Platte City job—and fired. The bullet tore through the back of Jesse's skull behind the right ear, and he fell to the floor, dead. He was thirty-four and had spent more than half of his life as a bushwhacker and a bandit, in the process becoming what he remains: The most famous outlaw in American history and legend—a legend enhanced by the manner of his death at the hands of "that dirty little coward who shot Mr. Howard."

Jesse's murder caused Frank, now thirty-nine, to realize that if he wished to reach forty, he had better make his peace with the law. After obtaining assurances from Crittenden that he would be given a fair trial, he surrendered to the governor at Jefferson City on October 5, 1882. Twice he stood trial, first in Gallatin for various crimes but not the murder of Sheets, and then in Alabama for a robbery committed in that state. Both times he was acquitted for lack of convincing evidence—convincing, that is, to openly sympathetic jurors. He lived out the rest of his life by trading on his celebrity status, dying in 1915 at his old family home near Kearney, where he had charged fifty cents a person for a tour. In certain respects he was the most successful of all of Bill Anderson's boys—or the luckiest.[28]

More than likely Tom Goodman had seen Frank James at Centralia, although of course he would not have known or cared who he was. To him Frank—and for that matter Jesse, supposing he was indeed with Bill Anderson on September 27, 1864—could only have been a face among the bushwhackers who slaughtered his fellow soldiers and who would have done the same to him had it not been for his two guards. Following his escape and return to Hawleyville, the big sergeant succumbed to the physical and psychological ordeal that he had undergone while a prisoner, becoming so ill that he was unable to return to Atlanta before the expiration of his thirty-day leave or before the First Missouri Engineers set forth in mid-November with the rest of Sherman's army on its March to the Sea. For a while the regiment's rolls listed him as "killed on the North Missouri R.R.," then as "absent without leave." Not until after Sherman reached Savannah late in December did the First Missouri receive word that he was "absent sick in Iowa since Nov. 5, 1864." And although he recovered his

Figure E.2 Tom Goodman's grave. COURTESY OF LORLEI K. METKE.

health by early 1865, it was impossible for him to rejoin the regiment while Sherman's legions spent the winter and spring tramping through the Carolinas, Virginia, and finally on to Washington, D.C., for the grand victory parade. Not until summer did Goodman at long last find himself again with his army comrades, and then only for the purpose of being discharged with them at Louisville on July 22, 1865, and receiving his pay "in full" at St. Louis six days later. Presumably both in travelling to Louisville and then back to Hawleyville he took a North Missouri Railroad train that passed through Centralia.

In Hawleyville he resumed his trade of blacksmith. He also wrote, or rather had written for him by "Captain Harry A. Houston," his *A Thrilling Record,* the booklet so often cited and quoted in this work. Published in 1868 by a job printer in Des Moines, it sold for fifty cents ("Liberal discounts made to booksellers") and could be procured by ordering it directly from Goodman. Probably it achieved only a modest sale, and that confined largely to Iowa and Missouri. In any event it did not make enough money to compensate Goodman for what one must assume was a stagnant, if not dwindling, income from his blacksmith business in what was becoming the moribund village of Hawleyville. So when he heard from two brothers living in California of its nice climate and good opportunities, he decided to go there as well. In 1875 he and his family trekked across the plains and mountains in an ox cart to Sonoma County, where they settled on a ranch near Santa Rosa.

Again he worked, along with his oldest son, James, as a blacksmith. Evidently he achieved a comfortable, if not affluent, living and became a respected member of the community, as did his sons and his brother George, with the result that an entire section of Santa Rosa became known as "the Goodman Place." He also joined the local Grand Army of the Republic post and perhaps handed some of his comrades copies of *A Thrilling Record* or showed them the coat that Bloody Bill Anderson had given him. But all the years of hard work, military service, and the ten days he spent as a captive of the bushwhackers took their toll. Early in February 1886, two weeks shy of his fifty-seventh birthday, Tom Goodman died, according to his death certificate, of "disease of heart." He was buried in Santa Rosa's Rural Cemetery. An iron grill fence, constructed by his youngest son, Daniel, also a blacksmith, surrounds the grave site. In 1899 his wife Mary—who had refused to believe he died in 1864—joined him. His headstone, toppled by the great California earthquake of 1906, now rests in a bed of withered oak leaves.[29]

Early in November 1864 some Union soldiers rode out to the Richmond cemetery to see where the remains of Bloody Bill Anderson lay. They found his grave decorated by a neat cairn and a bouquet. Outraged, they walked their horses back and forth across the grave, scattering the stones and trampling the flowers into the ground. Then they left, satisfied that it would be a long time before any secesh dared decorate the grave again.[30]

Today flowers still appear every so often on the tombstone that now marks the probable site of Anderson's grave in what since 1875 has been the Mormon cemetery in Richmond. Clearly there are those who see in him a heroic, romantic figure, a man driven by persecution and crimes against his family to wage a ruthless war of revenge until he died in a desperate, perhaps deliberately suicidal, charge.[31]

There is some truth in this view of Anderson. But not enough. What he was is revealed both by what he did while alive and the gruesomely fascinating photographs Kice took of him dead. They convey the essential and therefore the most terrible truth of all about Bloody Bill, a truth that should not be ignored, for it applies to the present and the future as well as the past.

Anderson was not unique. On the contrary, in war and peace, in all times and places, there are beings like him, or who become like him when given the stimulus and the opportunity: Savage.

In this sense his spirit still lives and will do so until the end of time.

Figure E.3 Bill Anderson's grave (note: date of birth should be 1839).
COURTESY OF DONALD R. HALE.

NOTES

PREFACE
1. George to Brownlee, November 26, 1958. Transcript in possession of author.

PROLOGUE: This is the Way We Do Business
This account of the fight at Fayette, Missouri, on September 24, 1864, is based on the following sources: *War of the Rebellion: A Compilation of the Official Records of the Union and Confederate Armies* (128 vols. plus atlas; Washington, D.C.: Government Printing Office, 1881–1901), Series I, Vol. 1, part 1, pp. 410, 418, 433, 448; part 3, p. 459 (hereinafter cited as OR, with all references from Series I unless otherwise indicated; whenever a volume consists of more than one part, the volume number will appear before the OR and the part following it); S. S. Eaton to Father, September 26, 1864, John Eaton Papers, Missouri Historical Society, St. Louis; W. H. Schrader, "Reminiscences of the Early History of Brunswick, Missouri," *The Brunswicker* (Brunswick, Missouri), September 30, 1982 (reprint of article first published in 1914 or 1915); James M. Jacks, "A Brush with Bushwhackers," *National Tribune,* September 29, 1910; Hamp B. Watts, *The Babe of the Company* (Fayette, Missouri: The Democratic Leader Press, 1913), pp. 18–21, 34; John McCorkle, *Three Years with Quantrill* (1914; reprint, Norman: University of Oklahoma Press, 1992), pp. 160–62; *St. Louis Missouri Republican,* October 3, October 28, 1864; *History of Howard and Chariton Counties, Missouri* (St. Louis: National Historical Company, 1883), p. 284 (for note accompanying Benton's scalp); John N. Edwards, *Noted Guerrillas, or, The Warfare of the Border* (1877; reprint, Dayton, Ohio: Press of the Morningside Bookshop, 1976), pp. 291–92.

CHAPTER ONE: The Last Man You Will Ever See
1. 41 OR 1:416; Watts, *Babe of the Company,* p. 21; Edwards, *Noted Guerrillas,* p. 292.
2. For the origins and nature of the Civil War in Missouri and along the Kansas–Missouri border, see: Albert Castel, *William Clarke Quantrill: His Life and Times* (New York: Frederick Fell, 1962); Thomas Goodrich, *Black Flag: Guerrilla Warfare on the Western Border, 1861–1865* (Bloomington: Indiana University Press, 1995); and Richard S. Brownlee, *Gray Ghosts of the Confederacy: Guerrilla Warfare in the West, 1861–1865* (Baton Rouge: Louisiana State University Press, 1958).
3. Castel, *Quantrill,* p. 184.

4. Ibid., pp. 110–15.

5. Richard Cordley, *A History of Lawrence, Kansas, from the First Settlement to the End of the Rebellion* (Lawrence: Lawrence Journal Press, 1895), quoted in Donald R. Hale, *They Called Him Bloody Bill* (Clinton, Mo.: The Printery, 1975), p. 2; *Liberty (Mo.) Tribune,* September 30, 1864.

6. U.S. Census, 1860: Kansas, Breckenridge County, Agnes City Township; William E. Connelley interviews with Eli Sewell, Charles Strieby, and B. F. Meunkers, July 7, 1910, Box 13, William E. Connelley Collection, Kansas State Historical Society, Topeka, Kansas; William Michael Shimeall, "Arthur Ingrham Baker: Frontier Kansas: (Master's thesis, Emporia State University, 1978), p. 117. The actual first name of Bill Anderson's youngest sister was Martha, the same as her mother's, but she was called Janie, presumably because her middle name was Jane.

7. Connelley interviews with Sewell, Strieby, and Meunkers, Box 13, William E. Connelley Collection, Kansas State Historical Society. The 1860 U.S. Census for Agnes City Township, Breckenridge County, Kansas, lists as a member of the Anderson family Charles, age one year and born in Kansas. In a phone conversation on January 23, 1998, historian Carolyn Bartels of Independence, Missouri, informed author Albert Castel that she knows of living descendants of Ellis Anderson.

8. Albert Castel, *A Frontier State at War: Kansas, 1861–1865* (Ithaca: Cornell University Press, 1958), pp. 214–15.

9. The account of Baker's career up to the spring of 1862 is based mainly on Shimeall's thesis, cited in note 6 for this chapter. It is supplemented by interviews, also previously cited, by Connelley of Sewell, Strieby, and Meunkers, Box 13, William E. Connelley Collection, Kansas State Historical Society. For the 1860–61 drought, see Castel, *Frontier State,* pp. 14–15.

10. Connelley interview with Strieby, Box 13, William E. Connelley Collection, Kansas State Historical Society.

11. Shimeall, "Arthur Baker," pp. 209, 212–216; Castel, *Frontier State,* p. 212.

12. Baker was on friendly terms with the Andersons prior to taking Bill and Jim with him into Missouri and while editor of the *Council Grove Press* extolled the hospitality to be enjoyed at the Anderson's home. Shimeall, "Arthur Baker," pp. 216–17.

13. The account of the killing of William Anderson Sr. and of the events leading up to and following it is based on these sources: *Emporia News,* May 17, 1862; *Junction City Smoky Hill and Republican Union,* May 22, May 29, 1862; Connelley interviews with Sewell, Strieby, and Meunkers; Shimeall, "Arthur Baker," pp. 217–23.

14. Some accounts assert that William Clarke Quantrill was a member of Anderson's party (see for example Ted F. McDaniel, ed., *Our Land: A History of Lyon County, Kansas* (Emporia: Emporia State Press, 1976), p. 42. As will be seen, not only did Anderson and Quantrill dislike each other, but in early July 1862 Quantrill was personally involved in western Missouri operations designed to assist a Confederate recruiting detachment. See Castel, *Quantrill,* p. 81.

15. Connelley interviews with Sewell, Strieby, and Meunkers, Box 13, William E. Connelley Collection, Kansas State Historical Society; *Topeka Tribune,* July 5, July 12, 1862; *Emporia News,* July 12, 1862; Shimeall, "Arthur Baker," pp. 223–27; Randall M. Thiess, "Bloody Bill's First Murder," copy of typescript graciously supplied by the author.

CHAPTER TWO: I'm Here for Revenge

1. William E. Connelley, Memorandum of Conversation with William H. Gregg, June 14, 1916, Box 1, William E. Connelley Collection, Kansas History Collection, Spencer Research Library, University of Kansas. Gregg was one of Quantrill's lieutenants until he left him in the winter of 1863–64 to join the regular Confederate army.

2. The account of the Yeager raid into Kansas is based on the following sources: *Council Grove Press,* May 11, 1863; *Kansas City Weekly Journal of Commerce,* May 16, May 23, 1863; *Leavenworth Daily Conservation,* May 7, May 30, 1863; *Leavenworth Daily Times,* August 30, 1863; George Pilson Morehouse, "Diamond Springs, the Diamond of the Plains," *Kansas Historical Collections* 15 (1915–18): 799–800; David Hubbard, "Reminiscences of the Yeager Raid, on the Santa Fe Trail, in 1863," ibid 7 (1903–1904): 169–70.

3. Castel, *Quantrill,* pp. 108–110; Castel, *Frontier State at War,* 112, 208, 215. According to reports in Missouri newspapers, Quantrill's band used "middle men" to sell in Leavenworth horses and mules acquired on both sides of the border. (*Lexington Weekly Union,* January 3, 1863, quoting the *Liberty Tribune* and the *Kansas City Weekly Journal of Commerce*). Since the Red Legs sold stolen livestock and other plunder in Leavenworth, it is conceivable that they acted as these "middle men." There may not be honor among thieves, but they will share profits when expedient.

4. Castel, *Quantrill,* pp. 110–11, 116–19.

5. 22 OR 2: 377–78.

6. Brownlee, *Gray Ghosts,* pp. 138–39; *Kansas City Weekly Journal,* May 13, 1865.

7. *Wyandotte Gazette,* August 1, 1863; *Leavenworth Daily Conservative,* August 2, August 4, August 8, 1863; *Kansas City Daily Journal of Commerce,* August 6, 1863.

8. Castel, *Quantrill,* 118–19.

9. The best study of the Kansas City prison collapse is Charles F. Harris, "Catalyst of Terror: The Collapse of the Women's Prison in Kansas City," *Missouri Historical Review* 89 (April 1995): 290–306, and the account presented here is based on it.

10. William H. Gregg Manuscript, p. 90, State Historical Society of Missouri.

11. *St. Louis Missouri Daily Democrat,* November 12, 1864.

12. For Quantrill's career prior to the Lawrence raid, see Castel, *Quantrill,* pp. 22–121.

13. Testimony of William Bullene in John C. Shea, comp., *Reminiscences of Quantrill's Raid upon the City of Lawrence, Kansas* (Kansas City, Mo.: Isaac C. Moore, 1879), p. 14.

14. Ibid. For a full account of the Lawrence raid and massacre, see Thomas Goodrich, *Bloody Dawn: The Story of the Lawrence Massacre* (Kent, Ohio: Kent State University Press, 1991).

CHAPTER THREE: Such a Damn Outfit

1. Castel, *Quantrill,* pp. 144–49.

2. Ibid., pp. 150–53; Thomas Goodrich, *Black Flag,* pp. 107–11.

3. Castel, *Quantrill,* p. 167.

4. Ibid., pp. 156–63.

5. Ibid., pp. 163–68.

6. Frank Smith, who joined Quantrill's band as a young member in 1863, states in his manuscript memoirs that he never heard of Anderson marrying her (Frank Smith

Manuscript, Notes and Extracts, Research Files of Albert Castel). On the basis of this, Castel, in *Quantrill*, p. 164, refers to her as his mistress, but as a result of subsequent research and reflection, he now believes that they were married.

7. Julia Lovejoy to her family, May 10, 1864, *Kansas Historical Quarterly* 16 (May 1948): 207–208.

8. Castel, *Quantrill*, pp. 168–69.

9. Reynolds to Quantrill, March 10, 1864, Thomas C. Reynolds Papers, Library of Congress.

10. Castel, *Quantrill*, pp. 169–71.

11. Ibid., 171–72. For additional information (and speculation) concerning Quantrill, Kate King, and Quantrill's stay in the Perche Hills, see Donald R. Hale, *We Rode with Quantrill* (Clinton, Mo.: The Printery, 1974), pp. 112–21.

12. Castel, *Quantrill*, pp. 175–76; Goodrich, *Black Flag*, pp. 129–30.

13. Castel, *Quantrill*, pp. 176–79.

14. Quoted in Goodrich, *Black Flag*, p. 135.

CHAPTER FOUR: Let the Blood Flow

1. 34 OR 1: 1001–1002; OR 2: Ibid., 76; *Kansas City Daily Journal*, June 16, 1864; Brownlee, *Gray Ghosts*, p. 138.

2. 34 OR 1: 1007–1008; 41 OR 2: 76.

3. 34 OR 4: 564–65; *St. Joseph Morning Herald*, July 8, 1864, quoting the *Lexington Weekly Union* of July 1, 1864.

4. *Carrollton Weekly Democrat*, July 8, 1864.

5. 41 OR 2: 75–77.

6. *History of Carroll County, Missouri* (St. Louis: Missouri Historical Company, 1881), pp. 343–45; *Carrollton Weekly Democrat*, July 22, July 29, 1864.

7. *Huntsville Randolph Citizen*, July 15, July 22, 1864, quoted in the *Columbia Missouri Statesman*, July 22, July 29, 1864; *Louisiana (Mo.) Journal*, July 23, 1864; *Kansas City Star*, December 3, 1912, Donald R. Hale, *They Called Him Bloody Bill: The Life of William Anderson, Missouri Guerrilla* (Clinton, Mo.: The Printery, 1975), pp. 18–22.

8. 41 OR 2: 367, 490, 496; *Kansas City Daily Journal*, July 28, 1864; *Columbia Missouri Statesman*, July 29, 1864.

9. 41 OR 1: 125; Ibid., OR 2: 367, 394; *Columbia Missouri Statesman*, August 5, 1864.

10. 41 OR 2: 421–23; *St. Joseph Morning Herald*, July 28, August 3, 1864; *History of Monroe and Shelby Counties, Missouri* (St. Louis: National Historical Company, 1884), pp. 769–71; Hale, *Bloody Bill*, pp. 23–24. For railroad bridge burning in 1861 by pro-Confederate civilian saboteurs and the consequent inauguration of a no-quarter policy toward guerrillas by Union military authorities in Missouri, see Brownlee, *Gray Ghosts*, pp. 23–25.

11. 41 OR 2: 479; *Huntsville Randolph Citizen*, quoted in *Macon (Mo.) Gazette*, August 11, 1864; *St. Louis Missouri Democrat*, November 11, 1864; *History of Carroll County*, 348–49.

12. *Macon (Mo.) Gazette*, August 11, 1864, quoting *Huntsville Randolph Citizen*; *Carrollton Weekly Democrat*, August 5, 12, 1864; *History of Carroll County*, pp. 350–51.

13. *St. Joseph Morning Herald*, August 10, 1864.

14. Ibid., August 13, 1864.

15. Ibid., August 10, 1864.

16. 41 OR 2: 479, 481–82, 506–10. For difficulty of Union forces in obtaining intelligence regarding the guerrillas, see Maj. R. Leonard to Brig. Gen. C. B. Fisk, ibid., pp. 80–81.

17. Ibid., p. 490. For a revealing description of the condition of Matlack's command, see ibid., pp. 656–57.

18. 41 OR 3: 424; Castel, *Quantrill,* pp. 178, 184.

19. 41 OR 2: 437–38. For plundering by the Seventeenth Illinois, see Brig. Gen. J. B. Douglass to Fisk, August 31, 1864, ibid., p. 963, in which Douglass states, "As to the Seventeenth Illinois, all reports from them are that they are almost worthless, and we cannot rely on them." The notion that the Missouri guerrillas tied down large numbers of Union troops who otherwise would have been employed in major campaigns east of the Mississippi is, to put it mildly, greatly exaggerated.

20. Hamp B. Watts, *The Babe of the Company: An Unfolded Leaf from the Forest of Never–to– be–Forgotten Years* (Fayette, Mo.: The Democratic–Leader Press, 1913), p. 6; William A. Settle Jr., *Jesse James Was His Name* (Columbia: University of Missouri Press, 1966), pp. 20–23, 26–27.

21. *Lexington Weekly Union,* January 28, 1865.

22. Jim Cummins, *Jim Cummins's Book Written by Himself* (Denver: Reed Publishing Company, 1903), quoted in Goodrich, *Black Flag,* p. 137.

23. 41 OR 1: 689–90.

24. 41 OR 1: 249–53; *Leavenworth Daily Conservative,* quoted in *LaGrange (Mo.) National American,* September 1, 1864; *History of Carroll County,* pp. 352–53; Settle, *Jesse James,* p. 27.

25. 41 OR 2: 795.

26. Ibid., p. 858.

27. Ibid., pp. 859–60. Throughout the summer and fall of 1864, Federal military reports and correspondence repeatedly referred to Quantrill as still commanding a large force of bushwhackers and even as being the supreme chieftain of all guerrillas in western Missouri. Many rank-and-file bushwhackers were themselves unaware of his true status.

28. 41 OR 1: 300; ibid, 2: 880–81; *Columbia Missouri Statesman,* September 16, 1864; Watts, *Babe of the Company,* pp. 11–12.

29. 41 OR 3: 8–9; *Columbia Missouri Statesman,* September 16, 1864; *Gallatin North Missourian,* September 22, 1864.

30. *Jefferson City State Times,* September 10, 1864.

31. Watts, *Babe of the Company,* p. 17.

32. 41 OR 3: 194; J. Thomas Fyfer, *History of Boone County, Missouri* (St. Louis: Western Historical Company, 1882), pp. 437–39.

33. Watts, *Babe of the Company,* p. 17.

34. 41 OR 1: 415, 432–33; ibid., 3: 348–49.

35. Watts, *Babe of the Company,* p. 18; Frank Smith Manuscript Notes and Extracts, pp. 124–26; William E. Connelley, *Quantrill and the Border Wars* (Cedar Rapids, Iowa: The Torch Press, 1910), pp. 452–53.

36. Watts, *Babe of the Company,* pp. 21–22. Quantrill did not participate in the attack but at least one of the few men who accompanied him did, that being Jim Little, who was badly wounded. Quantrill returned to his hideout in the Perche Hills immediately

after the fight, taking Little with him. Most of the bushwhackers never saw him again. See Castel, *Quantrill*, pp. 186–87.

CHAPTER FIVE: There are Guerrillas There

1. Unless indicated otherwise in a note, all the descriptions appearing in the text of Goodman's experiences, observations, and thoughts are derived from Thomas M. Goodman, *"A Thrilling Record"* (Des Moines, Iowa: Mills & Company Steam Book & Job Printing House, 1868; Facsimile Edition, with Introduction, Notes, and Appendix by Thomas R. Hooper, Marysville, Missouri: Rush Printing Company, 1960). This small book (fifty-eight pages of text) was written by Goodman with the assistance of "Captain Harry A. Houston," who "edited and prepared" Goodman's account.

2. Frederick H. Dyer, comp., *A Compendium of the War of the Rebellion* (Des Moines, Iowa: The Dyer Publishing Company, 1908), pp. 1320, 1332; 38 OR 1: 127, 136; Albert Castel, *Decision in the West: The Atlanta Campaign of 1864* (Lawrence: University Press of Kansas, 1992), p. 502.

3. Photocopies of Goodman's Mexican War service record and of his discharge from the Union army, National Archives; U.S. Census, 1860, Hawleyville, Page County, Iowa; Letters from Betty M. Pierce and Lorlei K. Metke to Thomas Goodrich, 1983–1992.

4. Thomas P. Lowry, *The Story the Soldiers Wouldn't Tell: Sex in the Civil War* (Mechanicsburg, Pa.: Stackpole Books, 1994), p. 77.

5. U.S. Census, 1850, Hardin County, Kentucky; U.S. Census, 1860, Hawleyville, Page County, Iowa; photocopy of Goodman's discharge; letters from Betty M. Pierce, Lorlei K. Metke, and Thomas R. Hooper to Thomas Goodrich, 1983–1992.

6. *Paris (Mo.) Mercury*, September 30, 1864, quoted in *The Canton (Mo.) Press*, October 6, 1864; 41 OR 1: 443; ibid., 3: 397, 488; Fyfer, *History of Boone County*, p. 453.

7. Goodman, *Record*, pp. 17–20.

8. 41 OR 3: 397; Watts, *Babe of the Company*, pp. 22–3; Fyfer, *History of Boone County*, p. 439; Edgar T. Rodemyre, *History of Centralia, Missouri* (Centralia: Fireside Guard, 1936), pp. 34–5.

9. Rodemyre, *Centralia*, p. 24.

10. *Paris (Mo.) Mercury*, September 30, 1864, quoted in *The Canton (Mo.) Press*, October 6, 1864; "Centralia Massacre," clipping from *Sturgeon (Mo.) Leader*, August 9, 1895, in Lewis M. Switzler Papers, Western Historical Manuscripts Collection, University of Missouri, Columbia, Missouri. *The Paris Mercury* account is the only known available contemporary account of Johnston's movements during the night of September 26–27, 1864, and presumably is based on the testimony of members of his command. The *Sturgeon Leader* article originally appeared in the Washington (D. C.) *National Tribune* and evidently was written either by a member of Johnston's command or by someone who interviewed surviving members.

11. Johnston's service record, microfilm, State Historical Society of Missouri, Columbia, Missouri; *History of Marion County, Missouri* (St. Louis: E. C. Perkins, 1884), pp. 517–18; *Louisiana (Mo.) Journal*, August 6, 1863; 13 OR: 271–72.

12. *Paris (Mo.) Mercury*, September 30, 1864, quoted in *The Canton (Mo.) Press*, October 6, 1864; "Centralia Massacre" clipping, Switzler Papers.

13. Possibly the force observed by Johnston consisted of a party of Confederate recruits commanded by Capt. G. W. Bryson of Boone County. The day before, mistaking Anderson's men for Federals because of the Union uniforms they wore, the recruits had fired some shots at the guerrillas before realizing their mistake. An angry Anderson told them to stay away from his outfit, which they did. This would account for them being to the northeast of Centralia. See Fyfer, *History of Boone County*, pp. 439–40.

14. Brownlee, *Gray Ghosts*, p. 24; Rodemyre, *Centralia*, pp. 24–27.

15. *Columbia Missouri Statesman*, September 30, 1864; Fyfer, *History of Boone County*, pp. 441–43.

16. C. B. Rollins, ed., "Letters of George Caleb Bingham to James S. Rollins," *Missouri Historical Review* 33 (October 1938): 48; *Columbia Missouri Statesman*, September 30, 1864; Rodemyre, *Centralia*, p. 27.

17. Goodman, *Record*, pp. 19–20.

18. "Statement of the Conductor of the Train," *St. Louis Missouri Democrat*, October 10, 1864. Hereinafter cited as Overall Statement. This statement also appears in Rodemyre, *Centralia*, pp. 56–60.

19. "Centralia Massacre" clipping, Switzler Papers.

20. James Clark, various newspaper interviews regarding the Centralia Massacre, newspaper clipping, Centralia Scrapbook, State Historical Society of Missouri, Columbia, Missouri. Hereinafter cited as Clark Interviews.

21. Goodman, *Record*, p. 21.

22. Clark Interviews.

23. Overall Statement.

24. Ibid.

25. Goodman, *Record*, p. 21; Overall Statement; Clark Interviews.

CHAPTER SIX: You All are to Be Killed

1. *Columbia Missouri Statesman*, September 30, 1864; Rodemyre, *Centralia*, pp. 26–27, Fyfer, History of Boone County, pp. 443–45, 447; Rollins, ed., "Letters of Bingham," p. 48, note 8. This last source refers to Rollins's hiding place as "Nancy's room," which would seem to indicate that it was the hotel maid's room.

2. Goodman, *Record*, pp. 21–22; Rodemyre, *Centralia*, p. 28.

3. Clark Interviews.

4. Goodman, *Record*, pp. 21–22; Clark Interviews; *St. Louis Daily Missouri Republican*, September 30, 1864; Fyfer, *History of Boone County*, 439–46; Rodemyre, *Centralia*, p. 29.

5. Goodman, *Record*, p. 22.

6. *Columbia Missouri Statesman*, September 30, 1864; Fyfer, *History of Boone County*, p. 446.

7. Goodman, *Record*, pp. 22–24; *Columbia Missouri Statesman*, September 30, 1864; *St. Joseph Morning Herald*, September 30, October 2, 1864; *Kansas City Daily Journal*, October 4, 1864; *Atchison Freedom's Champion*, September 29, 1864, quoted in *Manhattan (Kans.) Independent*, October 3, 1864; J. F. Benjamin to John Paddock, September 30, 1864, John and Diana Benjamin Letters, State Historical Society of Missouri, Columbia, Missouri; Fyfer, *History of Boone County*, p. 443; Rodemyre, *Centralia*, pp. 29–31.

8. Goodman, *Record,* p. 24; *St. Joseph Morning Herald,* September 30, 1864; Fyfer, *History of Boone County,* pp. 448–49.

9. Fyfer, *History of Boone County,* pp. 450–51. According to this account, which presents no source but was probably based on the testimony of one or more residents of Centralia, the bushwhacker Peyton Long persuaded Anderson not to search for Rollins, saying, "You can get another man just as good as he is, without half the trouble." Though plausible, this story lacks an authentic ring.

10. Clark Interviews; Fyfer, *History of Boone County,* pp. 449–51; Rodemyre, *Centralia,* pp. 31–32.

11. Goodman, *Record,* p. 27.

12. Clark Interviews; *St. Louis Daily Missouri Republican,* September 30, 1864.

13. Ibid.; Fyfer, *History of Boone County,* pp. 449–52. Rollins had been captured by guerrillas during the summer of 1863 but was released unharmed. Perhaps the bushwhackers feared that taking a United States congressman prisoner and killing him would lead to harsh Federal reprisals against their families and prominent Confederate sympathizers. See James Madison Wood Jr., "James Sidney Rollins: Civil War Congressman from Missouri" (master's thesis, University of Missouri, 1947), p. 109.

CHAPTER SEVEN: The Lord Have Mercy

1. Goodman, *Record,* pp. 28–31.

2. *St. Louis Daily Missouri Republican,* September 30, 1864; "Centralia Massacre" clipping, Switzler Papers: Fyfer, *History of Boone County,* p. 452; Rodemyre, Centralia, p. 35. According to a letter in the *Louisiana (Mo.) Journal,* October 8, 1864, that purports to report an interview with a member of Johnston's command who went to Centralia, Johnston's force first went to Sturgeon, where at noon it saw smoke arising from the area around Centralia and so marched there. This seems to be very compelling evidence that Johnston went to Centralia by way of Sturgeon, and it also would help explain why it took him so long to reach Centralia, which is only about twenty miles from Paris. All the other sources, however, both primary and those based on the testimony of participants and eyewitnesses, state that Johnston marched directly to Centralia; several of them also say that he entered Centralia from the east; and, finally and most conclusively, neither Clark nor anyone else who accompanied him to Sturgeon during the early afternoon mentions meeting or seeing Johnston's force while they were on the way to Sturgeon, something they surely would have done, especially since Johnston would have gone to Centralia from Sturgeon by way of the wagon road that paralleled the railroad. Either the writer of the *Louisiana Journal* letter misunderstood or misreported what the member of Johnston's command told him, or else that member garbled his account or for some reason lied.

3. Fyfer, *History of Boone County,* pp. 453–56; Rodemyre, *Centralia,* pp. 35–36; "Centralia Massacre" clipping, Switzler Papers.

4. Why he found this astonishing cannot be explained. Presumably he could see that the Federals were infantry equipped with rifles. The Enfield rifles carried by Johnston's men were close to four and a half feet long. To reload one after discharging its single shot, a soldier had to tear open a paper cartridge with his teeth, pour black powder down the barrel, press a lead bullet down into the muzzle with his thumb, withdraw an iron ramrod from beneath the barrel and use it to press the bullet down the barrel onto

the powder, remove and replace the ramrod, pull back the hammer to half cock, extract a metal cap filled with fulminate of mercury from a pouch attached to his belt, afix it to a nipple, full cock the hammer, and then—and not until then—would his weapon be ready to be fired again. To do all of these things rapidly and correctly while on a plunging, rearing, frightened horse in the middle of battle bordered on the impossible. And even if done, it was just as difficult to aim and fire the rifle accurately. The only way Johnston's troops could hope to repel the forthcoming guerrilla onslaught was to fight on foot.

Moreover, they were not necessarily at a disadvantage. Soldiers on foot possessed far greater killing power than those on horseback, so much so that Civil War cavalry as often as not fought on foot, employing carbines. Indeed, most Confederate troopers in the West, notably Nathan Bedford Forrest's "critter company," dispensed with sabers altogether and went into battle on foot and with long-barreled Enfields. By the same token, veteran infantry in both armies asked for nothing better than a chance to take on a mounted cavalry charge. Given time to fire their three shots a minute from the protection of either a natural obstacle (such as a thick hedge) or a man-made one (a stout rail fence would do), they could empty so many saddles that the surviving assailants would literally turn tail before they got close enough to use their pistols, much less slash anybody with a saber. Only if attacked at close range and while in the open, or from the flank and rear, did foot soldiers need to fear horse soldiers. This rarely happened, and a good, experienced commander would make sure not to let it happen.

5. 41 OR 1: 309, 417, 440–41; ibid., 3: 521; Goodman, *Record,* pp. 31–32, Frank Smith Manuscript Notes and Extracts, pp. 127, 130; *Paris (Mo.) Mercury,* September 30, 1864, quoted in *The Canton (Mo.) Press,* October 6, 1864; *Columbia Missouri Statesman,* September 30, 1864; *St. Louis Daily Missouri Democrat,* September 29, September 30, October 4, 1864; *Kansas City Weekly Journal,* October 1, October 8, 1864; *Liberty Tribune,* September 30, 1864; Fyfer, *History of Boone County,* pp. 457–58; Rodemyre, *Centralia,* pp. 36–38; Howard C. Conrad, ed., *Encyclopedia of the History of Missouri* (4 vols.; New York, Louisville, and St. Louis: The Southern History Company, 1901), 1: 555. Frank James, in an interview published in the *Columbia Missouri Herald,* September 24, 1897, asserted that his brother, Jesse, shot and killed Johnston. Given the circumstances, not only was it unlikely that anyone could have seen who shot whom at Centralia, there is reason to doubt that Jesse was even at Centralia. (See interview with Morgan T. Mattox, June 30, 1864, and William H. Gregg to William E. Connelley, in William E. Connelley Collection, Box 1, Kansas Collection, Spencer Research Library, University of Kansas.) Frank James was not a reliable source, especially when relating anything having to do with himself and Jesse.

6. Fyfer, *History of Boone County,* pp. 459–61; Rodemyre, *Centralia,* pp. 38–40.

7. Frank James Interview, *Columbia Missouri Herald,* September 24, 1897; Rodemyre, *Centralia,* p. 40.

8. Report of Lieutenant Colonel Daniel Draper, 41 OR 1: 440; Goodman, *Record,* p. 33. Only four of Johnston's men who took part in the battle on the ridge were not killed, and two of them were mortally wounded. 41 OR 3: 552.

9. John McCorkle, *Three Years with Quantrill* (written by O. S. Barton and first published in 1914; reprint with notes by Albert Castel and commentary by Herman Hattaway, Norman: University of Oklahoma Press, 1992), pp. 163–65, and Frank

Smith Manuscript Notes and Extracts, pp. 129–31, claims that George Todd planned and commanded the guerrilla ambush at Centralia; Rodemyre, *Centralia,* p. 36, states that George Todd and John Thrailkill were in command but also (p. 24) that Quantrill was present and played an influential role; and W. C. Todd, a bushwhacker who evidently was a relative of Tom Todd, claims that George Todd was in charge in a publication titled *Civil War in Missouri: The Centralia Fight* (n.p., n.d., copy of file at State Historical Society of Missouri, Columbia, Missouri), pp. 9–10. McCorkle, *Three Years with Quantrill,* p. 163, also asserts that George Todd disapproved of the slaughter of the Union troops in Centralia and "severely reprimanded Anderson for doing it." Given the murders and massacres perpetrated by George Todd and bushwhackers serving under him (cf. Baxter Springs), this is highly unlikely. In any case, Anderson received the credit (so to speak) for Centralia from the Federals, as witness the report of Lt. W. T. Clarke, aide-de-camp to Fisk, who, after investigating the Centralia massacres, notified Fisk on September 30, 1864, that "Anderson was in command; Todd was second." 41 OR 3: 521.

10. Clark Interviews.

11. 41 OR 1: 443; Fyfer, *History of Boone County,* pp. 463–64.

12. Goodman, *Record,* p. 34; Fyfer, *History of Boone County,* pp. 461–64; Rodemyre, *Centralia,* pp. 60–68.

13. Goodman, *Record,* pp. 34–35

CHAPTER EIGHT: Reserved

1. This chapter is, for obvious reasons, based on Goodman's account as presented in his *Thrilling Record.* It has here and there been supplemented by an interview he gave to the *St. Joseph Herald-Tribune* that appeared in the October 14, 1864, issue of that paper and was reprinted on pages 59–61 of the 1960 facsimile edition of his *Thrilling Record.*

2. *St. Louis Tri-Weekly Republican,* September 30, 1864; Fyfer, *History of Boone County,* pp. 465–67.

3. Along this line, Price's chief of engineers, Capt. T. J. Mackey, referred to Anderson as a "colonel" when giving testimony at a court of inquiry on Price's Missouri expedition of 1864. (41 OR 1: 888). However, there is no evidence that either Anderson or Quantrill ever received a Confederate colonel's commission as partisan rangers.

4. Ibid., 3: 395–96, 592.

5. For a full discussion of the tactics used by the bushwhackers, see Albert Castel, "Quantrill's Bushwhackers: A Case Study in Guerrilla Warfare," *Winning and Losing in the Civil War: Essays and Stories* (Columbia: University of South Carolina Press, 1996), pp. 133–44.

CHAPTER NINE: How Do You Like That?

1. Castel, *Price,* pp. 200–27.

2. *St. Louis Tri-Weekly Republican,* October 28, 1864.

3. *St. Louis Daily Missouri Democrat,* October 27, 1864; *St. Louis Tri-Weekly Republican,* October 28, 1864; *History of Monroe and Shelby Counties, Missouri* (St. Louis: National Historical Company, 1884), p. 769.

4. 41 OR 1: 632, 718, 888; ibid., 3: 893; ibid., 4: 854; *Kansas City Weekly Journal,* November 12, 1864; *St. Louis Tri-Weekly Republican,* October 8, October 14, 1864; Castel, *Price,* pp. 228–29.

5. Goodman, *Record,* pp. 56–67.

6. Ibid., pp. 11, 57.

7. Walter Williams, ed., *A History of Northeast Missouri* (2 vols.; Chicago: The Lewis Publishing Company, 1913), 1: 497; Conrad, ed., *Encyclopedia of the History of Missouri,* 3: 1260; Lewis to Fisk, August 21, 1864, 41 OR 3: 795.

8. 41 OR 1: 632–33, 656–67, 681–82.

9. *St. Louis Daily Missouri Democrat,* November 12, 1864. This contains the most detailed and accurate account of what happened to Lewis on the night of October 21, 1864, and is obviously based on the testimony of eyewitnesses.

10. 41 OR 4: 471; *St. Louis Daily Missouri Democrat,* November 12, 1864; *History of Howard and Chariton Counties* (St. Louis: National Historical Company, 1883), pp. 288–89.

11. *St. Louis Daily Missouri Democrat,* November 12, 1864.

12. 41 OR 1: 438–39, 444–45, 888; ibid., 3: 893; *St. Louis Daily Missouri Democrat,* October 20–22, 1864.

13. *St Louis Daily Missouri Democrat,* November 12, 1864; *Gallatin North Missourian,* November 3, 1864.

14. Genealogy of BenjaminWhitehead Lewis, Missouri Historical Society, Jefferson Memorial Library, St. Louis, Missouri.

CHAPTER TEN: Good Morning, Captain Anderson

1. 41 OR 4: 241, 255–56; Brownlee, *Gray Ghosts,* p. 228; interview with B. F. Meunkers, July 7, 1910, Box 13, William E. Connelley Collection, Kansas State Historical Society; *History of Carroll County,* pp. 362–64. For death of Todd and defeat of Price, see respectively Castel, *Quantrill,* pp. 197–98 and Castel, *Price,* pp. 228–36.

2. 41 OR 1: 442; ibid., 2: 362, 376; ibid., 4: 726–27; *Kansas City Star,* August 16, 1913 (obituary of Cox); Howard C. Grisham, *Centralia and Bill Anderson* (Jefferson City: Howard C. Grisham, 1964), pp. 12–13 (sketch of Cox's life).

3. 41 OR 1: 442 (Cox's report); Diary of Lieutenant Thomas Hankins, in *Richmond Missourian,* June 6, 1938; Report on Centralia battle by anonymous officer dated "Headquarters 33rd Regiment Enrolled Missouri Militia, Hamilton, Missouri, October 31, 1864," and addressed to "General Craig," in *Richmond (Mo.) Daily News,* December 19, 1986 (hereinafter cited as Anonymous Officer's Report); Kingston, Mo. *Caldwell Banner of Liberty,* November 18, 1864; *Liberty Tribune,* November 11, 1864; *Kansas City Weekly Journal,* November 5, 1864. Cox's report, as published in the *Official Records,* is dated Richmond, Missouri, October 27, 1864, and in it he refers to the encounter with Anderson as occurring "yesterday" (i.e., October 26). Either the October 27 date is a typographical error (rare in the *Official Records* but they do exist) or he misdated the report or (another possibility) wrote it so late on the night of October 27 that he thought of the fight as having taken place "yesterday." All other accounts, and in particular the Anonymous Officer's Report, state that the fight took place on October 27.

4. 41 OR 1: 442., ibid., 4: 334, 354, 726–27, 734; Anonymous Officer's Report (which contains the most detailed account of what was found on Anderson's body); statement by Adolph Vogel, *Moberly (Mo.) Evening Democrat,* August 15, 1924, quoted in Hale, *Bloody Bill,* p. 78.

5. Statement by Vogel in Hale, *Bloody Bill,* p. 79; statement by James S. Hackley, quoted in ibid; *Liberty Tribune,* November 4, 1864; Wiley Britton, *The Civil War on the*

Border (2 vols; New York: The Knickerbocker Press, 1898), 2: 545; *Richmond Missourian,* June 17, 1938.

6. *Liberty Tribune,* November 4, November 11, 1864; *Kansas City Weekly Journal,* November 5, 1864; Kingston, Mo. *Caldwell Banner of Liberty,* November 18, 1864; *The Richmond Missourian,* June 27, July 4, 1938.

EPILOGUE: The Spirit of Bill Anderson Yet Lives

1. 421 OR 4: 317. A Union officer stationed at Waynesville claimed on September 20, 1864, to have killed Anderson. Ibid., 1: 850.

2. *St. Joseph Morning Herald,* October 29, 1864; *Kansas City Weekly Journal,* November 12, 1864.

3. *History of Carroll County,* pp. 363–64; *St. Louis Daily Democrat,* November 12, November 16, 1864.

4. *St. Louis Daily Democrat,* October 28, 1864; *Liberty Tribune,* October 28, 1864.

5. *History of Carroll County,* p. 364.

6. Castel, *Quantrill,* pp. 201–207.

7. *Kansas City Daily Journal,* May 10, May 11, 1865; Castel, *Quantrill,* pp. 217–18.

8. *Kansas City Daily Journal,* May 10, May 11, 1865.

9. Ibid., May 10, 1865.

10. 48 OR 2: 349,. 351–53; *Kansas City Weekly Journal,* May 13, May 20, 1864.

11. *Kansas City Weekly Journal,* April 15, 1865, quoting the *Columbia Missouri Statesman,* n.d.

12. 48 OR 2: 371; Castel, *Quantrill,* p. 218.

13. Castel, *Quantrill,* pp. 216, 220–21.

14. 48 OR 2: 528–29

15. *History of Ray County, Missouri* (St. Louis: Missouri Historical Company, 1881), p. 304; 48 OR 2: 599.

16. 48 OR 2: 410, 785, 872; *The Messages and Proclamations of the Governors of Missouri* 4 (19 vols.; Columbia: State Historical Society of Missouri, 1922–61): 280–81. Interestingly, the proclamation announcing the reward for Clements describes him as "almost twenty-eight" and "about five feet eight inches high." He was at most twenty-one, and had he been five feet eight he would not have been called Little Archie because that was the average height of men then.

17. Castel, *Quantrill,* pp. 207–13. Quantrill was wounded and captured on May 10, 1865, and died in a Louisville prison on June 6, 1865.

18. 48 OR 2: 573, 609, 634, 797–98, 837, 1001; *History of Carroll County,* p. 364; James M. Jacks, "A Brush with Bushwhackers," *Washington (D.C.) National Tribune,* September 29, 1910, p. 7; *Kansas City Daily Journal,* April 14, 1866; William A. Settle Jr., *Jesse James Was His Name* (Columbia: University of Missouri Press, 1966), pp. 30–34; Hale, *Bloody Bill,* pp. 101–102.

19. Hale, *Bloody Bill,* p. 105; Brownlee, *Gray Ghosts,* 242.

20. Hale, *Bloody Bill,* pp. 105–106; Brownlee, *Gray Ghosts,* 242–43.

21. Hale, *Bloody Bill,* pp. 106–107.

22. Ibid., pp. 107–10.

23. Settle, *Jesse James,* pp. 30–40; Hale, *Bloody Bill,* pp. 110–11.

24. Settle, *Jesse James,* pp. 39–40.

25. *Jefferson City Missouri State Times,* May 10, 1867, quoting the *Glasgow Times,* n.d., in Hale, *Bloody Bill,* p. 106; Donald R. Hale to Albert Castel, January 7, 1998, stating that a source in his possession but which he had misplaced "said that George Shepherd cut [Jim] Anderson's throat on the courthouse lawn in Sherman, Texas, about September of 1868."

26. Hale to Castel, January 7, 1998.

27. It could be argued that since Frank and Jesse, just two men, robbed the Gallatin bank, and Jesse killed Sheets almost immediately after entering the bank, their purpose was not so much robbery as it was to murder Sheets, and they were motivated in doing so by a desire to avenge Bill Anderson's death. But why slay Sheets, who had nothing to do with Anderson's death? And if vengeance was their motive, why did Frank and Jesse not attempt to waylay and kill Cox? A more likely explanation of their conduct is that they were drunk, a surmise supported by Jesse's inability to mount his horse.

28. This book's account of the outlaw careers of Frank and Jesse James and the fame that they achieved is based on the relevant sections of Settle's *Jesse James Was His Name.* This work, which began as an master's thesis at the University of Missouri, was the first scholarly examination of its subject, and at the time of the writing of this book it remained the only published one. For a more detailed yet short account of the Jameses, see Albert Castel, "Men Behind the Masks: The James Brothers," *American History Illustrated* (Summer 1982): 10–18, an article also based mainly on Settle's book.

29. The account of Goodman's life and death, 1864 to 1886, is based on his service record (microfilm, State Historical Society of Missouri), U.S. Census records, and above all on reminiscences, documents, and photographs supplied by Betty M. Pierce, a descendant of Goodman, and on documents and data provided by Lorlei K. Metke, a professional historical and genealogical researcher, between 1989 and 1992 to Thomas Goodrich. The information about Goodman retaining the coat given him by Bill Anderson comes from a notation made by Thomas R. Hooper, who edited and published the 1960 facsimile edition of Goodman's *A Thrilling Record,* in a January 8, 1983, letter to him by Thomas Goodrich.

30. *Columbia (Mo.) Daily Times,* n.d., Centralia Massacre Clippings, Folder #2, State Historical Society of Missouri. See also *Richmond Missourian,* July 4, 1938.

31. Anderson's present tombstone was placed on his grave by Donald R. Hale and his father, Lester C. Hale, in April 1969. They obtained it, somewhat ironically, from the United States government, which provides such markers for the grave of any person proved to have served either the Union or the Confederacy in a military capacity. See Hale, *Bloody Bill,* pp. 114–15.

BIBLIOGRAPHICAL ESSAY

Perhaps there are fields or types of history wherein the sources are so ample in quantity and so reliable in quality that the historians employing them are able to tell the whole truth and nothing but the truth with absolute certainty that it is the truth. Were such a situation to exist (which is doubtful), it would be a enviable one, and few historians would envy it more than those who write what might be termed bushwhacker history. Their circumstances, when it comes to source material, borders on the direct opposite to the ideal state of affairs described above, especially if their subject happens to be a particular bush-whacker named William T. Anderson.

For all historians the most prized source materials are diaries, letters, and reports providing firsthand accounts of events by participants soon after they occurred. Unfortunately but understandably bushwhackers did not keep diaries, and while it is possible that some of them sometimes wrote letters, none to my knowledge survive. Likewise, with a single exception, guerrilla leaders never filed reports. The exception was William Clarke Quantrill, who in October 1863 sent a brief account of his victory at Baxter Springs to Gen. Sterling Price. Uniqueness, though, is its sole virtue, for it conceals more than it reveals, and from the standpoint of historical research it is of little value. Concerning Bill Anderson, it is of no value at all, because it does not mention him.

The lack of bushwhacker diaries, letters, and reports forces the historian to make all possible use of Federal sources of the same type. But even here there is a shortage of diaries and letters—a shortage so great that one is tempted to con-clude that Union soldiers serving in Missouri and Kansas were not, by and large, of a literary bent. That is why it was a sheer delight to obtain from the Missouri Historical Society in St. Louis a photocopy of Lt. S. S. Eaton's September 26, 1864, letter to his father describing the bushwhacker attack on Fayette, Mis-souri, where he commanded the garrison. By the same token, it was a joy to locate in the *Richmond Missourian* of June 6, 1938, an excerpt from the diary of Lt. Thomas Hankins recounting the fight with Anderson's band near Albany,

159

Missouri, on October 17, 1864, and to find in the *St. Louis Missouri Democrat* of October 10, 1864, the statement by Richard Overall, conductor of the train that Anderson's men waylaid at Centralia on September 27, 1864. If only there were more such historical gems! As it was, heavy reliance for primary source material had to be placed on the Union military reports and correspondence gathered in the pertinent volumes of the *Official Records of the Union and Confederate Armies*. These contain much valuable, indeed indispensable, information. Generally they are reliable with respect to such things as Federal troop movements and casualties, and they provide insights into the attitudes, plans, and reactions of the Union commanders engaged in combating the guerrillas. Yet they need to be used with care and discernment. They almost always exaggerate bushwhacker numbers and losses, tend (as do all military reports) to minimize failures and defeats, and sometimes are hilariously inaccurate when locating and identifying guerrilla bands. Finally, by their very nature they present a biased, one-sided view of the bushwhackers and their operations that, in the interest of accuracy and fairness, calls for consulting the best available substitute for guerrilla diaries, letters, and reports—namely, guerrilla memoirs.

Sad to say, they are small in number, for the most part low in quality, and in some cases of dubious authenticity. Moreover, the two best ones are unpublished, and in the case of one of the two, unobtainable. They are, respectively, William H. Gregg's manuscript, "A Little Dab of History Without Embelishment [*sic*]," in the Joint Collection of the State Historical Society of Missouri and the Western Historical Manuscript Collection, Columbia, Missouri; and an untitled manuscript by Frank Smith, which is available solely in the form of notes and extracts made in 1958 by Albert Castel and in his private collection. Gregg was an early member of Quantrill's band, and his memoirs are the best source on that band's history until he left it in the winter of 1863–64. It contains little about Anderson, however, and most of that little is strongly biased against him. Smith, on the other hand, did not join Quantrill until 1863, when he became seventeen, and he served under him and George Todd until the Price raid in the autumn of 1864, at which point his narrative ends. He offers important information, not to be found in any other source, about Anderson and his quarrel with Quantrill in Texas during the winter of 1863–64, but after that his only contact with Anderson occurred at Fayette and Centralia, concerning which his accounts are brief and of little value.

The best of the published bushwhacker memoirs is John McCorkle's *Three Years with Quantrell* [*sic*], first printed in 1914 and most recently republished, with notes by Albert Castel and commentary by Herman Hattaway, by the University of Oklahoma Press (hardbound edition, 1992; paperback edition, 1998). Actually written by a Missouri lawyer named Oswald S. Barton "as told" to him by McCorkle, this book provides an "insider's view" of the Quantrill–Todd band by McCorkle, who joined it in 1862 and remained with it until late 1864, when he accompanied Quantrill to Kentucky. It offers data and details unavailable elsewhere but magnifies the prowess of the bushwhackers, ignores or glosses over such things as Todd's supplanting of Quantrill as chieftain, and is more critical than informative regarding Anderson.

Only two members of Anderson's band left memoirs: Hamp B. Watts, *The Babe of the Company* (Fayette, Missouri: The Democratic Leader Press, 1913), and Jim Cummins, *Jim Cummins's Book Written By Himself* (Denver: Reed Publishing Company, 1903; various reprints, some with title of *Jim Cummins, Guerrilla*). Watts's book was very useful on events leading up to the attack on Fayette and for the attack itself (which, oddly, he misdates despite Fayette being his hometown!) but provided little of value on Centralia and virtually nothing about events following that affair. Cummins's book, which despite its title was probably *not* written by him, mainly relates his putative postwar exploits as an outlaw and furnished only a quotation.

Thus, ironically, the most important memoir pertaining to Anderson comes from a Federal sergeant. It is, of course, Thomas M. Goodman's *A Thrilling Record* (Des Moines, Iowa: Mills & Company Steam Book & Job Printing House, 1868; facsimile edition, with introduction, notes, and appendix by Thomas R. Hooper, Marysville, Missouri: Rush Printing Company, 1960). Although written for Goodman, who lacked the education required to do it himself, by "Captain Harry A. Houston," it is an authentic account of what he witnessed and experienced while he was Anderson's captive and as such provides the most revealing view of Bloody Bill and his followers that exists. Both the text and the endnotes of this book testify to its great—indeed, unique—value.

Owing to the absence of bushwhacker diaries and letters, the inadequacies of guerrilla memoirs, and the inherent limitations of the *Official Records,* the most useful and therefore most used sources were contemporary newspapers and local Missouri histories. The former contain interviews, or accounts based on interviews, with participants and eyewitnesses that offer much vital information that can be found nowhere else and is on the whole highly reliable. In particular, reports in the *Emporia News, Council Grove Press, Leavenworth Daily Times,* and *Lexington Weekly Union* shed light on Anderson's hitherto obscure career prior to his emergence as a guerrilla chieftain in the summer of 1863. For what he did during the summer and fall of 1864, the most informative newspaper sources were the *St. Louis Missouri Democrat,* the *St. Louis Missouri Republican,* the *St. Joseph Morning Herald,* and the *Kansas City Daily Journal* (which published a weekly edition).

Like the newspapers, certain local histories contained important data derived from the testimony of people who took part in or beheld the events described. Chief among them were Thomas Fyfer, *History of Boone County,*

Missouri (St. Louis: Western Historical Company, 1882); the anonymously authored *History of Carroll County, Missouri* (St. Louis: Missouri Historical Company, 1881); and Edgar T. Rodemyre, *History of Centralia, Missouri* (Centralia: Fireside Guard, 1936). All are, to be sure, pro-Union in viewpoint, yet there is no reason to doubt the essential accuracy of their narratives when describing personal experiences.

As for secondary sources, John N. Edwards's *Noted Guerrillas, or, The Warfare of the Border* (1877; reprint, Dayton, Ohio: Press of the Morningside Bookshop, 1976) could have been the bedrock history of its subject, for Edwards was an ex-Confederate major who possessed the friendship and trust of many former bushwhackers, notably Frank and Jesse James, and therefore had access to information that only they could have supplied. But he was not interested in writing a history; instead, he sought to create a legend. Consequently, to quote from B. James George Sr.'s 1958 letter to Richard Brownlee, he "saw Quantrill and his men through the mist of partisan comradeship, and in poetic prose magnified their victories, tossed aside their defeats, and over-excused their shortcomings." As a result, his book, although fascinating reading, is a mixture of fiction and fact—and not to be relied on for the latter.

William E. Connelley's *Quantrill and the Border Wars* (Cedar Rapids, Iowa: The Torch Press, 1910; many reprints) is as intensely biased on the pro-Union side as Edwards's *Noted Guerrillas* is on the Confederate, but it does contain an immense amount of documentary material from which much valid information about the bushwhackers can be extracted. Little of this material, however, relates to Anderson. Connelley planned to write a book about him, and although he never did so, in July 1910 he interviewed several men who had known Anderson and his family when they resided near Council Grove, Kansas, during the late 1850s and the early 1860s. The record of these interviews, neatly typed and preserved in the William E. Connelley Collection at the Kansas State Historical Society in Topeka, constitutes, despite some vagueness and vagaries in the testimony of the interviewees, the best source of information about what in certain respects was the most decisive phase of Anderson's life.

For the collapse of the Kansas City military prison, which resulted in the death of one of Anderson's sisters and the crippling of another, the best account is Charles F. Harris's article, "Catalyst of Terror: The Collapse of the Women's Prison in Kansas City," *Missouri Historical Review* 89 (April 1995): 290–306. Much otherwise unobtainable information was found in Donald R. Hale's *They Called Him Bloody Bill: The Missouri Badman Who Taught Jesse James Outlawry* (Clinton, Missouri: The Printery, 1975) and William A. Settle Jr.'s *Jesse James Was His Name* (Columbia: University of Missouri Press, 1966), the first and still the only scholarly study of its subject. For the relationship between Quantrill and Anderson, the Lawrence and Baxter Springs massacres, and Confederate military operations in Missouri in the fall of 1864, the authors relied on, for obvious reasons, Albert Castel's *William Clarke Quantrill: His Life and Times* (New York: Frederick Fell, 1962; hardbound reprint, The General's Books, 1992, 1995), Castel's *General Sterling Price and the Civil War in the West* (Baton Rouge: Louisiana State University Press, 1968; paperback reprint, 1992), and Thomas Goodrich's *Bloody Dawn: The Story of the Lawrence Massacre* (Kent, Ohio: Kent State University Press, 1991) and his *Black Flag: Guerrilla Warfare on the Western Border, 1861–1865* (Bloomington: Indiana University Press, 1995).

INDEX

(Page numbers in italics indicate illustrations)

A Thrilling Record (Houston), 143

Agnes City, Kansas, July 3, 1863 events in, 11–18

Albany, Missouri
October 26, 1864 events in, 123–24
October 27, 1864 events in, 125–27

Alexander Mitchell and Company Bank, Lexington, Missouri, robbery of, 137

Allen (Moberly), Missouri, 47

Anderson, Bush, 35, 36

Anderson, Charles, 12

Anderson, Ellis, 11, 12

Anderson, Janie, 11, 26, 27

Anderson, Jim, 11, 14, *14,* 22–23, 46, 48–49, 131, 133, 134, 136–37
Baker killing, 16–18
death of, 139–40
Lexington and Warrensburg operations, 19

Anderson, Josephine, 11, 26
death of, 27

Anderson, Martha, 11, 12

Anderson, Mary Ellen, 11, 15, 26, 27

Anderson, William, Sr., 11–12
death of, 16

Anderson, William T. "Bloody Bill," *10,* 12–13, *14,* 22–23, 38, 39, 97
Baker killing, 16–18
Baxter Springs massacre, 32–33
becoming guerrilla "captain," 24
being known as "Bloody Bill," 96
Centralia massacres, 73–74, 79–86
death of, 125–27
emergence of, 27
escape from Federals, 100–3
Glen Eden raid, 119–22

Goodman's description of, 87
grave of, 143–44, *144*
jayhawking, 13
Johnston column ambush, 89–92, 95
Lawrence massacre, 29
letter to newspaper editors, 42–44
Lexington and Warrensburg operations, 19
marriage of, 36
motives of, 15
photographs of, after death, 127–30, *128,* *129*
pony business, 13
Price orders, 114–15
rank of, 34
at Rocheport, 57–58
scalping as trademark of, 41
separating from Price, 123–24
silken cord of, *127*
wounding of, 55
at Young's Creek, 69

Anderson homestead, 12

Baker, Arthur Inghram, 13–16
death of, 16–17

bank robberies, 136–42

Barnum, Bill, 81

Baum, Solomon, 44

Baxter Springs, Kansas, massacre, 31–33

Benton, Tom, 1, 4

Berry, Ike, 119

Big Shanty, Georgia, 64

Bingham, George Caleb, 26, 27

"Bleeding Kansas" troubles, 12

Bluff Creek, Kentucky, 12

Blunt, James G., 32

Boone County, Missouri, September 28 to
    October 8, 1864 events in, 99–109
Boonville, Missouri, October 11, 1864 events
    in, 111–15
Border Ruffians, 7
Bradford, J. H., 20–21
Bridger, Jim, 124
Brown, Egbert, 41, 44
Brownlee, Richard S., viii
Burns, Dick, 138
Burris, Milton, 42
bushwhackers, viii, 1–2, 3, 9–10
    Centralia massacres, 79–86
    conference, 60–61
    escape from Federals, 100–3
    Fayette defeat, 60–61
    fighting amongst, 33–36
    military order and discipline of, 105–6
    outfits of, 10–11
    rendezvous of, 106
    scalping as trademark of, 41
    turning into bandits, 136–42
    weapons of, 11
    Young's Creek camp, 69–70, 87–88,
        97–98

Carroll County, Missouri, 124
    "the Gourd" area of, 49–50
    massacre, 44–45
Carson, Kit, 124
Centralia, Missouri, 36, 70
    September 27, 1864 events in, 88–89,
        96–97
    September 27, 1864 events southeast of,
        89–92, 94–96
    massacres, 73–74, 79–86
    raid on, 93–94
Chariton County, Missouri, 49
Chiles, Jim Crow, 36
Clark, James, 76–78, 79–80, 84, 85–86, 96
Clark, John B., Jr., 117
Clay County Savings Bank, Liberty, Missouri,
    robbery of, 136
Clements, Archie, 24, *25*, 47, 93, 96, 124,
        131, 133–35, 136
    Centralia massacres, 79–86
    death of, 137
    scalping as trademark of, 41
    wounding of, 55

Colt Navies, 11
Columbia, Missouri, raid on, 56
Comer, Josh, 69
Committee of Safety for Montgomery
        County, letter, 57
Confederate States of America, 8
    collapse of, 133
"contributory tax," 58
Council Grove, Kansas, 20–21
Council Grove Press, 13, 20
Cox, Samuel P. "Cob," 124–27, 138
Craig, James, 124
Crittenden, Thomas T., 141
Cummins, Jim, 54
Curtis, Samuel Ryan, 115

Damon, George, 45–46
Danville, Missouri, 120
Daviess County Bank, Gallatin, Missouri,
        robbery of, 138–40
Davis, Berryman K., 134–35
Denny, Lieutenant Colonel, 69–70
Diamond Springs, Kansas, raid on, 21
District of the Frontier, 32
Dodge, Grenville, 134
Draper, Daniel, 2
Dunnica, W. E., 118

Eaton, S. S., 2
Edward, John N., 127
Ellington, Richard, 104
Emporia News, 15
Ewing, Thomas, Jr., 26, 31, 113

Fayette, Missouri
    bushwhackers defeat at, 60–61
    raid on, 1–5
Federal counterguerrilla campaign, 54–61, 132
Fifteenth Kansas Cavalry, 53
Fifty-first Missouri Militia, 124
First Iowa Cavalry, 53, 76
First Missouri Engineers, 64–67
Fisk, Clinton B., 52, 54, 67, 105, 124
    extermination party, 54–61
Flannery, Ike, 136
Ford, Bob, 141
Ford, Charles, 141
Forrest, Nathan Bedford, 133
Fourth Missouri State Militia, 57–58

Fredericksburg, Missouri, raid on, 54
Freestaters, 12

George, B. James, Sr., viii
Glasgow, Missouri
    battle at, 117
    October 21, 1864 events in, 117–22
    raid on, 118
Glasgow Road, September 24, 1864 events
    on, 7–11
Glen Eden, Glasgow, Missouri, *119*
    raid on, 118–22
Goodman, Mary, 116–17
Goodman, Thomas Morton, 64–67, *65*, 68–
    69, 75, 77, 78, 79, 80, 81, 82, 115–16,
    142–43
    capture of, 85
    escape of, 108–9
    grave of, *142*
    observations of, 105–6
    as prisoner, 87–88, 97–98, 100–9
Gordon, Si, 60
    Johnston column ambush, 89–92
Grant, Ulysses S., 63
Gray Ghosts of the Confederacy: Guerrilla War-
    fare in the West (Brownlee), viii
Griffin, Lee, 15, 17
guerrillas. *See* bushwhackers

Hale, Donald R., vii
"half-and-halfs," 64
Hannibal & St. Joseph Railroad, 48, 115
Harding, Chester, 134
Hart, Charley. *See* Quantrill, William Clarke
Hawleyville, Iowa, October 14, 1864 events
    in, 116–17
Hilly, Jim, 66
Hite, Wood, 141
Holden-Kingsville raid, 133–34
Holtzclaw, Cliff, 60, 120
Houston, Harry A., 143
Howard County, Missouri, September 28 to
    October 8, 1864 events in, 99–109
Howard County Courthouse, Fayette, Mis-
    souri, *3*
Hughes and Wasson Bank, Richmond, Mis-
    souri, robbery of, 137–38
Huntsville, Missouri, raids on, 45–46, 48, 56
Huntsville Randolph Citizen, 49

Jackson County, Missouri, 19
    April to May, 1864 events in, 36–38
    raids on, 23
James, Frank, 54, 55, 93, 133, *139,* 140, 142
    Centralia massacres, 79–86
    wounding of, 56
James, Jesse, 54, *56,* 133, 139, *139,* 140
    death of, 141
    wounding of, 55–56
James-Younger gang, 140–42
Jaynes, Thomas, 93
Jefferson City, Missouri, 113
Jefferson City State Times, 58
Jennison, Charles "Doc," 9, 53
Jewell, William, 136
Johnston, Ave, 70–73, *72,* 76, 88–89
    column, ambush of, 89–92, *92,* 94–95
    death of, 92
    march, *90*
    scalping of, 95
Johnston, Joe, 133

Kansas
    eastern, May to July 1863 events in, 23–24
    map of, *8*
    see also individual counties; individual
        towns
Kansas City, Missouri, August 13, 1863 events
    in, 26–27
Kansas City Daily Journal of Commerce, 26
Kansas City Journal, 137
    Holden-Kingsville raid editorial, 134
Kansas conflict, 7–8
Kansas jayhawkers, 9
Kansas "Red Legs," 23
Kentucky, central, September 25, 1864 events
    in, 63–67
Kice, Robert B., 127–30
King, Kate, 37, 133
Kingsville, Missouri, massacre, 41, 133–34
Kirker, John, 50

Lafayette County, Missouri, raids on, 23–24
Lakenan, Missouri, raid on, 48
Lane, James H., 9, 15
Lawrence, Kansas, raid on, 27–29
Leavenworth Daily Bulletin, Anderson editor-
    ial, 95
Lee, Robert E., 133

Leonard, Reeves, battalion, 2
letter to editors, Anderson's, 42–44
Lewis, Benjamin, 117–22, *118*
   death of, 122
Lewis, Eleanor, 118
Lexington, Missouri, 42
Lexington Weekly Union
   on Anderson, 23
   bushwhackers editorial, 19–20
Liberty Tribune, 132
Liddil, Dick, 141
Lincoln, Abraham, 8, 113
Little, Jim, 138
Little, Tom, 138
Litton, Hiram, 104
Long, Peyton, 133
   Centralia massacres, 79–86
Lovejoy, Julia, 36
Lyons, Cyrus, 45

McClellan, George, 113
McCulloch, Henry, 33–36
McDowell, James L., 21
McDowell, William, 138
McFerran, James, 42, 44
McGee's Addition, Kansas City, Missouri, 26
   collapse of, 26–27
Macon County, Missouri, 48–49
maps
   Johnston column ambush, *92*
   Johnston's march, *90*
   Kansas, *8*
   Missouri, *8, 22*
Matlock, Lucius, 52, 56–57
Maupin, John, 50
Mexico, Missouri, September 27, 1864 events
   in, 75–76
militiamen, 52–53
Missouri
   maps of, *8, 22*
   northern, summer of 1864 events in,
      41–61
   prairie of, September 27, 1864 events in,
      70–73
   western, July 1862 to July 1864 events in,
      19–20, 23–24, 38–39, 41–61
   see also individual counties; individual
      towns
Missouri guerrillas. *See* bushwhackers

Missouri Statesman, bushwhackers editorial,
   134
Missouri Unionists, 9, 72

Neosho Rapids, Kansas, raid on, 12
New York Tribune, 15
Ninth Missouri State Militia Cavalry, 1, 59
   Leonard battalion, 2
North Missouri Railroad, 115, 120
   attack on, 47
   between Mexico and Young's Creek, 76–78
Noted Guerrillas (Edward), 127

*Official Records of the Union and Confederate
   Armies,* 24, 44
Ogden, William, 24
Order No. 11, 31, 135
The Outlaw Josey Wales (film), vii
Overall, Richard, 75–76, 77

Pace, Ed, 66
Paris, Missouri, September 26, 1864 events in,
   67
partisans. *See* bushwhackers
"Paw Paws," 53
Perche Hills, Missouri, 56
Peters, Valentine, 66, 69, 83
Pilot Knob, Missouri, 113
Platte County, Missouri, raid on, 51
Pleasonton, Alfred, 115
Police Gazette, 140
Poole, Dave, 31, 60, 90, *94,* 103, 133, 134,
   137
   Johnston column ambush, 94–95
   surrender of, 135
Poole, John, 137
Poole, William, 139
Price, Sterling, 9, 28, 34, 39, 60, 70, 97,
   111–15, *112*
   Missouri campaign, 112–13, 123
   recruiting Anderson, 114–15

Quantrill, William Clarke, vii, 19, *21,* 34–35,
   36–38, 60, 115, 118, 136
   Baxter Springs massacre, 31–33
   in Kentucky, 132–33
   Lawrence massacre, 27–29
   rank of, 34
   Todd confrontation, 37

Rains, Captain, 125
Rains, James S., 125
Ratcliffe, John, 14
Republicans, 8
Reynolds, Thomas C., 37, 112, 114
Richmond, Missouri
    October 27 to 28, 1864 events in, 124,
        127–30
    raid on, 138
Robinson, Charles, 13
Robinson, Jim, 69
Rocheport, Missouri, 47, 105
    encounter at, 57–58
    raid on, 56
Rollins, James Sidney, 74, 79, 84, 86
Rose, Cass, 66
Rosecrans, William S., 39, 44
Russellville, Missouri, raid on, 50–51

St. Charles, Missouri, September 27, 1864
        events in, 68–69
St. Joseph, Missouri, October 13, 1864 events
        in, 115–16
St. Joseph Herald and Tribune, 116
    on Anderson, 51
    Anderson editorial, 52
    on Federal counterguerrilla campaign, 132
St. Louis Democrat, on Anderson death,
        131–32
St. Louis Republican, on Anderson, 100, 123
Santa Fe Trail, 12
    May 1863 events on, 20–23
scalping, as bushwhackers trademark, 41
Second Colorado Cavalry, 37, 53
    Todd encounter, 38–39
Segur, Annis, 15
Segur, George, 17–18
Segur, Ira, 16
Seventeenth Illinois Cavalry, 47, 53, 56
Sewell, Eli, 16
Sheets, John W., 138
Shelbina, Missouri, raid on, 47–48
Shelby, Jo, 42
Shepherd, George, 139
Shepherd, Ol', 138
Sherman, William Tecumseh, 26, 63
silken cord, Anderson's, *127*
Smith, A. J., 115
Smith, Bush. *See* Anderson, Bush

Smith, Edmund Kirby, 133
Sneed, A. F., 88–89, 93
Sneed, Thomas, 79, 84
Stafford, J. E., 93
Strieby, Charles, 15, 16, 17, 115
Sturgeon, Missouri, September 27, 1864
        events in, 96

tax collectors, Anderson's, 58–59
Taylor, Fletch, 51, *139*
Texas, northern, March 1864 events in, 33–36
Theiss, Adam, 89
They Called Him Bloody Bill (Hale), vii
Third Missouri Militia, ambush of, 59
Thirty-ninth Missouri Infantry, Companies A,
        G, and H, 67, 70–73
Thirty-third Missouri Militia, 124
Thrailkill, John, 60, 87, 97, 103, 133
    Johnston column ambush, 89–92, 95
Todd, George, 10, *32,* 33, 35, 36, 87, 97,
        103, 123, 132
    Baxter Springs massacre, 32
    Fayette defeat, 60–61
    Johnston column ambush, 89–92, 95
    Quantrill confrontation, 37
    rank of, 34
    Second Colorado Cavalry encounter,
        38–39
Todd, Thomas, 60, 95
    Johnston column ambush, 89–92

Union District of North Missouri, 52

Vaughn, Jim, 26
Vogel, Adolph, 128

Wakenda River, 55
Wales, Josey, vii
Watts, Hamp, 58, 59
Waverly, Missouri, 41–42
Wellington, Missouri, 41
Westport, Missouri, raid on, 26
Williams, George, statement of, 57
Wyandotte County, Kansas, raid on, 24–26
Wyatt, Cave, 59, 82

Yager, Dick, 20–21
    death of, 54
Younger, Bob, 140

Younger, Cole, 140
Younger, Jim, 140
Young's Creek, Missouri

guerrilla camp, 87–88, 97–98
September 27, 1864 events in, 69–70